PRAISE FOR
PHIL

"Alan Shipnuck didn't know his biography of Phil Mickelson would become the most anticipated and newsworthy release of a golf book since his 2011 collaboration with Michael Bamberger, *The Swinger*, a work of fiction that was a thinly disguised version of Tiger Woods. . . . The big difference is that *Phil* is true—difficult as it may be to believe some of the exploits, stories, and anecdotes packed into the book. . . . Shipnuck vividly tells the story of a walking, talking, shot-making contradiction."

—**Gary Smits,** *Florida Times-Union*

"A thoroughly readable portrait of a man who, for good *and* ill, shatters every stereotype of golfers as personality-deficient cyphers."

—**Bill Ott,** *Booklist*

"I devoured every win, wager, and ounce of Mickelson mischief in this unflinching portrayal of golf's most complicated character. Hero? Gentleman? Jerk? Shipnuck's masterful reporting is packed with inside information (the legal sort) that lets the reader decide. Thumbs up, indeed."

—**Tom Coyne,** *New York Times* **bestselling author of**
A Course Called America **and** *A Course Called Ireland*

"Alan Shipnuck has spent his whole career writing about and thinking about Phil, and that palpable fascination for his subject has fueled a superb biography. Anecdotes fly off the page, made rollicking and weighty by engaged and perceptive sources. Mickelson's golfing genius, charisma, and foibles are tracked with a high-wire blend of irreverence and dispassion. For all of that, it's Shipnuck's unflinching pursuit of Phil's complexity that will most endure."

—**Jaime Diaz, Golf Channel commentator**
and #1 *New York Times* **bestselling coauthor**
(with Hank Haney) of *The Big Miss*

"As juicy as one might expect, chronicling in extraordinary detail Mickelson's exploits on the golf course, and off the golf course, where he built a reputation as a big-time gambler—and a habitual loser."

—*Detroit News*

"It is terrific fun, 19 chapters that read like Mickelson's swashbuckling back nine in the final round of the 2004 Masters. Any fan reading it will be able to tell Mickelson stories for the rest of their lives. . . . Shipnuck charts his subject's journey through golf with Mickelson-like enthusiasm."

—*The Sunday Times* (**London**)

"*Phil* is not a hatchet job. Mr. Shipnuck, who has been reporting on golf since 1994, has more than enough stories, insights and details to create a fascinating read without taking sides.

—**John Paul Newport,** *The Wall Street Journal*

"For the golf geek, there's a wealth of golf lore. For the casual fan, there's a whole host of wonderfully-told stories that flesh out this compelling character. It gets to the heart of the gifted pro and a unique talent. . . . Whether hero or anti-hero, it's testament to the heart of the book that Mickelson holds such appeal, his flaws making him seem ever more interesting as a character in his own sporting soap opera."

—*Irish Daily Mail*

"As if I needed to tell you, go buy this book. You'll enjoy revisiting the glory days of the southpaw, but be warned: you won't feel the same about him when you turn the final page."

—**Golf WRX**

"One of the best sporting biographies in years—a rip-roaring, thoroughly fair portrait of the golfer Phil Mickelson. The opening chapter, in which Shipnuck gets 30 golf personalities to tell their best Mickelson story, is worth the cover price alone."

—*Irish Times*

© ABIGAIL SHIPNUCK

ALAN SHIPNUCK is the author of eight books, including the national best-sellers *Bud, Sweat, & Tees* and *The Swinger* (with Michael Bamberger). Shipnuck has received twelve first-place awards from the Golf Writers Association of America, breaking the record of Dan Jenkins, a member of the World Golf Hall of Fame. After more than two decades at *Sports Illustrated* and *GOLF* magazine, Shipnuck is now a partner at the golf media company the Fire Pit Collective, where all his writing, podcasts, and video storytelling can be found. Shipnuck lives in Carmel, California.

PHIL

**The Rip-Roaring (and Unauthorized!)
Biography of Golf's Most Colorful Superstar**

ALAN SHIPNUCK

AVID READER PRESS
New York   London   Toronto   Sydney   New Delhi

AVID READER PRESS
An Imprint of Simon & Schuster, Inc.
1230 Avenue of the Americas
New York, NY 10020

First Avid Reader Press trade paperback edition May 2023

AVID READER PRESS and colophon are trademarks of Simon & Schuster, Inc.

For information about special discounts for bulk purchases, please
contact Simon & Schuster Special Sales at 1-866-506-1949
or business@simonandschuster.com.

The Simon & Schuster Speakers Bureau can bring authors to your live event.
For more information or to book an event contact the Simon & Schuster Speakers Bureau
at 1-866-248-3049 or visit our website at www.simonspeakers.com.

Interior design by Wendy Blum

Manufactured in the United States of America

1   3   5   7   9   10   8   6   4   2

Library of Congress Cataloging-in-Publication Data has been applied for.

ISBN 978-1-4767-9709-0
ISBN 978-1-4767-9710-6 (pbk)
ISBN 978-1-4767-9711-3 (ebook)

This book is dedicated to
the memory of my mom,
Barbara

INTRODUCTION

Just throw the first punch."

Phil Mickelson is standing so close to me I can smell his breath. (Gamy, perhaps from a dry mouth?) We are crowded into a tunnel beneath the eighteenth-hole grandstand at Medinah Country Club, outside of Chicago. Moments earlier, he had put the finishing touches on a final-round 77 at the 1999 PGA Championship, one more indignity in what would be the first winless season of his PGA Tour career. I watched Mickelson play out the string, waving to the adoring fans as he ambled up the final fairway. There was no indication that only two months earlier his heart had been broken by Payne Stewart on the final green at Pinehurst. Or that his nemesis, Tiger Woods, was already tearing up the front nine at Medinah, on his way to what Mickelson was serially incapable of doing: winning a major championship. No, with his perma-grin and goofy thumbs-up, Mickelson appeared utterly carefree . . . but with him, looks are often deceiving. As I was about to find out.

This was the dawn of the internet age, and I was writing a weekly reader mailbag for CNNSI.com, the nascent *Sports Illustrated* website. Mickelson was the subject of much fascination and more than a little scorn. With his maniacal work ethic and ruthless excellence, Woods had thrown into sharp relief the flaws in Mickelson's flashy game, and Phil's fleshy physique became a kind of shorthand for his apparent lack of commitment. With a nod to the recent birth of Amanda Mickelson, one wag asked in the mailbag, "Was it Phil or Amy who was pregnant?" Another reader referred to him as Full Mickelson. Unbeknownst to me, this had wafted back to Mickelson, and he was pissed. I'm not sure if he conflated the readers' words and made them mine or if he was miffed that I was giving a platform to such sophomoric discourse (in retrospect, a valid objection);

either way, Phil was spoiling for a fight when, back at Medinah, I asked him a benign question for a Ryder Cup preview story.

"I'm not going to answer that because I don't respect you as a writer," he snapped.

We were in a small scrum of reporters and a couple seconds of awkward silence ensued. Interview over. The other scribes drifted away, but I was frozen in place, still stunned and more than a little embarrassed, when Phil wheeled in my direction. There was a hardness in his eyes that was utterly different from the gauzy gaze he wore coming up the eighteenth fairway.

"Do you have a problem with me?" he asked.

"Not really."

"Come over here and let's talk about it."

He motioned toward the more private tunnel under the grandstand and started drifting in that direction, eyes locked on mine. If you're a reporter long enough and you're doing the job properly, it's inevitable that one of the subjects you write about is going to be upset; sometimes the truth hurts. It's an unwritten rule that, when confronted with such a person, you have an obligation to let them blow off steam. After all, you've already had your say. So I followed Mickelson into the darkness, not knowing what to expect.

"Some of the stuff in your little web column is bullshit," he said. It was the first time I'd ever known him to employ profanity.

I offered a highfalutin explanation that I was leading a revolution in golf journalism by giving a voice to the casual fan. Phil wasn't having it.

"That's bullshit, too," he said. "If you have a problem with me, just throw the first punch." He stepped a little closer. "Just throw the first punch."

I was suddenly aware that the heat in Mickelson's voice had attracted an audience: stray tournament officials on either end of the tunnel were stealing glances and a couple of fans had peered over the stands and were watching upside down like red-faced bats. I could feel my pulse pounding in my temples.

Unlike Phil, I had important work to do on this major championship Sunday; the story I would write that night about Tiger's victory landed on the cover of *SI*. Also, he's a big dude and I hadn't been in a fistfight since fifth grade. (For the record, I won that little scuffle and retired with a career record of 1-0.) When I heard my own voice it was surprisingly calm: "I don't think that would be a good idea for either one of us."

"That's what I thought," Phil woofed, and then he stalked off.

Even in his mid-eighties, Gary Player is a keen observer of professional golf, and he doesn't hesitate when asked to name his favorite contemporary player. "Phil Mickelson," Player says. "He is good-looking and neatly dressed. He is a fierce competitor, but he's always smiling, and that happiness is contagious. He never forgets to take his hat off and he signs autographs until his arm nearly falls off. He is excellent in victory and even better in defeat. For me, he is the consummate professional." This is the Mickelson that the golfing public has always known, and it explains why for most of his career he has been maybe the most popular player since his hero, Arnold Palmer. But as I observed at Medinah, there are other sides to Phil, too. This book is an attempt to reconcile the multitudes within Mickelson.

The evolution of our own relationship is revealing of how mercurial Mickelson can be. He is blessed to have one of the most effective PR people in the game: his charming and chatty wife, Amy, who greets most every reporter she knows with a hug. Beginning in the early aughts, Amy and I have walked countless holes together, discussing kids and life as a way to find common ground. (When her hubby would make a mistake on the course, or do something particularly crazy, she would simply sigh, "Oh, Philip.") It surely helped that we spoke the same language: I'm about the same age as the Mickelsons and we share California roots. With Amy as a moderating influence, Philip became less combative with me and I was able to glimpse this shape-shifter in many different settings. I've been to the family home in Rancho Santa Fe, California, a faux-Tuscan village of stone buildings featuring one helluva backyard practice facility. Phil and I have had brunch at his swanky nearby club, the Bridges. (We're not millennials, but each of us ordered avocado toast.) We have munched on donuts together in the manager's office at a Target in a scrappy corner of San Diego, where the Mickelsons were hosting Start Smart, a program that buys school supplies and clothes for a couple thousand kids bused in from economically disadvantaged neighborhoods. (At the end of the day, Phil simply handed a credit card to one of the overwhelmed cashiers.) After Mickelson's epic victory at the 2013 Open Championship, I drank champagne with him and Amy at a private party in the shadow of the Muirfield clubhouse. A month earlier, while doing interviews following the second round at Merion, Mickelson eyed the horizontal stripes of my polo and cracked that it accentuated my budding dad bod. I laughed, but at 3:34 a.m., he texted an apology that concluded: "I won't be such a smartass next time. Even though it's against my nature."

This is the ever-present tension in Mickelson's life: he is always battling his inherent tendencies. He is a smart-ass who built an empire on being the consummate professional; a loving husband dogged by salacious rumors; a gambler who knows the house always wins but can't help himself, anyway; an intensely private person who loves to talk about himself and at such a volume you can often hear him from across the room. In an unguarded locker room moment, Steve Elkington once called Mickelson "the biggest fraud out here—a total phony." Paul Goydos, among the most thoughtful of Tour pros, describes Mickelson as "just about the most engaging person you can imagine, given his level of stardom." Who is the real Phil Mickelson? I often think of something he said during our confrontation at Medinah. It was meant as a taunt but became the challenge that animated this book: "You think you know me, but you don't."

CHAPTER ONE

So, what's your best Phil Mickelson story?

"A year or two after I retired," says Tom Candiotti, a big-league pitcher from 1983 to '99, "I played Whisper Rock [Golf Club] with Phil and Jason Kidd. Afterward, we were sitting around the clubhouse, talking shit. Phil went on this whole riff about how if he hadn't been a golfer he could have played Major League Baseball. Oh boy, okay. I just rolled my eyes, because I've heard that so many times; every professional athlete thinks they could have been great in another sport, even though it's never really true. But Phil wouldn't shut up about it. He kept saying, 'I could have been a really special player.' Finally, I said, '*Okay, let's see it.*' So we drive to my house and get all this gear—bats, balls, helmets—and then go to the baseball field at Horizon High School. I start throwing batting practice and Jason pops a few home runs right away. He's a great athlete. Now it's Phil's turn. Imagine driving by and seeing a Hall of Fame basketball player shagging fly balls and a Hall of Fame golfer at the plate . . . wearing golf spikes, a Titleist glove, and a right-handed batting helmet, with the flap on the wrong side. I'm just throwing easy fastballs and Phil is swinging out of his shoes. He's so determined to hit one over the fence, but he can't even get it to the warning track. He's getting more and more pissed off and me and Jason are trying really, really hard not to laugh. Eventually Jason got so bored he just laid down in the grass in centerfield. Phil never did hit a home run."

"There was a period in 1989 and 1990 when Phil and I played a lot of golf together because we were on Walker Cup and World Amateur teams together," says David Eger. "At the 1990 U.S. Amateur, we faced each other in the semi-finals and he beat me pretty good [5 & 3]. We were always friendly, but over time we just kind of lost touch, which happens. Fast-forward to 2017, when the PGA Championship was at Quail Hollow, where I'm a member. Phil came out early for a practice round and I heard about it. It'd been at least ten years since we had last seen each other, so I grabbed my wife and we jumped in a cart so we could go say hello. We found him putting on the fifth hole. We walked up onto the green and I introduced him to Trish, and literally the first thing Phil said was 'Did David tell you what an ass-whooping I put on him at the Amateur in 1990?' It had been twenty-seven years."

"When my wife was diagnosed with breast cancer in '16, I caught Phil outside the scoring tent in Baltusrol," says Ryan Palmer. "I took him aside and told him about Jennifer, and before I said anything else he just pulled me in for a hug. It lasted a really long time. Then he said, 'Here's what's going to happen—I'm going to put you in touch with Dr. Tom Buchholz of MD Anderson [Cancer Center in Houston], he's gonna get you the best doctors and surgeons in the world. They're gonna take care of you guys and Jennifer is going to be okay.' That night I was on the phone with Dr. Buchholz, and everything Phil said came true. I've never stopped being grateful for what he did for me and my family."

"The last time the Open Championship was at Royal Birkdale," says Johnny Miller, "there was a sixtieth birthday party for Nick Faldo. It was thrown by his lady friend at the time, in a really nice house on the eighteenth hole. There were TV people there and some players and past Open champions [including Tony Jacklin, Mark O'Meara, Stewart Cink, Henrik Stenson, and Paul McGinley]. Nice crowd. Faldo is sitting at the head of this big table and just loving all the attention. He's having a great time. Then Phil sits down next to him and starts talking, and he literally doesn't stop. He starts saying some kind of outrageous things: 'Nobody can hit the shots I can hit.' I'm thinking, *Yeah, buddy, because they end up in the wrong fairway.* He just keeps going like that, saying a lot of things you shouldn't really say in front of players of a similar stature, but Phil was doing that Phil thing. At some point, [my wife] Linda leans over and says, 'Is this guy ever going to stop talking?' Poor Nick Faldo is just sinking deeper and deeper into his chair. He looks miserable, like all his thunder had been stolen. It was a total alpha move by Phil and undeniably entertaining. Shows how confident he is, how much he believes he is the best to ever do it. The record doesn't reflect that, but don't tell Phil."

"At the 2003 Presidents Cup," says Jack Nicklaus, who captained the U.S. team, "Phil went 0-5, but I called him my MVP. I did that because most guys, if they go 0-5, they will be down in the dumps and take the team with him. Phil did not do that. He had a great attitude all week and never stopped cheering for his teammates. That's not easy to do when you're losing match after match. Told me a lot about his character."

"For many years I've played in the same fantasy football league as Phil," says Jim Nantz. "He takes it very seriously and he's good at it—he has won the league championship a couple of times. We hold the draft in person every year in a hotel conference room during the Northern Trust [tournament] and Phil has never missed one. In 2013, he was staying at a different hotel in Jersey City a couple of blocks away, so he walked over . . . carrying the Claret Jug. Some good wine was drank out of it that night. But the best story is from 2020. Phil had Alvin Kamara as his running back when he went for six touchdowns in Week 16. That gave Phil such a commanding lead in the standings it was a virtual certainty he was going to win the title. I'm talking a 99.999 percent probability. He sent out an email to the whole league, gloating. I mean, he went on and on, really laying it on thick. Well, the team that was in second place had Josh Allen as their quarterback, and in the last game of the season, on Monday night, Allen went for thirty-nine points and Phil lost the title by one point. He was crushed. Absolutely devastated. He took it so hard I honestly believe it affected his play on the West Coast swing."

"I remember one time, me, Phil, Larry Barber, and Stricky [Jim Strickland] were gonna play a 'hate game' at Grayhawk," says Gary McCord. "A hate game is, whoever you're paired with, you hate the other two guys really bad. There's no rules. The verbal sword fights get bloody. Anyway, Phil said he had a photo shoot in the morning, so we agreed to play at one o'clock. We get to the twelfth hole, a short par-4 with a cluster of bunkers around the green. You know that backward shot Phil hits, where it goes over his head? He says, 'You see that bunker there? I bet I can put a ball on the [steep grass] face and hit it backward to within the length of the flagstick on the first try.' It's a twenty- to thirty-yard shot, off the side of a hill, to a sloping green. Seems almost impossible, but with Phil, when you make a bet, you gotta go through all possibilities, because he'll always try to trick you into somethin'. So we talk it out in great detail and finally all bet him a hundred dollars he can't do it. He throws down a ball and takes a mighty swing and hits to about six feet. We go ape shit. It was just incredible. Well, remember the photo shoot that morning? He had spent three hours hitting that exact shot from that exact spot over and over and over again for *Golf Digest*. The rat bastard got us and got us good." (Years later, Mickelson would play an over-the-shoulder backward shot in competition, from a steep downslope in the back bunker on the fourth hole at Pebble Beach; he hit it to twelve feet.)

"About fifteen years ago, I was playing in a fundraiser for the Wounded Warriors," says Chip Beck, "and Phil was playing in it, too. My kids absolutely loved Phil Mickelson. So at the banquet that night I brought them over to meet him, and he says immediately, 'At one of my first tournaments on the PGA Tour, I was walking down the hill at Riviera and I saw your dad talking to a group of reporters. He said to them, "I need thirty minutes to go to the range and figure something out and then I'm going to come back and find you guys and answer all your questions." He was so nice to the reporters, and I stood there and watched how he handled them and the mutual respect they shared, and it never left me. I've always tried to emulate your dad.' I was floored. I never knew any of that. Made me feel like a million bucks, in front of my kids and everything."

"I wasn't even in the room when it happened, but I've heard this story so many times it's become my favorite," says Paul McGinley. "The 2016 Ryder Cup was right after the Olympics, and Matt Kuchar, who is a bit of a court jester, wore his bronze medal around everywhere he went, just to wind people up. He was slagging Phil and Tiger, saying they'd won all these majors but they didn't have an Olympic medal. So for one of their team meetings, the Americans bring in the swimmer Michael Phelps to have a chat. Of course, he has twenty-one or twenty-two gold medals, or whatever it is. Phelps gets a standing ovation, he's high-fiving everyone, and just before he's about to address the players, Phil speaks up: 'Hey, Kuch, why don't you show him your bronze medal—he probably hasn't seen one before.' That's just great comedic timing."

"Not so much anymore, but for a long time Phil was an astonishing eater," says Nick Faldo. "I remember moons ago in player dining seeing Tiger with a grilled skinless chicken breast and a plate full of broccoli and Phil had a triple bacon cheeseburger and a huge pile of french fries, and thinking that right there was the difference between them. At Firestone one year, Phil came to dinner with a bunch of the CBS guys. He was talking about what a strong constitution he has and that he can eat almost anything. This restaurant was almost like a little bowling alley and they had these sauerkraut balls on the table. Phil is drinking red wine and holding court on everything from politics to the best way to change a nappy [diaper], and he keeps popping in these sauerkraut balls. He must've had a dozen of them. Maybe more. Well, the next day he shot about 82 and had to run to the bathroom as soon as he putted out on eighteen, so I guess he can't eat *anything*."

"At the Wells Fargo Championship in 2012, Phil threw a party for select players, caddies, and a few media at Del Frisco's," says Steve DiMeglio, long-time golf writer at *USA Today*. "We had the basement all to ourselves. It was in celebration of his induction into the World Golf Hall of Fame. One long wall was packed with TVs showing the NBA, NHL, and pay-per-view boxing, so of course there was lots of betting. Mayweather was fighting Cotto in the main event. One of the fights on the undercard had a thirty-to-one shot. Of course, Phil was the only one to bet him, and the guy knocks out the heavy favorite. So there's Phil sitting at a table and everyone is throwing cash in front of him to pay off their bets. 'What are these?' Phil said as he lifted twenty-dollar bills off the table, like he only lives in a world of hundred-dollar bills. Big laughs."

"This happened ten years ago, but I remember it like it was yesterday," says TV announcer Jerry Foltz. "The Barclays was at Liberty National, and on the thirteenth hole, Phil drives it into the fairway bunker. He's playing to a kidney-shaped, two-tier green and the pin is all the way in the back left. Phil's got a hundred-and-twenty-yard bunker shot. . . . Nobody wants that. He takes his gap wedge, opens the face way up, and plays this huge slice. His ball lands on the lower tier and then spins dead left, *up the hill*, and cozies next to the hole. No one else on earth could hit that shot. They couldn't even think of it, and if they somehow did, they certainly wouldn't try it in competition, and if they did try it there's no way they could pull it off. I just looked at him and said, '*Fuuuuuck me*.' And Phil was like, 'What? It was just a little side sauce.'"

"You remember there was that period when we were having our equipment tested for legality and it was other players who were making the allegations?" asks Paul Casey. "There was a player who accused Phil of having an illegal club. We won't use his name, but he wasn't as accomplished as Phil, put it that way. The club was tested and it passed, of course. Phil left a note in this gentleman's locker that said, 'You'll be glad to know it's legal and, by the way, good luck at Q School.'"

"The first time I ever met him I was an amateur playing the Open at Carnoustie [in 1999]," says Luke Donald. "Back then, for practice rounds they just had a tee sheet where you signed your name. I was looking and saw that Phil was scheduled to play with Mark Calcavecchia and Billy Mayfair. It was just the three of them and I was like, 'Hey, why not?' I figured they might see my name and play at a different time or something like that, but they all turned up at the appointed hour. Phil arrives on the first tee so energetic and outgoing, asking me lots of questions. I was pretty wet behind the ears and he made me feel so welcome. He says to the other guys, 'Me and Luke will take you on for two hundred bucks.' That's a lot of money for a college kid and I think he could sense I was feeling a little uneasy, so Phil says, 'Don't worry, Luke, I got you covered.' I can't confirm or deny that any NCAA violations occurred that day. But what a great first impression. There is a larger-than-life element to Phil that has always been there."

"Right after Phil won the British Open in 2013, the Tour was in Akron," says Brandt Snedeker. "On Tuesday night I'm driving to dinner, and at a stoplight Phil pulls up next me. What are the chances, right? We roll down the windows and he yells, 'Hey, buddy, where are you going to dinner?' I told him I was meeting some people. He asks if I want to join him, but I say I can't. He's like, 'That's too bad because we're going to be drinking something special out of this.' He starts waving around the Claret Jug, smashes the gas, and then takes off. I'm just sitting there shaking my head and laughing like, *Man, you can't make this stuff up.*"

"The first time I saw him in action was a clinic at Grand Cypress, in Orlando," says Paul Azinger. "Phil had just turned pro. This had to be the greatest clinic ever: Nicklaus was there, Palmer, Trevino, Hale Irwin, Freddy [Couples]. Heavy hitters. During the clinic, Phil pulls a guy out of the crowd and has him stand right in front of him and then hits a full-swing flop shot right over his head. These days you see stuff like that on social media, but thirty years ago? It was like a bolt of lightning hit the driving range. The crowd was freaking out, everyone screaming. When the clinic was over and all the people had left, Jack and Arnold and Trevino—especially Trevino—gathered around Phil and said, 'Son, don't ever do that again. You're gonna get yourself sued, you're gonna get the Tour sued.' And Phil says, 'Guys, you don't understand, there's no way I can't pull it off. What I do is . . .' He goes into this whole long spiel about the mechanics of the shot. I looked at Calc"—Mark Calcavecchia—"and said, 'This guy is gonna be gooooood.' I mean, he's not even on Tour yet and he's giving Jack Freaking Nicklaus a full-blown lecture."

"There was a rain delay at the 2008 PGA Championship," says Brian Gay, "and we were sitting around and Phil started talking about how he was going to take a trip to the moon. He said it was still ten years away, and it would probably cost him a million dollars, but he was definitely going to do it. He was dead serious—he had it all mapped out. It was like, *Okay, Phil, whatever.* But now guys are on the verge of going to the moon for fun for a few million dollars. He actually knew what he was talking about! No doubt he's first on the list and someday we're all gonna wake up and he will be doing fireside chats from the moon. That's classic Phil. People ask me what he's like and I say, 'If you ask Phil Mickelson what time it is he'll tell you how to build a watch.'"

"When Phil was still in college I wrote the first *Sports Illustrated* feature on him," says legendary golf writer John Garrity. "I told him I'd take him out to dinner anywhere he wanted and it was my treat. From a college kid, you'd expect a hamburger joint, or maybe a steakhouse. Phil said he wanted to go to this fancy new French restaurant on Scottsdale Drive. I thought that was different and interesting. So we go, and the first thing Phil does is order escargot, saying he's always wanted to try it. He's got a plate full of snails and those little tongs—it's like the scene in *Pretty Woman*. Of course, at this point he has a pretty high profile around town, so there was this sense that the whole restaurant was watching discreetly, and sure enough one of the snails goes flying and he just gives that Eddie Haskell grin of his. I think I knew then he was going to be a different kind of character than the typical Tour pro."

"One day right after he got his pilot license we went up in a small plane," says Jim Strickland, a college teammate and still a close friend. "Phil was gonna fly us to Laughlin to gamble for a couple hours. We were up in the air for six or seven minutes and Phil says, 'Uh-oh, we don't have any gas.' It was like, *What?* He says, 'Yeah, the guy was supposed to fill it up. But don't worry about it, I can put this thing down anywhere.' I look down and we're flying over canyons and mountains. There is nowhere to land. My heart starts pounding. I am panicking. I am literally sweating. But Phil was so calm it was almost scary. He went through the backup systems, he communicated with the folks in the tower, and it turned out we did have gas, but it was an instrument malfunction. But the coolness and calmness was something to see."

"Phil was always trying to talk me into flying with him," says Charles Barkley. "No fucking way, dude. Fuck that shit. I thought his total confidence was funny. He was like, 'C'mon, man, I'm a good pilot.' No, you're a great golfer. There's a difference. I'm a firm believer that you only get to be good at one thing in life. You don't see any United Airlines pilots on the PGA Tour, do you? I rest my case. But Phil argued that point all day long."

"One year at Bay Hill, we're on the eighth tee and he's talking to [his former caddie Jim "Bones" Mackay] about what club to hit," says Justin Leonard. "There's a fairway bunker down there and Bones says, 'Your stock driver will get to it.' I had never heard that term before, *stock driver*. Phil asks, 'Where will my 3-wood leave me?' Bones says, 'Maybe 178 out.' That's more than Phil wants, so he says, 'What if I take four yards off my stock driver?' At this point, I'm laughing out loud. I can't believe this is a serious conversation, but it is. Bones says, 'Yeah, take four yards off the stock driver.' That's just the way they did things. And by the way, his drive wound up ten yards short of the bunker. I guess he took too much off of it."

"This whole 'bombs' thing, this guy is like fifty-one or fifty-two or whatever it is, like, c'mon, he's not going to hit it *that* far," says Harry Higgs, recalling his thinking ahead of his first competitive pairing with Mickelson at the 2021 BMW Championship. "Phil says aloud to Tim [Mickelson], his caddie, 'Tim, do you like stock or nasty here on this tee shot?' This comes out of his mouth. [My caddie] and I are just looking at each other like, *Are you kidding? No one has ever said this on a golf course in a professional golf tournament in their lives.* But that's just Phil. And Tim's like, 'Stock is good here, Phil. We can get there with a good stock one.' He goes through his routine, swings . . . and grunts. This is not stock. He audibly grunted as he struck the golf ball. That's one of the nasty ones. To Phil's credit, it went nine miles."

"Phil likes to go to Augusta ahead of the Masters and I've been lucky to go with him a bunch of times," says Keegan Bradley. "The first time we go, we're having lunch in the champion's locker room. We're just wearing regular golf clothes. At some point Phil excuses himself. I figure he's going to the bathroom. But he comes back and he's wearing his green jacket, and with this huge shit-eating grin he says, 'Sorry, I got a little chilly and needed another layer.'"

"One time at Pebble," says Kevin Streelman, "there were a bunch of guys at dinner, including Phil and Gary McCord. As you can imagine, none of the other nine of us got a word in. Phil and McCord spent the whole time talking about astronomy and geology and the big bang and the expansion of the universe. Phil was really going deep, to the point he was trying to text a buddy at NASA to clarify some point about the start of humanity. I was like, *Hey, pass the wine.*"

"At Pebble Beach one year," says Peter Kostis, "McCord and I are at the house of a guy named Ernie Garcia. It's a great house with a formidable wine cellar, and we dug around pretty deep. The last bottle we had before Phil came to join us was an '82 Petrus [a Bordeaux that can retail for low five figures per bottle]. Knowing Phil was coming, we got some '86 Silver Oak"—a perfectly good cabernet that sells for around $120—"and poured it into the Petrus bottle that we had just emptied. We put the cork back in with a corkscrew in it so that it looks like we're in the middle of opening it up. Phil arrives, and he says, 'What are we drinking, boys?' And I say, 'Well, it's '82 Petrus.' Phil's an expert on everything in his own mind, so he's excited, because he knows this is a big bottle of wine. We pour him a glass, he takes a sip, and he smacks his lips and goes, 'Ah, nectar of the gods.' To this day, Phil doesn't know that we switched it out. And you know he's out there telling the whole world that '82 Petrus is the best wine he's ever had."

"In 2003, the U.S. Open was at Olympia Fields and Phil went in early to see the course," says Jeff Rude, a former writer at *Golfweek*. "Him and Bones go to a little breakfast place in Homewood, Illinois. He leaves the waitress a hundred-dollar bill for a small check, but that's not the point of the story. A woman who works at an eye-care center across the street comes in and recognizes Phil and asks for an autograph. He politely says he'll do it when he's done eating. Well, she can't wait around, she has to get back to work. After breakfast Phil goes to Olympia Fields, and then after playing eighteen holes, he drives back across town to the eye-care place to sign autographs for this woman and all the other people at her office."

"We played together in a thirty-six-hole qualifier for the U.S. Junior," says Michael Zucchet, a onetime San Diego city councilman who competed against Mickelson in high school. "It was sixty boys for three spots at Singing Hills. Phil had his own caddie, which was kind of unusual back then, but what was more interesting was that all they did for thirty-six holes was gamble on every shot. The caddie would say, 'I bet you can't hook your ball around this tree and have it land in the fairway.' Or, to a front pin, 'I dare you to land the ball at the back of the green and suck it all the way back.' They literally screwed around for all thirty-six holes, and of course Phil was the medalist. I worked my ass off to shoot 77-78 and never had a chance. He was just from another planet."

"I went out to Torrey Pines in 2007 to work on a preview piece," says Scott Michaux, formerly the golf writer at the *Augusta Chronicle*. "This was the era when Phil had introduced the term 'subcutaneous fat' to the golf lexicon and was talking in press conferences about how he had changed his diet and was way more fit than anybody was giving him credit. He had agreed in advance to do the interview, so he says, 'Hey, let's talk in my car, it will be quiet in there.' Sure, whatever. So we walk to this black Ford Explorer and I open the passenger door and the seat is covered in McDonald's wrappers. Just buried. He rakes them off the seat and the look on his face was priceless, like, *Oh, shit, busted.*"

"There are so many stories," says Stewart Cink, "but they all have one thing in common: juice. Doesn't matter what form the juice takes. Needling in the locker room is juice. Money games during practice rounds is juice. Trying to pull off crazy shots with a tournament on the line is definitely juice. Criticizing Tiger's equipment when he's on a historic run is a lot of things, but it's also juice. Phil loves math and computations, and where that stuff meets juice is Vegas, so of course Phil loves it there. When you know you don't have an advantage, but you still want to bet large amounts? That's juice. Phil is an all-time juice guy."

"This shot was totally insignificant to the outcome of the tournament, but I've always remembered it," says Mark Brooks. "It was Phil's first year on Tour and we were paired together at TPC Avenel. The first hole was a pretty easy par-4, just driver-wedge, but somehow he got hung up in rough and ended up thirty yards short of the green. You might remember that back then Avenel was having trouble with their fairways. There wasn't much grass. Walking to the green I had to go right by Phil's ball, so I took a peek at the lie and it was horrendous: ball was sitting down, and there was more dirt than grass. Where the flag was, to get it close he would have to go over the corner of this big bunker. Given the lie, I would say ninety-nine out of a hundred touring professionals would have aimed thirty feet from the flag, taking the bunker out of play. But Phil is that one player out of the hundred, and next thing you know he is taking these big old long practice swings and staring down the flag. I'm thinking, *Holy smokes, this rookie might make a triple bogey right out of the box.* Well, he plays this kind of explosion shot and hits it to a foot. It's one of the best shots I've ever seen. It wasn't even so much that he pulled it off, but more impressive was that he was willing to try it in the first place. What kind of prep did it take to be able to do that, especially on the first hole? How many thousands of similar shots did he hit like that in practice? How many times did he fail and what did he learn from it? That one shot told me everything I needed to know about Phil Mickelson. But where did that shot come from? There's a story there, for sure."

CHAPTER TWO

For the longest time, there were whispers that Phil Mickelson's grandfather Al Santos had killed a man. It wasn't out of the realm of possibility. Santos was as tough as a two-dollar steak, a man's man with big calloused hands and the briny demeanor that came from having been at sea for weeks at a time. Only recently did his daughter Mary—Phil's mom—set the record straight: "Pirates were shooting at his boat, trying to steal his catch, and he shot back at them. He might have killed one of them. He didn't want to stick around and find out."

So, maybe Santos killed a man, maybe he didn't. Either way, it's an instructive story. When the young Mickelson began winning tournaments with an upturned collar and rakish grin, there was befuddlement at how this pretty boy could harbor such a ferocious killer instinct. That was Santos's DNA.

He was born in 1906 in Monterey, California, the son of a Cannery Row fisherman who had emigrated from Portugal. John Steinbeck, born four years earlier, would memorialize that grimy world with the greatest opening paragraph in the English language:

Cannery Row in Monterey in California is a poem, a stink, a grating noise, a quality of light, a tone, a habit, a nostalgia, a dream. Cannery Row is the gathered and scattered, tin and iron and rust and splintered wood, chipped pavement and weedy lots and junk heaps, sardine canneries of corrugated iron, honky tonks, restaurants and whore houses, and little crowded groceries, and laboratories and flophouses. Its inhabitants are, as the man once said, "whores, pimps, gamblers, and sons of bitches," by which he meant Everybody. Had the man looked through another peephole he might have said, "Saints and angels and martyrs and holy men," and he would have meant the same thing.

Santos harbored ambitions of transcending his grubby circumstances. He had a head for numbers and fancied a career as an engineer. But Santos was the third of eleven children, and when he reached the eighth grade, his father informed him that it was time to get a job and help support the family. To avoid the pungent canneries, he began caddying at the Hotel Del Monte golf course in Monterey, in 1919. But Santos couldn't resist the siren song of the open road—he ran away from home at sixteen and spent six months riding freight trains, panning for gold, and exploring the West. Not long after he returned home, Pebble Beach Golf Links opened and he joined the caddie corps. A photo from that era shows Santos in a newsboy cap, a collared shirt, and a blazer and trousers that look like they're made of burlap.

He earned thirty-five cents a loop, often going around twice in a day. For his efforts, one appreciative golfer gave Santos a Morgan silver dollar, circa 1900. It became a talisman he refused to spend, no matter how much his belly ached from hunger. Santos would rub the coin in his pocket for good luck. He came to think of it as a tangible sign that better days were ahead. For the rest of his life he had a simple mantra about the value of saving money: "As long as you have a silver dollar in your pocket, you'll never be poor." (Shortly before his death, Santos gave his prized silver dollar—rubbed as smooth as a marble countertop—to his grandson, who uses it as a ball marker whenever he competes at Pebble Beach; this may or may not account for Phil's record-tying five victories at the Crosby Clambake.)

Santos married a dark-eyed beauty of Portuguese descent named Jennie. They had three daughters, with Mary being the eldest. In the early years of the Great Depression, the Santos family moved down the coast to San Diego. Al became what was known locally as a "tunaman." He worked long hours and saved his money and eventually bought his own boat, the *Sacramento*. His brothers toiled alongside him in the vastness of the sea. When they pulled into the harbor after their long expeditions they would be hauling as much as 150 tons of tuna. Santos later bought a second boat, the *Julia B*. The Santoses owned and lived in a two-bedroom house near the commercial piers, at the bottom of what was Grape Street. Later they moved to a bigger home in the Mission Hills neighborhood. That was every fisherman's dream, to live on higher ground, far from the stinky air of the harbor that was redolent of Cannery Row.

To Santos, family was everything. He doted on Jennie and the girls. When they were teenagers, he took a graveyard shift on the assembly line at Convair, a division of General Dynamics. He didn't love the job but he wanted to be home more.

Mary inherited her father's warmth and big laugh and ability to spin a yarn. She was an athlete, excelling at any sport she tried, though options for girls were limited in those days. She married a navy pilot named Philip Anthony Mickelson. (Their son isn't a Jr. because his middle name is Alfred.) Mickelson grew up in tiny lumber towns in the Sierra. He was a gymnast and competitive water-skier who went on to captain the downhill ski team at Chico (California) State. After serving his country in Vietnam, he became a commercial airline pilot and channeled his athletic passion into golf. He often teed it up with his father-in-law around the public courses in San Diego.

There was no doubt that the Mickelsons' first son was going to be a golfer. (Same goes for their firstborn, Tina, who is now a teaching pro, and their youngest, Tim, would later join the family business, too.) Phil's parents sent out a birth announcement that had a sketch of a baby with a golf bag slung over his shoulder and this cheeky write-up:

> Introducing the Mickelsons' 'fourth.' Phil Alfred hurried to join the Mick-elson threesome on the first tee at Mercy Hospital for a 3:45 p.m. starting time on June 16, 1970. Using all of his 8 lbs., 13 ounces in a powerful swing, Philip proudly equaled his height with a tee shot of 21 inches. Philip's first message: "Let's play golf at my new home in San Diego."

As a toddler, Mickelson loved to sit in the backyard and watch his dad hit chips on the lawn. (This is eerily similar to the young Tiger Woods being parked in a high chair to stare at his father, Earl, as he pounded balls into a net in their garage.) Around the time of Phil's second birthday, his dad cut down a fairway wood and handed it to him to test. Phil was right-hand dominant, but in that moment he swung the club lefty, perhaps to mirror what he had been watching from his dad. The elder Mickelson tried to correct his son, but Phil kept swinging left-handed and his old man was impressed by the smoothness and soundness of the action.

"We'll just change the golf club instead," he told Mary.

He returned to his workbench, did some sawing and grinding, and—voilà!—a left-handed club was born. Phil never looked back. Much later, he would explain what he considers to be the advantages of this happy accident: "I'm right-handed in everything else I do, so it's very easy for me to play golf left-handed and especially chip because my right hand is dominant and just leads the shot. But when you're a right-handed golfer and that right hand is flipping over, I think it's very difficult to control the club. I actually think it's easier to play left-handed if you're right-handed in everything else. It's like the backhand in tennis. Especially short-game, where you're essentially creating a slice backhand, it's much easier to chip when your dominant hand is leading the stroke." Ben Hogan would agree. So would Jordan Spieth, who as a kid had a sweet lefty jump shot and a nasty curveball as a left-handed pitcher.

Around Christmastime of 1973, when Phil was three and a half, he tagged along to Balboa Park Golf Course for a tee time with his dad and grandfather, whom he called Nunu. Santos was slightly peeved. "This won't last," he grumbled.

But Phil powered through the first seventeen holes, swinging with abandon. Walking up the steep fairway of the home hole, the kid whined, "Do we have to play this hole?"

Feeling vindicated at last, Nunu said, "See?"

"If we play it, that means we'll be done."

Little Phil didn't want the round to end. Surely Santos, of all people, could appreciate that kind of grit.

CHAPTER THREE

The putting green in the Mickelson backyard was an oval maybe a dozen steps across at its widest point, garnished with a shallow bunker. On the merits, it was not particularly special. Then again, neither was Bobby Fischer's chessboard or the piano in the Mozart living room in Salzburg. This little practice green, built and lovingly maintained by Phil's dad, is where genius was made, not born. It is fashionable to call Mickelson one of the most naturally talented players ever to pick up a golf club, but that misses the point. "Ah, *talent*," says Bryson DeChambeau, placing a finger on his temple and pretending to blow his brains out. "I hate that word. No one is born with an intrinsic talent for anything. What people call talent is just a skill that has been mastered through hard work."

It's true that Mickelson came from athletic stock. Perhaps as a child his hand-eye coordination was better than most. Being tall for his age (he would top out at six feet, three inches) certainly conferred certain advantages. But the magical chipping and pitching skills that would come to define Mickelson—a monumental advantage around which he built his swashbuckling style of play—was the product of repetition, not some ephemeral gift handed out by the golf gods.

Mickelson was nine when his dad built the putting green in the backyard of their nice-but-not-flashy house in the Del Cerro neighborhood of San Diego. He already had a love affair with the game. It is a treasured piece of family lore that at age three, after being told he couldn't accompany his father to the golf course, Phil ran away from home, carrying his golf bag and a suitcase crammed with golf balls, his favorite blanket, and a stuffed animal named Flopsy. A neighbor spied his escape and instructed him to make four left turns to find the golf course; Mickelson wound up back at his house, where his mom, having been tipped off, was waiting in the driveway. Just shy of his fifth birthday, Phil attended a weeklong junior clinic. On the last day, he won the putting contest against much older kids. That earned Mickelson his first trophy, which he slept with that night. (Having already inculcated how golfers were supposed to look, he insisted on wearing plaid pants and a striped shirt so he looked extra snazzy when his photo was printed in the *San Diego Union-Tribune*.) By the time Mickelson was six, he was spending long days at Presidio Hills, a par-3 course. The owners of the facility were family friends and they watched out for him. It was a user-friendly layout, which gave Mickelson an early taste for going low; he thinks he was seven the first time he broke par. A year later, he was picking the range two or three nights a week at Navajo Canyon so he could have unlimited access to the course. (It would later be renamed Mission Trails.) Mickelson has a favorite story from those days: "Rainy days were my favorite time because nobody else would be there. So I'd put on my rain gear, grab a bucket of balls, and go out under a palm tree. I'd have the entire place as my private driving range—free to hit the ball wherever I wanted. One time, it really started to pour and one of my friends who worked in the pro shop came out and asked me what I was doing. 'This extra practice right here is going to help me win a couple of Masters someday.' That's a true story."

But it was the creation of the backyard green that changed everything. Mickelson would spend hours on end hitting chip after pitch, usually alone, sometimes with his dad. He was so obsessive that eventually his parents installed floodlights so he could practice into the night. There was no swing analysis, no computer spitting out spin rates, just a very curious boy digging the game's secrets out of the dirt: "After a while, I began to notice that the ball would react different ways depending on how my club struck it. So I started to experiment. If I hit it just right, I could make [the ball] back up, or bounce right, or bounce left. I could de-loft the club and watch it roll along the ground. I'd hit it below the equator of the ball and above the equator just to see what would happen. Sometimes my dad and I would try some crazy shots and then talk about why the ball did what it did. It was just fascinating to me." This echoes the naturalistic way another golfing genius, Seve Ballesteros, taught himself the game, as a boy in Spain, by sneaking out of his humble home under the moonlight and onto the grand course across the street where he caddied, Royal Pedreña. "It was a very strange experience to walk around a golf course at night, because all the reference points that help estimate distances vanished," Ballesteros wrote in his autobiography. "I knew where the shot was heading from the way my hands felt the hit and from the sound the ball made when it hit the ground. By practicing at night I learned to feel the grass under my feet, to measure distances intuitively and adjust the power of the strokes I wanted to make."

Mickelson and his dad would play a game in which each had twenty balls and they amassed one point for every shot that settled within a flagstick's length of the hole and two points for a hole out. To make it more challenging, they often threw their balls behind bushes, under trees, or hard against the fence. (The backyard was long enough to accommodate forty-yard pitches.) When his parents weren't around, Mickelson began trying to hit shots over the house, or bend them around corners, which inevitably led to the neighbors having a window and then a sliding door smashed by errant shots; the Peters family took it in stride because they understood the depth of the kid's obsession. Though chipping was Mickelson's favorite activity, he spent a ton of time putting, too. He could also work on his iron game, launching balls over the back fence into the canyon beyond. (Mickelson is careful to point out that these were beat-up range balls that otherwise would have been discarded.)

When the young Phil ventured out of his backyard, he stepped into the best competitive scene imaginable. San Diego had a long history of supporting junior golf, with an engaged community of organizers and financial help from the Century Club, the charitable arm of the annual PGA Tour stop. While the nearby megatropolis of Los Angeles has produced only two players of note (Anthony Kim and Collin Morikawa, though Max Homa is on the verge), San Diego golf's excellence is passed down from generation to generation. "What Phil was doing at a young age, that drove me to be a better player," says Chris Riley, the future Ryder Cupper, who was three and a half years younger than Mickelson. "He pushed a lot of people. But that's what's amazing about this place. I can promise you Phil was chasing Craig Stadler and Scott Simpson, just as they were chasing Billy Casper and Gene Littler. Then Charley Hoffman and me and Pat Perez were chasing Phil. Just like Xander [Schauffele] is chasing those guys now. It just feeds on itself."

From the very beginning, Mickelson had an intense rivalry with Harry Rudolph, a ball-striking savant who a lot of local folks thought had the brighter future of the two. Phil also got to test himself against top international talent: the Junior World Golf Championship, played every summer in San Diego, was without question the premier tournament on the planet for young golfers. It was also a prime opportunity to catch the eye of the college coaches who made up a substantial portion of the gallery. "In those days, you'd get off the plane in San Diego and it felt like you were arriving at the Masters," says Ernie Els, who made an annual pilgrimage from South Africa.

The oldest age division (fifteen to seventeen) competed at Torrey Pines, but younger kids were scattered to different courses around the city. Mickelson's last year to compete in the ten-and-under division was 1980. It was contested at Presidio Hills, a short course with a long history: future Masters champions Casper and Stadler learned to play there, and the first time Tiger Woods competed in the Junior Worlds, at age six, he signed an incorrect scorecard and was disqualified. Presidio consists of eighteen par-3 holes, none longer than seventy-nine yards, which was right in Mickelson's wheelhouse. He won his age group in 1980, what he once joked was his first major championship victory. Surprisingly, Mickelson never won another Junior World title. (In a clash of future titans, he finished runner-up to Els in 1984 in the Boys 13–14 division. Other age-group winners that year included Woods, David Toms, and future LPGA winners Leta Lindley and Joan Pitcock.)

Mickelson loved baseball and still brags about his Little League no-hitter. When he was eleven, he made a local all-star team, which would have entailed a lot of summertime travel, cutting into his planned slate of junior golf tournaments. That was the end of his baseball career . . . at least for a couple of decades. (More on that later.)

By the time Mickelson was a tween, he had already established the contours of an enduring persona. On the golf course he had serious swag—gold chain, popped collar, putter twirls. But he was also noted for his sportsmanship. His father, a taciturn Swede with the discipline of a navy man, didn't brook profanity or displays of ill temper. In the Mickelson family, golf was the carrot and the stick for the young Phil: when he was eleven, he was supposed to play in three junior events across a long Easter weekend, but his parents yanked him out of all of them when he slacked off on his household chores. After that, the Mickelsons rarely had any problems with their son.

He was an extrovert like his mom and had Nunu's gift for gab. Phil delighted in the attention that his early golf success brought. "I still laugh thinking about those San Diego Junior Golf Association awards banquets," says Riley. "Phil won player of the year every time. The other kids who got awards would get up and barely say a word—they were so awkward and shy. Phil worked the room. He would give these three- or four-minute speeches thanking the organizers, the corporate sponsors, the other parents. He was like a little CEO, so polished. He was just different from everybody else his age."

That was especially true on the course. American golf in the 1980s was the epoch of the grinder. The biggest stars—Hale Irwin, Tom Kite, Curtis Strange, Mark O'Meara—plodded their way from point to point, with an emphasis on control and precision. Mickelson, even as a youngster, played a very different game, inspired in part by his hero Ballesteros, whose hot-blooded, imaginative style tipped golf's balance of power to Europe, away from the anodyne Americans. Mickelson was entranced by Ballesteros's victory at the 1980 Masters and used his VCR to watch Seve's swing over and over. This charismatic champion didn't seem bothered by missing fairways, so why should he? Long before Shot-Link data and math nerds would confirm it, Mickelson intuited that the best strategy was to smash a driver on every hole. If he was in the fairway he could pin seek. If he drove it off-line, he could still escape with a short game that was already more Harry Houdini than Harry Vardon. The recovery shots that would become his trademark, and which were often ascribed to God-given talent, were actually the product of intensive trial and error. By thirteen, Mickelson was working at Stardust Country Club. (It would later be renamed Riverwalk.) His parents were members, but the attached driving range was open to the public, so Phil took a job there to have access to free practice balls. "We would hit four or five or six large buckets a day, even when we were supposed to be working," says Jason Peterie, a fellow range-picker and future high school golf rival. "We never tried to do the same robotic swings over and over—we were obsessed with hitting creative shots, weird shots. We spent a solid month hitting 5-irons at the same time, trying to get our balls to collide at their apex. People used to sit there and watch us do it. We came close so many times, and when we finally did it we went absolutely crazy." He remembers sitting in the Mickelson living room watching the 1985 U.S. Open. (As a diversion they would stack golf balls on top of each other; Mickelson, as dexterous as a neurosurgeon, could make a tower of five balls.) When T. C. Chen suffered his infamous double chip, "Phil and I just looked at each other," Peterie says, "and automatically it was like, 'Ohmygawd, we gotta go out there and try that.' It was pouring rain, but we didn't care, we just stood out there getting soaked trying to figure out how to double-hit a chip." Every year they attended the San Diego Open, but they rarely lasted very long at Torrey Pines. "We just wanted to run home and try to hit the shots we had just seen," says Peterie. He is now a teaching pro and he always makes a point to watch when his old friend is in contention on the PGA Tour. He says, "I love how when Phil pulls off some crazy shot and the announcers always say, '*That was one in a million!*' They make it sound like luck. But Phil has spent his whole life practicing and preparing for that exact shot."

As a middle school graduation present, Mickelson traveled to Pinehurst, North Carolina, for a weeklong golf camp. When celebrated instructor Jim McLean gave a bunker clinic, he asked a couple of kids to step into the sand for a demonstration. After their timid efforts, Mickelson volunteered. McLean was beginning to smooth the sand when young Phil dropped a ball into the remnants of a footprint. "That's okay, Mr. McLean, it doesn't matter," he said, and then proceeded to hit his shot stone dead.

"I guess you're right, it doesn't matter," said an amused McLean.

Mickelson also caught the eye of another of the featured instructors, Dean Reinmuth. This wasn't an accident. Already a schmoozer and a networker at four-teen, Mickelson wanted to attend the camp in part so he could get an audience with Reinmuth, who was based in San Diego. "He walked up to me and said, 'When we get back I'd like you to work with me,'" recalls Reinmuth. "I didn't know anything about him, but he carried himself with so much confidence I was intrigued."

After the camp, they jumped right in, focusing on the wild child's long game. Mickelson's handsy swing was highly reliant on timing. He made it work with his irons, but the flaws were magnified when wielding his driver. Reinmuth reshaped his action so it was shorter and more on plane. (Tightening the swing was made more challenging because Mickelson is "the most naturally flexible player I've ever seen," Reinmuth says. "His arms, shoulders, elbows, wrists—he is freakishly flexible.") They also worked extensively on learning how to play a fade off the tee. Mickelson had always favored a hard draw, trying to squeeze out every extra yard. Of course, a draw can easily turn into a fatal hook, which is why Ben Hogan once said of drawing a driver, "It's like a rattlesnake in your pocket." A favored venue for San Diego junior events was Chula Vista Municipal Golf Course, which has a creek that runs down the right side of many of the holes. "We always knew Phil was going to hook two or three balls into that creek every round," says Peterie. "That was the only thing that gave the rest of us a chance. I'll never forget when he started playing that fade. It was like, *Oh crap, it's all over now.*"

But Mickelson didn't have the discipline to employ the safe, conservative shot over and over. It didn't help that another of Reinmuth's teenage pupils, Keith Sbarbaro, was more mature physically than Mickelson and crazy long for his age. Not for the last time, Phil became obsessed with chasing distance. On the golf course a battle raged within, and this tension was often expressed when he stepped to the tee. "Phil has always had beautiful rhythm with his irons," Reinmuth says. "The great drivers of the golf ball, they have a rhythm that never changes. Think about a long tennis rally—what breaks the rhythm is usually one player taking a chance. Phil was capable of hitting fairways, but then he'd go after it and try to hit the equivalent of a winner in tennis. Sometimes it worked, sometimes it didn't. It's just a different mentality of how to play the game."

Mickelson matriculated to the University of San Diego High School in Del Mar. Uni, as it was always called before being renamed Cathedral Catholic, had more than a passing resemblance to the fictitious Ridgemont High that lit up silver screens a couple years before Mickelson reached high school. Amid the flip-flopped surfers and beach bums, the cut of Mickelson's jib was unforgettable: polyester slacks, stiff-collared polo, belts with ostentatious buckles, visor. Every day right after school, Mickelson proceeded directly to the golf course, so he figured he might as well save time and dress like a PGA Tour player on school mornings. Throw in his perennially good grades, his predilection for brownnosing teachers, and the fact that he didn't drink alcohol or go to parties (his father is a teetotaler), and the conclusion is inescapable: "I hate to say this," says Peterie, "but he was kind of a nerd."

Mickelson's single-minded devotion—he was already fond of quoting the Ben Hogan maxim "Every day that you don't practice is one day longer before you achieve greatness"—was already paying big dividends. In 1985, when he was fifteen, Mickelson won his first AJGA tournament, announcing that he was a national and not just a provincial talent. Mary had gone back to work as a marketing director at a retirement home to help subsidize her son's golf dreams. Phil was able to fly for free to the out-of-state tournaments on account of his dad being a commercial pilot, but, he says, "Problem was, you could always get bumped. If I called ahead to see whether a flight was open, by the time I got to the airport, maybe it wasn't open. If the flight before was canceled because of weather or whatever, all the overflow would go on the flight I wanted, so I was out. I spent a lot of nights sleeping in those hub cities like Detroit, Minneapolis, and Memphis. I was big in the Memphis airport."

Even the teenage Phil's love life had a golf angle, as he began dating Tana Rey Figueras, who was good enough to play on the Uni boys' team. She would go on to represent California in the Junior America's Cup and twice compete in the U.S. Girls' Junior Championship. They would often practice together, and Mickelson delighted in breaking down her game in granular detail. Says Reinmuth, "Phil once said to me, 'Tana asked me how to hit a shot, so I told her you have to do this, this, this, and this. And she said, *Oh, I can't think of all of those things during the swing.* So I showed her how to hit it and explained it a different way, but she didn't get it. I kept trying, but I don't think she ever got it.'" This was his version of flirting.

Among San Diego high school golfers of a certain age, Figueras still stirs feelings. "Ah, Tana Rey," says Michael Zucchet, who played for crosstown La Jolla High School. "She had an otherwise normal body, but absolutely gigantic breasts. You take a bunch of teenaged boys and we were just mesmerized how she could swing a club around them." That Tana Rey was Mickelson's girlfriend only added to his aura as he dominated the local high school scene. "Think about the Phil that won the Phoenix Open when he was in college," says Zucchet. "You know that tan, smart-ass, cocky, putter-twirling, shirt-collar-up fucker who won a Tour event in college? That was Phil Mickelson in high school. He had so much swagger but, unfortunately, he could back it up. He would show up at matches holding hands with Tana Rey and with a big, cheesy grin, and that just added to the annoyance of it all when he went out and beat us."

The summer before his senior year, in 1987, Mickelson cemented his standing as the best junior golfer in the country, tying the AJGA record by winning four tournaments in a season. (Woods would match the feat in 1991 and '92.) He had already crushed the spirit of his putative crosstown rival, Rudolph, who much later would say, "You don't realize at the time the guy's going to be a Hall of Fame player. I was constantly being compared to him and that got old. I'd play some pretty good golf. I'd shoot a 69 and he'd shoot a 65, and people would say, 'You got beat by the Mickelson kid again.' I wish I could go back in time and tell those people, 'See, I was losing to the Jack Nicklaus of my era.'"

Mickelson's senior season was turbocharged by the arrival of Manny Zerman, a squat, intense South African who enrolled at Uni for his final year of high school. In the preceding four Junior Worlds, Zerman had two third-place finishes and a pair of runner-ups. Along the way he became close with his host family and they invited him to live with them full-time as a senior to facilitate the college recruiting process. Zerman had none of Mickelson's flair, but he brought a monk-like dedication to practicing, often going to the range at six a.m. before school. "That's going to help the team immensely," Mickelson said at the time about his new teammate's fervor. "It was easy for me to slack off on easy matches, but he'll push me. To beat him, I'll have to play as well as I can. He inspires me. He practices all the time. If I'm not, I know I'm losing ground."

So Mickelson's game was razor-sharp when the PGA Tour rolled into town for the 1988 San Diego Open. (Aficionados of over-the-top corporate names will be delighted to hear that the tournament was officially known as the Shearson Lehman Hutton Andy Williams Open.) To the surprise of no one, Mickelson played his way into the field through open qualifying. He would be making his Tour debut, at seventeen.

Ever the maneuverer, Mickelson lined up a practice round with the great Ballesteros, who recognized the kid's duende. "I was impressed with him," Ballesteros said. "If somebody hadn't told me he was seventeen, I would have thought he was twenty-one or twenty-two." But in what sounded like a self-referential critique, he added, "So often, a young golfer will do the difficult things good and do the easy things bad."

Figueras served as Mickelson's caddie for the first round. His gallery included his parents, Reinmuth, and various cousins and neighbors. Riley was there, too. He says, "Phil was standing on the [practice] putting green and he looked so confident. He wanted people to notice him. He wanted to be great. That's a big part of it. I didn't have that at all."

On Torrey's challenging South Course, Mickelson buried a thirty-five-footer on the second hole and stood two under par through ten holes. But he wobbled coming home, missing a three-footer on sixteen and then a two-foot tap-in on the next hole, leading to a double bogey. After his 74, Mickelson said, "I don't really know what happened on those short putts. I do know that I was getting a little tired at the end. I didn't feel nervous, but . . ."

The next day he shot 71 to miss the cut. His first brush with the big time hadn't gone exactly as he'd imagined, but the young master left Torrey Pines feeling undeterred. "The takeaway for Phil wasn't that he missed the cut," says Reinmuth. "It was how comfortable he felt out there. He felt like he belonged."

CHAPTER FOUR

Steve Loy played on the football and golf teams at Eastern New Mexico University, a most unusual combination. After graduating in 1974, Loy worked as an oil wildcatter. A year later he drifted back to golf, taking a coaching position at Scottsdale Community College. Over eight seasons, he built a mini-dynasty with the Fighting Artichokes (we're not making this up), winning two national championships and with Loy twice being named the national junior college coach of the year. In 1984, Loy finally got his big break, getting hired as the head coach at Arkansas. That same year, another golf-football hybrid arrived in Fayetteville. This kid was a punter and place-kicker on a championship high school football team in Missouri, as well as the state amateur champion in golf. But John Daly looked like he had swallowed a beach ball whole when he arrived at Arkansas. Loy told him he had to lose sixty pounds if he ever wanted to suit up for the Razorbacks. The coach offered some old-school dieting advice.

"He was a smoker," Daly says now, "so he told me to start smoking cigarettes because it would kill my appetite. It worked—I lost the weight. And I got addicted to smoking. Great, huh? It'll probably kill me, but I don't think I could ever stop, to be honest with you. But I don't know, if I hadn't started smoking I would not have lost the weight and gotten to play. I guess it's a catch-20/20."

Daly had a drinking problem to go with his nicotine addiction and he clashed often with Loy. But he retains a grudging respect: "He was a helluva coach. He was strict. Very organized, very army-like. It couldn't have been easy dealing with a bunch of shitheads like us."

Loy loved to make his players run wind sprints at six a.m., or have them fill their golf bags with rocks and walk eighteen holes as punishment for sub-standard play. In addressing his team, he channeled Mike Ditka, not Tony Jacklin. "His speeches were crazy," says Daly. "Eyes poppin' out, spit flyin' everywhere. It was like we were goin' to war, not playing golf against the Texas Fucking Longhorns, you know what I mean?"

Loy was just crazy enough to think he had a shot at recruiting Phil Fucking Mickelson. He first approached him at an AJGA tournament when Mickelson was fifteen. Loy spotted him walking down a fairway and tried to summon all of his oily charm. "Hi, Phil," he said in his gentle voice. "I'm Steve Loy, the new golf coach at the University of Arkansas."

Mickelson, the golden boy from the Golden State, couldn't even pretend to be interested in going to Arkansas. "Riiiiiight," was all he said in return, without ever breaking stride.

Loy's kicker to the story: "I guess we both knew that was probably the last time I'd be talking to Phil Mickelson."

But during the phenom's senior year of high school, Loy snagged the head coach position at Arizona State. Nearly sixty schools recruited Mickelson, but from the beginning he was intrigued by the notion of taking his talents to the desert. He wanted to get out of the fishbowl of Southern California, but not be too far from home. There was already a pipeline of talent flowing from San Diego to the Arizona schools, including Manny Zerman and Harry Rudolph, both of whom committed to the U of A. They were joined there by a fero-cious grinder with a ridiculous swing—Jim Furyk. If Mickelson had gone to Arizona it could have been a team for the ages, but there was a complicating factor: Tana Rey Figueras. She was on her way to Arizona State to play for the women's team. And so Loy did, in fact, get another conversation with Mickelson. A few of them, and eventually Phil the Thrill committed to the Sun Devils.

College golf would never be the same.

Mickelson joined a talented, eclectic squad in Tempe. The team leader was senior Jim Strickland, a dandy and a dedicated skirt chaser. Per-Ulrik Johansson was another prized freshman but couldn't have been more different from Mickelson, in both his game and constitution. A native of Sweden, Johansson played with a Scandinavian rectitude, carefully maneuvering around the golf course. While teammates slept in and ate leftover pizza for breakfast, Johansson started every morning with a thousand sit-ups and two hundred push-ups and subsisted on a diet that seemed to consist of twigs and berries. The rest of the roster was brimming with blue-chip talent. (If you can't recruit at Arizona State, you can't recruit.) Practice had the energy of stags rutting. "Our version of team spirit was trying to beat each other's brains in every day," says Scott Frisch. "We figured if we could beat each other, we could beat every other team out there."

Money games in practice were common, and a standard bet was a $20 Nassau with one-down automatic presses. Birdies paid out $5, eagles $25, hole outs $50. "Press when pissed" was the team rule. The betting could get so out of hand that after one player lost $500—a monumental sum for a college kid—a team meeting had to be called to turn down the temperature. Little wonder that Mickelson thrived in this hypercompetitve environment. In his first college tournament, at LSU, he shot 71-69-72 to finish second.

"I was so proud of him," says Strickland. "What an accomplishment for an eighteen-year-old kid playing in his very first college tournament. I went up to him and said congratulations and I'll never forget the look he gave me. It was piercing. He practically growled at me: 'How could you possibly think that second place is good?' He was just a complete outlier from the rest of us."

Mickelson still possessed his all-world short game, but now he was maturing physically. "Phil's swing was so long and flowing and his ball just stayed in the air forever, like a Frisbee," says teammate John Bizik. "He generated effortless speed."

Over the final three tournaments of the fall season, Mickelson went third-second-third. As they did at the end of every semester, the Sun Devils gathered for what they called the Beer Bash Scramble. They would travel to an out-of-the-way public course and pay the greens fees, like regular customers. To avoid getting busted, ASU logos were verboten. (Most players wound up shirtless anyway.) The roster was split into two-man teams to play better ball, and the rules were simple: each player had to drink one beer per hole. A team bogey meant each player had to take an additional shot of Jose Cuervo. Mickelson, the high school square, had yet to acquire a taste for alcohol. He was paired with the clean-living Johansson, a future Ryder Cupper and six-time winner on the European Tour. "They were already two of the best players in college golf," says Frisch, "but they were going up against professional drinkers." No one can remember exactly how many holes it took for Mickelson to puke, but it wasn't many. He never played in another Beer Bash. "You can't be good at everything," Frisch says. At least one player wound up walking through the desert barefoot. Somehow the winning score was a 59 or 60; which team actually took possession of the oversized trophy has been lost to the sands of time.

Amid all these hijinks there was a larger culture clash brewing between Loy and his players. He had imported some of his hard-ass coaching techniques from Arkansas; sometimes in practice matches, if a player lost a hole he was made to carry his teammate's bag down the next fairway. On a squad of freewheelers, Loy tried to institute a rigid course management system in which he ordained how certain holes were to be played. This went over like a fart in church, especially because as the season wore on players at the bottom of the roster began to notice that Mickelson was given more latitude in how he attacked a golf course. "Yeah, Phil was treated different," says Strickland, "because he is different."

This extended to his wardrobe. Thanks to John Ashworth and others, golf fashion had begun to evolve; even Oklahoma State was now rocking Ralph Lauren for its team uniforms. But Mickelson was stuck in a different sartorial era. "He dressed like Ed Fiori," says Rob Mangini. On a campus in which the unofficial uniform was shorts and a T-shirt, Mickelson was still strutting around in Sansabelt slacks and hard-collared polos in colors so garish Liberace would have blushed. Strickland begged Mickelson to loosen up. "He was hurting the reputation of the entire team!" he says.

But on the golf course, Mickelson was in full flight. At the 1989 natty, he was the only player to break par on a brutal setup at Oak Tree Country Club, becoming one of only five freshmen to win the individual NCAA Championship. It had been a helluva season and his teammates were in the mood to celebrate. Led by Strickland, a few of them broke into Mickelson's dorm room and nabbed the most offensive garments in his wardrobe. They marched down to a fire pit near the volleyball courts and set them all ablaze.

Mickelson came out smoking for his sophomore year, winning two of the first four tournaments. He was still dating Figueras, but his teammates began to discern a pattern. "Every time Phil won a tournament he would dump poor Tana Rey," says Frisch. "There are a lot of fish in the sea at ASU. I guess he wanted to see if the golf success would translate. It must not have, because he always wound up back with her." The ASU women's team was stacked, with a roster that included future LPGA winners Brandie Burton and Pearl Sinn. In part because of the Mickelson-Figueras union, there was a strong connection between the teams. They would occasionally have coed competitions in practice and host joint parties on the weekend.

The men's team further embraced the rituals of male bonding. Late-night gin games were common, usually instigated by Mickelson. They played many different sports together. "We had some sneaky-good athletes on that team," says Mangini. Pickup games of "two-hand shove" football were common, and Mangini offers this scouting report on Mickelson: "Elite thrower of the football, but can't run for shit." There were sand volleyball courts on campus and the golf team regularly haunted them. Mickelson had a jump serve that was almost impossible to return, but he only got about one-in-five in play, which is extremely on-brand. Mangini and Dave Cunningham had been decorated high school basketball players, so the pickup hoop was cutthroat. Mickelson towered over most of his teammates, but it should come as no surprise that he liked to hang out around the arc and hoist three-pointers. He could do damage on the rare occasions he ventured into the paint. "I don't think you can use this expression anymore, but he's what we used to call 'retard strong,'" says Mangini. "Look at Phil's hands. They look like DeMarcus Ware's—he can grab you like a defensive end and just envelop you."

On the golf course, ASU was emerging as a powerhouse. At the Sun Devil Thunderbird Invitational, the host school entered two different squads . . .

and the B-team won the event. At the Pac-10 Championship, ASU won by a whopping fifty-four shots, with Mickelson taking individual honors. By the spring of 1990, Tempe was the center of the college golf universe, as both ASU's men's and women's teams were at the summit of the top-20 polls. The women came through first, winning the first golf national championship in school history. "The energy was amazing," says Mangini. "The whole place was on fire. You couldn't have had a better college experience." Two weeks later, the men brought home their own national title, though it wasn't without a little controversy: the team got busted for hitting golf balls off the balcony of their tenth-story hotel rooms into the parking lot below. (Perhaps they should not have used ASU logo balls?) Mickelson tamed Innisbrook, site of the PGA Tour's annual Valspar Championship, to join Ben Crenshaw as the only players to win the NCAA individual crown as a freshman and sophomore. He was already on the short list of the greatest college golfers ever. But there was still a gaping hole in Mickelson's résumé that needed to be filled.

The 1990 U.S. Amateur was played at Cherry Hills in Denver, famous as the venue where Arnold Palmer—Mickelson's spiritual forebear in both style of play and fan interaction—won his only U.S. Open, in 1960. That Phil had never claimed a USGA event to that point in his career was a head-scratcher, given the scale of his success. For amateurs, USGA events were, and remain, far and away the most prestigious championships. (In 1991, Tiger Woods—five and a half years younger than Mickelson—would win the first of three straight U.S. Juniors, which would be followed by three straight U.S. Amateurs, a match play winning streak that might be the single most impressive accomplishment of a legendary career.) Mickelson was the overwhelming favorite at Cherry Hills, and during the second round of thirty-six-hole stroke-play qualifying, he shot a then-record 64, adding to the feeling of inevitability. "If I play the way I've been playing, I don't think I'll get beat," Mickelson woofed. "I'm playing as good as I've ever played. Every facet of my game is one hundred percent right now. Whoever I play, I'd be intimidated (if I were them). Why shouldn't they be?"

In the second round of match play, Mickelson faced Jeff Thomas, a New Jersey legend. Thomas was a brawler and a boozer, and his had been a hard-knock life. His mom died when he was young and he had to scrape to survive; he got fired from a caddie job at Plainfield Country Club while in high school for having stolen a member's Ping putter. Thomas grew into a rebel in pleated pants. A victory in the U.S. Mid-Am got him invited to the Masters, where he snuck groupies into his accommodations within the Augusta National club-house for dangerous liaisons and sold his caddying job to the highest bidder. On the thirteenth hole of the first round, he left himself a fifteen-footer for eagle but had to putt with his 2-iron because his clueless looper had abandoned his putter next to the twelfth green. By the time Thomas roared down Magnolia Lane in his beat-up old Cadillac after missing the cut, the green jackets had made it clear he would never be invited back, no matter which tournaments he won. Thomas had enough of an edge that he didn't fear a pretty boy like Mickelson, regardless of how outsized his reputation might be. "Jeff was brash and fiery and he loved the mental aspect of match play," says John Doherty, his caddie at the 1990 U.S. Amateur. "He was always angling for an advantage. He would try to get underneath your skin, push the rules, whatever he could get away with. He loved the gamesmanship." Doherty recalls standing on the range with Thomas, watching Mickelson warm up. "He had the collar up, his college coach was on the bag, he carried himself like a Tour player," Doherty says. "I could see in Jeff's face he knew he was going to have to play his best. He was fired up for the challenge." But on the very first hole, a short par-4 that Palmer famously drove in the final round to begin his comeback at the Open, Thomas left himself a very long par putt, while Mickelson had stuffed his approach shot to four feet for birdie. In an all-time alpha move, Phil conceded Thomas's putt. "I'll never forget the look he gave me," Mickelson says. "It was just funny. Why did I do that? Well, he took like two minutes to hit the chip shot and hit it forty feet by the hole. Then he started the process again, and I just thought, *Pick it up.*"

Mickelson had chosen psychology as his major at ASU, and he had to know the concession would have a larger effect than just speeding up play. He poured in his birdie putt to win the hole and went on to thrash Thomas, 6 & 5.

"That was the biggest dose of mental intimidation I've ever seen in my life," says Doherty, who would go on to caddie in more than seventy USGA events. "Jeff was never the same after that. Talk about confidence. Talk about backing it up. What Jeff always strived to do to other players, Phil did it to him."

"There has always been gamesmanship in match play, but this was something else," says John Garrity, who covered that Amateur for *Sports Illustrated*. "This was emasculation. Phil psychologically destroyed his opponent on the first hole, and at that point the match was essentially over. Word of what happened traveled very quickly among the other competitors. There was a mixed reaction. Some thought it was kind of a snotty thing to do, that Phil was a show-off. But there was also total admiration that any player could have the confidence, or you might say the balls, to pull it off."

Thirteen years later, Thomas's body was found in the cheap hotel room he had been living in on the outskirts of Palm Beach, Florida; he died from a drug overdose. No one is suggesting Mickelson bears any responsibility, but the humiliation at Cherry Hills shadowed Thomas until his dying breath. "Everybody always asked him about it," says Doherty, who remained Thomas's close friend. "He would be berated and battered about it. He tried to blow it off, but it always bothered him. It became part of his identity. It was just one more bad thing in a life that had a lot of dark spots."

Mickelson faced Mike Swingle in the third round of the Amateur. He was a steady, fairways-and-greens kind of player, and Swingle led 1-up through fifteen holes. Number sixteen is a long par-4 with a creek that cuts across the fairway and then meanders left of the green. Mickelson hooked his tee shot into the gnarly rough, and his path to the putting surface was stymied by a tree. So he aimed at the creek left of the green and, with a 7-iron, played what he called a sixty-yard hook, leaving his ball twenty feet from the hole. "It was crazy how much that ball curved," Swingle says. "For a long time Phil called it the best shot he ever hit in competition. I was in the middle of the fairway and he put his ball inside of mine." Then Mickelson made the putt to win the hole.

On the tee of the par-5 seventeenth hole—where Ben Hogan lost the 1960 U.S. Open by spinning his third shot back into the fronting pond—Mickelson unsheathed his secret weapon. In shades of things to come, he had put in play a forty-five-inch driver, which was a full inch and a half longer than most other competitors' of that era. His logic was simple: "I could reach that par-5 [seventeenth] and no one else could and I needed to take advantage of that." Swingle elected to lay up with a 1-iron off the tee. "That fairway was so narrow and I didn't think it was reachable anyway," he says. "Phil was taking a big risk late in the match." But Mickelson smashed a perfect drive and then got home with a 3-wood, setting up an easy two-putt birdie that won the hole; he closed out the match on eighteen. "Bottom line, he hit three incredible shots in a row when he had to," says Swingle, who today is the owner of Issaquah Coffee Company, a popular café on the outskirts of Seattle. "Any of those go sideways, he's in trouble. I played the smart shots and it didn't work out. That's probably why he's Phil Mickelson and I'm selling coffee."

In the quarterfinals, Mickelson fought off a game Bob May—who ten years later would engage Woods in an unforgettable tussle at the 2000 PGA Championship—and then in the semis he overwhelmed David Eger, 5 & 3. That set up a juicy thirty-six-hole final versus Manny Zerman, his onetime high school teammate and now archrival at the University of Arizona. Mickelson was not exactly collegial: he won four holes in a row starting at number two to put a ton of pressure on Zerman. But the gritty South African fought back in the afternoon round, and after coming within inches of an ace on the sixth hole, Zerman was only 1-down. Two holes later, he was poised to square the match after chipping in for birdie. But Mickelson topped him with a twenty-footer that was good as soon as it left the putter blade. Looking back, Zerman offers a succinct play-by-play: "Fuckin' A, same shit as always." An ensuing burst of birdies by Mickelson ended the match, 5 & 4. The 1960 U.S. Open at Cherry Hills was where Jack Nicklaus announced himself to the golf world, pushing Palmer to the brink as a chubby twenty-year-old amateur. Now Mickelson had joined Big Jack as the only players in golf history to win the NCAA Championship and U.S. Amateur in the same year. He was the Bear apparent.

Mickelson won the first tournament of his junior year, assuaging any concern around Arizona State that he might grow complacent. But even as he continued to dominate college golf, he had his eye on a bigger prize: the PGA Tour's Tucson Open. As a sophomore, in 1990, Mickelson had been given a sponsor's exemption and he finished a very solid nineteenth. His game had gone to another level since then. "Phil had that tournament circled on his calendar for a long time," says Dean Reinmuth. "He knew in his heart he was good enough to win it."

The Tucson Open was a sleepy event played at the tail end of the Tour's West Coast swing, but it had a rich history dating to 1945. In a twelve-year stretch beginning in 1967, the champions included Palmer, Tom Watson, Lee Trevino twice, and Johnny Miller three times, including a signature nine-stroke blowout in '75. Mickelson became obsessed with joining the ranks of these champions and, in the months before the '91 tournament, often made the hour-and-a-half drive from Tempe to learn the nuances of the host venues, Starr Pass and Tucson National.

"A few months before the tournament I went out for a quick twilight round at Starr Pass," says Gary McCord, who was then winding down his long and unfruitful playing career. "I'm on the fifteenth green and this tall, skinny kid walks up. It's Phil. I knew who he was, of course, but we'd never met. He says, 'I've been out here all day working on my game, but since it's getting dark, why don't we have some fun?' He proposed that we play the last three holes with him using my clubs and me using his. For a hundred dollars a hole. I should've known right then it was a bad bet, because what college kid can afford to play for a hundred dollars a hole? But I had been working with Mac O'Grady"—the famously ambidextrous (and eccentric) Tour pro turned teacher—"and I was pretty good left-handed, so I took the bet. Well, Phil won the sixteenth hole, the seventeenth hole, and the eighteenth hole. He cleaned me out, shook my hand, and disappeared, probably to have a nice dinner with my money. It wasn't until later that I learned he's naturally right-handed."

When the tournament proper began, Mickelson roared to the top of the leaderboard with an opening 65. He wobbled a bit in the second round, with a 71, but caught fire on Saturday, playing the front nine in a mere twenty-nine strokes. After Mickelson drove the green of the par-4 sixth hole, Hal Sutton whispered to the omnipresent Steve Loy, who was serving as a caddie, "You know, Coach, I'll sure be glad when he grows up and gets a little fear in his blood." Mickelson's 65 staked him to a two-stroke lead.

On Sunday he would have to tangle with seasoned veterans. Mickelson was paired with future U.S. Open champion Corey Pavin. Also in the mix was Bob Tway, winner of the 1986 PGA Championship, and Tom Purtzer, whom the cognoscenti considered to have one of the sweetest swings in the game. Mickelson was clinging to a one-stroke lead when he arrived at the par-5 fourteenth tee. His ASU teammates had driven over and were part of a large, raucous gallery trying to carry him home. But Phil is Phil and it was never going to be a boring stroll to victory. On the fourteenth tee, he uncorked a wild hook that sent his ball into the recesses of a deep, dark canyon. It was playing as a lateral hazard, so he took a penalty drop . . . and then smothered a 3-iron into another unplayable lie. When the hole mercifully ended, Mickelson had taken an 8, pretty much the only way to make a snowman in the desert. He tumbled into a tie for fifth, two shots behind Purtzer. But Mickelson rallied to make a birdie at sixteen to stay in the fight. Up ahead on the eighteenth hole, Purtzer hit a perfect tee shot, but was left between a pitching wedge and a three-quarter 9-iron. "I shoulda hit the wedge," he says now with a sigh. He took too much off the 9 and his ball fluttered into the front bunker. Purtzer tried to get too cute with the ensuing shot and left it in the sand. Double bogey. Tie ball game.

The crowd was in full throat when Mickelson arrived at the home hole. He hit a good drive and then rifled a wedge at the flag, leaving himself ten feet for the win. Otherwise, a playoff with Purtzer and Tway loomed. Loy lumbered over to ask his man if he needed help with the read.

"No thanks, Coach," Mickelson said. "I've got this. Just get out of the way."

Purtzer and Tway gathered by the green for their denouement. "Back then he putted like a god," says Purtzer, one of many to invoke the almighty in describing the young Mickelson's supernatural gifts. "It was a big moment for an amateur, sure, but I would've been shocked if he missed it. Well, he rolled it in like it was nothing. Me and Tway looked at each other, shook hands, and said, 'We'll get him next time.' But I think both of us knew that wasn't going to be easy."

Pavin, rightfully celebrated as one of the game's grittiest, guttiest grinders, was dazzled by the kid's perseverance after the brutal triple bogey. "I've never seen anyone come back from something like that," he said.

Three decades later, as various tributes to the win were popping up on social media, I asked Mickelson what emotions they stirred. He focused not on any particular shot, but on the cringey nature of his post-round interviews. "I can't believe how babyish I sounded," he said.

As an avowed amateur, Mickelson had to forfeit the $180,000 winner's check, but he kept the coveted three-year exemption onto the PGA Tour, securing his place in the firmament. A couple of months after Tucson, he made his Masters debut, cashing in the invitation that came with winning the U.S. Amateur. Mickelson shot 69 in his first competitive round at Augusta National, which left him tied for ninth, one shot behind a fella named Nicklaus. The audacious debut only added to the feeling that Mickelson was born to play that golf course. In the ensuing months, he would also make the cut at the U.S. Open and Open Championship, further cranking up the hype machine. Mickelson was building a solid-gold brand and he knew it was about a persona that was as flashy as his game. "A golfer is an entertainer, much like an actor," he said at the time. "People pay money to go out and watch you play, and I don't think they pay just to watch you hit a drive down the middle, hit a shot on the green, and two-putt. That's why Lee Trevino and Fuzzy Zoeller are so popular. They are entertainers as well as golfers." Mickelson's future was unlimited . . . as long as he could avoid saying something stupid.

The 1991 Walker Cup was always going to be overheated. It was being played for the first time in Ireland, at Portmarnock, a stern links outside of Dublin. Three Irish lads led the team, headlined by future major champion Padraig Harrington and Paul McGinley, who would go on to be a Ryder Cup hero as a player and captain. In the previous playing, Great Britain & Ireland had claimed the Cup for the first time since 1971. The Americans were hell-bent on revenge, most especially Mickelson, who had gone a disappointing 1-1-2 in '89. The U.S. team touched down in Ireland with maybe its best team

ever: Mickelson, David Duval, Bob May, future PGA Tour winner Tom Scher-
rer, Allen Doyle (who would go on to win eleven tournaments on the Senior
Tour), and cocktail circuit legend Jay Sigel, who was playing in his record-
tying eighth Walker Cup. "We knew it was going to be a war," says Paul Mc-
Ginley, but no one expected it would play out in the tabloids. Then, following
a practice round, Mickelson was asked by a TV reporter about having hit an
errant drive into the gallery. He replied, "That's not a place I want to be. The
Irish women are not that attractive."

Hooo boy.

"That comment went ripping through the press tent like a virus," says Garrity, once again the man on the ground for *Sports Illustrated*. "It was like a scene
in the movies, with everyone in the press room rushing to their phones to call
back to their paper." The Irish headline writers pounced: "BAD BOY PHIL!"
screamed one. Another blared, "MASTERFUL MICKELSON DRAWS
IRISH IRE." It became an actual international incident; as the U.S. team was
leaving the course, their bus ground to a halt and Mickelson had to disembark
to film an apology being demanded by the Irish consulate. "He was very, very
distraught about the whole thing," says May. "He didn't mean to hurt people.
It was just Phil being Phil, but obviously this time it didn't work out very well."
Among the tweedy golf officials at Portmarnock, only David Fay of the USGA
had any sense of humor about the incident, as he spent the week humming the
Beach Boys: "*I wish they all could be California girllllllls. . . .*"

Never a shrinking violet, Mickelson created more of a stir during a first-
day singles match against Andrew Coltart, a future European Tour winner
whose on-course visage evoked Ebenezer Scrooge. On the ninth hole, Coltart
didn't concede a putt of around eighteen inches. With a typically rakish grin,
Mickelson held his putter parallel to the ground to make clear that his ball was
"inside the leather." Unmoved, Coltart made him putt the putative gimme
and afterward went off on Mickelson, calling him an "arrogant so-and-so."
But Mickelson had the last word, winning 4 & 3. "To this day we kid Coltart
about that," says McGinley. "If someone has a short putt, a fellow in the group
will invariably say, 'That wouldn't be a gimme if you're playing with Mickelson, would it?' Thirty years later he's still sore about it."

At the Walker Cup there are twenty-four points up for grabs. The U.S. led 8–4 heading into the second of two days of competition, but GB&I mounted a spirited rally, taking three of the four points in the morning foursomes. In the ensuing singles session, Mickelson was sent out first to blunt the opposition's momentum, and his point became crucial with the U.S. losing three of the four matches immediately behind him. Playing the eighteenth hole, he was clinging to a 1-up lead over Jim Milligan, who had been the hero of GB&I's upset two years earlier. Mickelson missed the final green on the short-side left, his ball settling in a recessed collection area. The pin was cut just a few paces beyond a swale he would have to negotiate. He had a slightly downhill lie on firm, closely cropped turf. "At that stage, pretty much every other player who has ever lived would have reached for the putter," says McGinley. That was the smart play. Mickelson snatched his 60-degree wedge and a murmur went through the Irish women, and men, in the gallery. If he didn't clip his ball absolutely perfectly, it would likely roll back to his feet, a titanic embarrassment that could also cost his country the Walker Cup. "It was madness, really," says McGinley. "But that's the kind of balls he had." Mickelson took an almighty swing, sending his Titleist toward the heavens. It landed gently two feet from the hole. Game over. Mickelson won the match and the U.S. wrested back the Walker Cup.

"You can't imagine the pressure he was under, because of the accumulated strain of being portrayed as the Ugly American for the whole week," says Garrity. "Inevitably, his became the crucial match. You think about the reputation he brought into that event, the scrutiny he had put himself under, the degree of difficulty of the shot he was facing with the whole Walker Cup potentially riding on it. . . . Goodness, that flop shot has to rank as the greatest pressure shot I've ever witnessed."

Mickelson would have instantly been among the biggest stars in the game if he had turned pro after the Walker Cup, but he returned to Arizona State for his senior year. He had promised his parents he would earn a degree. He was also influenced by a chat he'd had with Nicklaus, who left Ohio State at the age of twenty. For decades, the PGA Tour printed phone book–sized media guides that listed a player's basic data, including their college affiliation. Those who earned a degree had it noted next to the school name. Nicklaus had always been nettled that he didn't have a bachelor of arts to display in the media guide. The schoolwork wasn't onerous because Mickelson has what he likes to call a photographic memory. "He would take my notebook," says Mangini, "and study it for a while and then get a 100 on the test. Then he'd look at all the questions I missed and, without ever looking at the notebook again, tell me exactly where I could find the right answer: 'You dumbass, it's in your notes midway down the third page. It's right there in your own handwriting, dickhead.'"

Anyway, Mickelson was having too much fun in Tempe to think about leaving it behind prematurely.

"After he won Tucson I asked him if he was gonna drop out of school and go play the [PGA Tour's] Florida swing," says Strickland. "He said, 'Hell, no. All I won is a hundred and eighty grand—who cares? I'm going to have plenty of money. But you can never get back your college years.'"

Mickelson was also juiced by the growing rivalry with Arizona. In the spring of his junior year, the Wildcats and Sun Devils were locked in a shoot-out at the Golf Digest Collegiate Invitational, at the Woodlands outside of Houston. On the last hole, Mickelson drove it down the middle of a rain-saturated fairway. Matched against Zerman, per usual, he asked for a free drop from casual water. "What he really wanted was to wipe the mud off the back of his ball when taking the drop," Zerman says. He didn't see any puddles and denied the drop. Mickelson took his stance and, pressing down with his size 13 clodhoppers, was able to get some water to ooze out of the turf. Zerman said that Mickelson's squatting and bouncing did not constitute his normal stance and reiterated that no drop was forthcoming. Pissed, Mickelson whipped out his 7-iron, calculated the effects of the glob of mud on his ball, and promptly holed out his approach shot from 160 yards. Arizona coach Rick LaRose sidled up to Zerman and said, "The next time Phil Mickelson wants a drop, give it to him. Don't make him mad." Aided by the mic-drop eagle, Mickelson won the individual crown, but Arizona nabbed the team title.

The Wildcats and Sun Devils went at it again at the 1992 NCAAs, the swan song to Mickelson's college career. He was a first-team All-American for the fourth straight season and about to win his third straight Haskins Award as the male college player of the year. He shot a career-low 63 in the first round, pretty much ending any suspense as to whether or not he would join Ben Crenshaw as the only three-time NCAA individual champ. (The sixteenth career win was a collegiate record.) But on the final day, Mickelson stumbled to a closing 74 and Arizona raced by ASU to steal the national championship, a bittersweet end to an incomparable undergraduate career.

Mickelson turned pro for the 1992 U.S. Open at Pebble Beach. In the opening round, he shot a smooth 68 to surge into a tie for third. With the previous two Opens at Pebble having been won by Nicklaus and Watson, many of the Friday papers trumpeted the arrival of American golf's next generational talent. But Mickelson went out and shot 80 to miss the cut, the perfect beginning to his star-crossed, love-hate relationship with the national championship.

Mickelson was still living in the desert, and not long after the U.S. Open he ventured to a Guns N' Roses concert in a remote location in West Phoenix. A freak flash flood turned the dirt parking lots and egress roads into quagmires, so Mickelson and his buddies slept in their car. They pulled into his friend's apartment complex the next morning, looking a little rough. Bounding down the stairs was a perky blonde who lived above the friend's apartment. Mickelson had heard a lot about this ASU coed—the romance with Tana Rey was finally kaput—but they had not met. (Phil's excuse: "I never took the time because I wasn't into going to parties and, besides, I was always too busy playing golf.") She introduced herself and Mickelson, rendered nearly mute by her beauty, could squeeze out only one syllable: "Hi."

Amy McBride continued on her way to class. Their paths would cross again.

CHAPTER FIVE

A my McBride grew up with parents who stressed the same values as Nunu: family, faith, hard work. Her childhood was split between Northern California and Salt Lake City. She matriculated to the University of Utah, but found the atmosphere stifling and transferred to Arizona State after one year. At a notorious party school, she brought a sobering dedication to her studies, and the former high school cheerleader worked two jobs to put herself through school: teaching dance lessons for kids and firing up the crowd as a member of the Phoenix Suns dance team. The latter gig compelled her to work at a Special Olympics event during the 1993 Phoenix Open. Phil Mickelson was playing in the tournament at the outset of his first full year on the PGA Tour. (Following his sour pro debut at Pebble Beach, he acquitted himself well in ten ensuing events, including a runner-up finish at the New England Classic.) Phil attended the Special Olympics shindig, and when he spotted Amy he locked on to her like a heat-seeking missile. After a half hour of flirting, she agreed to a tennis date a few days later. Their chemistry was instant, and she wound up going to visit him the following week at the Bob Hope Classic. Thus distracted, Mickelson missed the cut.

He has lamented through the years that, when it came to women, he had no game. To woo Amy, he turned to his textbooks. "One thing I learned as a psychology major," Mickelson says, "is that the physiological response of the human body for fear is the same as it is for arousal. So when you're afraid, your heart pumps faster and your lungs expand and your nostrils flare and your senses become much more acute. And that's what happens when you're aroused. So what I would do is I would take Amy to a suspenseful movie—not a horror movie, a suspenseful movie. And during this suspenseful time, I would grab her hand and I would rub it like this. [He demonstrates a creepy, unctuous rub.] And she would displace her fear as arousal or attraction for me. And that's how I was able to, when I didn't have as much to work with, land such a gem."

The Tour barnstormed into Mickelson's hometown of San Diego the week after the Hope. He played well enough to earn a spot in Sunday's final pairing. Even at this early juncture in his pro career, he knew he had something to prove. The previous autumn, at the B.C. Open, Mickelson was in the final group alongside John Daly, but shot 76 and Long John blew him away. ("I still love to give him shit about that," says Daly.) In his 1993 season debut, defending his title at Tucson, Mickelson again played in the last group, but he shot 75 and got run over. "I could close with a low score to win in college, but I hadn't proven that at this level," Mickelson said back at Torrey Pines. "When I didn't win at Tucson this year, it was hard to swallow."

Heading to the final nine holes at the San Diego Open, he trailed Dave Rummells by a shot, but Mickelson roared home in 31 strokes to win by four. On the final green, as he was hurrying through his routine, Payne Stewart cracked, "Why don't you wait? It's your show. Enjoy the moment." Turning to the crowd, he added, "Kids—you can't teach 'em anything."

Mickelson had hit sixteen greens in regulation and birdied all four par-5s, but Rummells was most dazzled by his work with the flat stick. "Phil Mickelson can roll that golf ball," he said. "He's probably the best putter I've ever played with. Every one of his putts goes right in the middle of the cup. They're not falling in the side door."

In the hours after his victory, Phil called Amy to ask if she had watched his triumphant moment on TV. She had blown it off, preferring to sunbathe by the pool with girlfriends.

Before leaving San Diego, Mickelson stopped by the Santos home to present his biggest fan with a flag from the tournament. For Nunu, he signed it, *To Champ, I'll love you forever.* His beaming grandfather pinned the flag to the wall in the kitchen, the beginning of an enduring tradition.

The Mickelson brand already had enough currency that three months after this breakthrough win he was invited to tee it up at the Tournoi Perrier de

Paris. A trip to the City of Light was the perfect opportunity to further dazzle Amy . . . or so he thought. Her very traditional parents were already wary of a romance with a jet-setting professional athlete, so Amy insisted Phil call her father to seek his permission. Gary McBride was unimpressed: "You know, that phone call kind of hit me wrong. Phil was very, very nice, but dads are pretty protective of their daughters. And when he said they would have separate rooms I was thinking, *Right—like there are no hallways*." Amy didn't make the trip. (Phil won the tournament.) She would have to wait until her fortieth birthday to finally visit Paris with her beau.

Amy knew little about golf but was aware that the Phoenix Suns' star player, Charles Barkley, was falling in love with the game. "She kept saying I needed to play with her boyfriend and I kept blowing that shit off," says Barkley. "I was at the peak of my situation, coming off the Dream Team. I was always getting invited to play golf, so I kept telling Amy no—I assumed she was dating some old dude who worked at an investment bank or some shit like that. Finally she told me who her boyfriend was and I was like, 'Sheeeeeee-it, set that shit up for tomorrow.' That's how me and Phil first became friends." Mickelson became a regular sitting courtside at Suns games. The Ken and Barbie vibes were strong: the dreamy young Tour star and the gorgeous cheerleader, making eyes at each other.

But Amy wasn't the only foundational relationship in Phil's life; Steve Loy had resigned from Arizona State to become Mickelson's agent. All the top management companies put the full-court press on Mickelson during his senior year, but from the beginning Loy took control of the recruiting process. (The sharpies at industry behemoth IMG largely disqualified themselves when they would not agree to hire Loy, who was suddenly part of a package deal.) Remember when Dick Cheney was put in charge of finding a vice president for George W. Bush and he named himself the best candidate? Loy pretty much invented that move. Right off the bat, Mickelson and his agent showed they were going to do things their own way, signing a blockbuster endorsement deal with Yonex, a Japanese company that had almost no presence in the U.S. market. Mickelson had been a gearhead at least as far back as when he employed the extra-long driver shaft that helped him win the U.S. Amateur.

Yonex's lightweight graphite shafts and larger driver heads made of composite materials opened up a world of possibilities for a player already obsessed with chasing distance. But quality was an ongoing issue, signified by the Tour bag Yonex supplied—the shoulder strap routinely broke, leaving Mickelson's beleaguered looper, Jim Mackay, to carry the bag down the fairway by its handle, as if it were a briefcase. Phil also began playing graphite shafts in his irons, which to that point was unheard-of on the PGA Tour.

Mackay quickly became an indispensable teammate to Mickelson. He was born in England to a Scottish father, but the family immigrated to New Smyrna Beach, Florida, when Jim was eight. The local muni, designed by Donald Ross, let kids play for free after three p.m. and Mackay showed up almost every day. He earned a scholarship to Columbus (Georgia) College, now known as Columbus State. In his senior year, Mackay was a third-team Division II All-American. "We had a match at the University of Florida's Gator tournament," says his coach, Earl Bagley. "Jim was playing Gary Nicklaus [of Ohio State] and Jack was in the gallery. I caught up with Jim and he said to me, 'Coach, I can't even bring the club back. Greatest golfer in history is here watching.' I told Jim, 'He's not watching you.' "

Mackay had dreams of playing professionally until he tangled with Davis Love III in U.S. Amateur qualifying. "I knew I had to get a job," he says. As an undergrad he had worked at Green Island Country Club, where 1987 Masters champ Larry Mize hung out. "I wound up shagging balls for him before or after class," Mackay says. Upon graduation, he landed a job at the financial services company Synovus, but before his first day of work Mize offered him a caddie gig. Mackay negotiated a two-year leave of absence from the straight world and then lit out for the 1990 Bob Hope. ("James Blanchard was the [Synovus] CEO," says Mackay. "He's a member at Augusta National. Every April at the Masters, he asks me when I'm going to report to work.") Back then he was six foot four and maybe 150 pounds. Fred Couples took one look at Mackay's tall, skinny, gangly frame and tagged him with an enduring nickname: Bones.

By 1992, Mackay was on Scott Simpson's bag, but when the '87 U.S. Open champ skipped the Tucson Open, Bones moonlighted for Curtis Strange. That tournament week he crossed paths with Steve Loy. The big money had yet to arrive on Tour and caddying was still largely the province of ruffians and scoundrels. The clean-cut Bones had a different vibe, which may be why Loy chatted him up, looking for looper recommendations for when Mickelson turned pro that summer. Phil was already on Bones's radar screen. Just weeks earlier, he had been driving to his favorite record store in Tempe, Arizona, when, rolling past the driving range where Arizona State practiced, he spied a big left-hander smashing the ball. He noted that it had to be the local phenom he had heard so much about. After buying a handful of CDs, Mackay was driving home and the same lefty was still grinding on the range. The golf nerd in Bones couldn't resist; he pulled over and introduced himself to Mickelson and watched him hit balls for a while. So, back at the Tucson Open, he was happy to help Loy but stopped midsentence when Strange arrived at the course. Mackay hustled off to perform his duties. Later, he sent Loy a handwritten letter of apology for prematurely ending the conversation. Mickelson saw the note and was deeply impressed. He arranged a practice round with Simpson and Bones at the ensuing Players Championship. They had just shaken hands on their first tee box when Mickelson blurted out, loud enough for Simpson to hear, that he wanted to hire Mackay as his caddie. Bones was mortified, but ultimately couldn't say no.

They made their debut at the 1992 U.S. Open. From the very beginning, there was no denying Bones's love for the game or dedication to his job. Mickelson didn't qualify for the 1992 Open Championship but Mackay traveled to Muirfield anyway, to soak up the experience and prepare for Mickelson's future assaults on the auld sod. "We ended up with seven or eight caddies in a tiny apartment," says Mackay. "I remember guys were sleeping in the kitchen, and things along those lines." Somehow, it could have been worse. "There's a great story about a caddie in the same spot we were in, who couldn't find a place to stay," says Bones. "He literally went to a guy who had a farm with a little metal caravan out on the property and he asked the guy if he could stay in the metal caravan. The guy goes, 'Well, yeah, sure.' And there was no electricity in there. None of us could figure out how he could wake up in the morning and make his early tee times. This caddie went down to the local store and bought some birdseed and put it on the roof of the caravan. In the morning, the birds would land on the roof of the caravan, peck the roof, and it would wake him up. And he would go to work."

In those early days, before he was a brand unto himself, Bones took to heart the old-school mandate for caddies to "show up, keep up, and shut up." Especially the last bit. If you were a reporter, a typical conversation would go like this: "Hey, Bones, how's Phil hitting it?"

"Is this off the record?"

"Yeah, sure, whatever."

"He's hitting it good."

But Bones brought a boiler room intensity to crunching the numbers, filling his yardage guides with detailed notes and minutiae. This proved particularly useful at the 1993 International, a Tour event played at a course built on the side of a mountain outside of Denver. The constant elevation changes and the differing yardage the ball flies in the mile-high air bedeviled many players and caddies, but Mickelson was locked in all week and won going away. For American golf, this was an era of parity and diminished expectations, so two wins counted as a banner year. Then Mickelson kicked off the 1994 season with a victory at the Tournament of Champions, defeating Couples in a playoff. The hype began to crest, and Mickelson just kept coming: top tens at Tucson and Phoenix and a near miss at Torrey Pines. "It felt like every time you looked at a leaderboard, his name was near the top," says Davis Love. "The way Phil came out of the box [to start his career], you just felt like the sky was the limit." Nothing could break his momentum, or so it seemed.

Mickelson grew up on the ski slopes, learning at the knee of a father who once harbored ambitions of competing in the Olympics. Justin Leonard, who now lives full-time in Aspen, has carved up a few mountains with Mickelson through the years, and he says, "He's a good skier, I can vouch for that."

If skiing had a handicap system like golf, what would Phil's index be?

"He's single digits," says Leonard. "Probably a four or five . . ."

Pause.

". . . who thinks he's a plus-two."

Shortly after the rousing final-round 64 that propelled him to third place at Torrey Pines, Mickelson went skiing with his old college teammate Jim Strickland. They drove Phil's 4Runner to Snowbowl in Flagstaff, Arizona. Conditions were a little icy. On their last run before lunch—it's always the last run—Mickelson and Strickland stood at the very top of the mountain and pointed to a warming hut far down below. They decided to race to it and the loser had to buy lunch. "Classic Phil, he says, 'Okay, you're five seven with 185s [length skis], I'm six three with 235s, so I'll give you a twenty-five-yard head start,'" says Strickland. "I tuck and go and I'm flying down the mountain. Down near the bottom there was a lot of ice. I started to break up and then just yard-saled it."

It took Strickland a while to collect his skis, poles, sunglasses, hat, and gloves. He assumed that while he was supine, Mickelson had raced past to win the bet. Strickland wandered around the chalet but couldn't find his friend. He went back outside and that's when he glimpsed a couple of ski patrolmen whoosh by to join a group of their colleagues who had gathered in a grove of trees a little down the mountain. With a pit in his stomach, Strickland hustled over. Mickelson was at the center of the circle of ski patrolmen, his left leg twisted into an awkward angle. He had lost control and blown past the lodge and careened down an embankment at high speed. His ski got wedged between two trees, creating enough shock and tension to snap in half his femur, the largest bone in the human body. "Think about the amount of force it takes to break that bone," Mickelson says in what sounds like a perverse boast. He had narrowly missed colliding with a tall tree that, says Strickland, "certainly could have killed him." He adds, "Seeing Phil's face, I got nauseous. I tried to say something positive, but he leaned in and said, in a really sad voice, 'I'm not gonna be able to play the Masters.'" That hurt as much as the leg.

Mickelson would miss three months of tournament play. Inspired by his dad, the onetime Top Gun, Phil decided to work toward his pilot's license. (This is not unlike Tiger Woods's cosplay with Navy SEALs in an attempt to feel closer to his late father, a onetime Green Beret.) Mickelson earned his license, but upon returning to the course he appeared rudderless, failing to cop a victory for the rest of the season.

Mickelson returned to his winning ways in his second start of the 1995 season, at Tucson, which was fast becoming an annual annuity. Amy had now graduated Arizona State and the cameras always found her in the gallery. They would be engaged before the end of the year. Mickelson also possessed what was already one of the most recognizable shots in the game, his famous flop. In describing how to play it, he made it sound almost routine: "I want the club to go underneath the ball. The bounce kicks the club into the ball and that's how I get it to pop up. I open up the face almost flat, so the toe is almost touching the ground. And I put my weight forward, which helps me drive the club into the ground and keep it underneath the ball. Now, if I stop my arms and let my wrists flip, the leading edge starts coming off the ground and I blade it. So I have to make sure my arms and club are accelerating through impact. It's not a high-percentage shot, but because I've hit it so many times I do feel comfortable with it to hit it in pressure situations." Years later, a launch monitor would be aimed at Mickelson while he was practicing his flop shot, and the clubhead speed for his lob wedge touched 102 miles per hour, a fantastical number given that Brendon Todd, a three-time winner on Tour, swings his much longer, much lighter driver only a couple of miles per hour faster.

The young Mickelson was earning respect on Tour not just with victories but also his performance in practice-round money games. "Man, Phil was so hard to beat," says Paul Azinger. "He just cleaned us out." At Bay Hill one year, he and Payne Stewart took on Mickelson and Ben Crenshaw. It all came down to the eighteenth hole. The other three players missed birdie putts, leaving Mickelson with a do-or-die fifteen-footer. If he were to make it, Stewart and Azinger would be out $1,600 apiece. Stewart was so confident Mickelson would hole the putt, he negotiated a buyout for $400. Azinger eyed the downhill, right-to-left slider and decided to take his chances, telling Mickelson, "Putt it, bitch." He drilled it dead center. Says Azinger with a sigh, "He had big ol' balls. Even as a new guy on Tour, he had no fear. When someone puts it on you like that, it tells you a lot about them."

The on-course highlight of Mickelson's '95 season was his first Ryder Cup, at Oak Hill. The biennial grudge match between the U.S. and Europe had reached a fever pitch. Four years earlier, the Americans prevailed in "The War by the Shore," inarguably the most overheated golf event of all time. In '93, this corps of battle-hardened Yanks went to England and retained the Cup against a European squad that boasted six future Hall of Famers. Mickelson, twenty-five, was by far the youngest U.S. player in '95, but he thrived in the combative atmosphere. In the first match of his Ryder Cup career, he and Pavin destroyed Bernhard Langer and former Sun Devil Per-Ulrik Johansson, 6 & 4. The next day, Mickelson stared down his hero Seve Ballesteros in a taut four-ball victory. The U.S. led 9–7 as the team gathered that night to hammer out the singles lineup. Mickelson stood up and looked around the room at all of the crusty veterans, among them Curtis Strange, Tom Lehman, Ben Crenshaw, Fred Couples, Davis Love, and Peter Jacobsen. He addressed his glowering captain, Lanny Wadkins.

"I want to be in the last group," Mickelson said, and it got so quiet you could've heard a pat of butter drop. "I want to be there at the end if you need me, because I'm gonna win my match."

The room erupted.

"Wow, that was ballsy," Jacobsen says now. "We had some tough characters on that team and none of them were volunteering for the anchor match. To do it as a rookie? That's a stud move."

Mickelson got his wish and was sent out last. But in what came to be known as Choke Hill, the Americans lost six of the first eight matches and halved another. By the time Mickelson closed out Johansson 2 & 1 to remain undefeated, it was too late; the Cup had been lost. Still, it was one helluva debut, and the U.S. appeared to have found a Ryder Cup cornerstone for the next couple of decades.

The accrued confidence carried Mickelson into the 1996 season. He won back-to-back at Tucson and Phoenix and then finished second at Torrey Pines. He shot an opening 65 at the Masters en route to third place and then won the Byron Nelson. He was playing a very different game from most of his peers. "Phil doesn't get credit for it, but he might be the guy who invented bomb 'n' gouge," says Jacobsen, referring to the modern Tour template of smashing the ball as far as possible off the tee and not really worrying if it winds up in the rough. "It was such a different era then. The balls were spinny, the driver heads were tiny, and there were still guys using persimmon! We had all been taught to swing under control and hit it straight. And here comes Phil with that Yonex driver, just swinging out of his shoes. He attacked relentlessly and he played with no fear because he knew he could always bail himself out with his wedge and his putter. He had the imagination and creativity to make it work."

In August 1996, Mickelson took the biggest tournament of his career, the World Series of Golf. It was his fourth victory of the year. Couples never won that many in a season. Neither did Love, Crenshaw, Strange, Wadkins, Lehman, Pavin, or Jacobsen. Or Tom Kite, Payne Stewart, Mark O'Meara, Hal Sutton, Paul Azinger, or Mark Calcavecchia. (More than half of these players are in the Hall of Fame.) All of the predictions had come true: Mickelson was the most prolific winner in the game. The world was his oyster. Nothing could could stop him now.

Four days after the World Series of Golf, Tiger Woods made his pro debut.

CHAPTER SIX

At a long-ago Masters, when Tiger Woods was just an intriguing amateur prospect and Phil Mickelson a hotshot young pro who was being billed as the Next Nicklaus, Woods sneaked a reporter into the Crow's Nest, the tiny dormitory perched atop the Augusta National clubhouse. Tiger was monitoring the Masters telecast when Mickelson appeared on the screen. Employing a putting stroke that was much too long and loose for the slippery greens, Mickelson characteristically charged a putt past the hole. As the ball trickled farther and farther from the cup, Woods offered only one word of commentary: "Roll."

The antipathy was born on the playing fields of junior golf. Tiger and Phil grew up in Southern California suburbia, separated by a hundred miles but linked by their talent. Older by five and a half years, Mickelson loomed over Woods's early golfing life. "Phil was an icon to us," says Chris Riley, one of Tiger's good friends from junior golf.

Woods's father, Earl, received most of the credit for his son's competitive spirit, but it was his mom, Tida, who sharpened Tiger's killer instinct. With her it was personal. (Years later, after her son beat Davis Love in a playoff, she famously said, "Tiger took his heart.") Any player as talented as the young Woods was considered not just a competitor but also an existential threat, so Tiger erased Phil's numerous junior records with a single-minded disdain. Mickelson won a Junior World at age ten? Woods took his first one when he was eight . . . and then five more. Phil could claim one U.S. Amateur? Tiger would win three in a row. Mickelson had sixteen NCAA victories across four years? Woods won eleven in two years and then got bored and dropped out of Stanford. In 1996, when Phil was enjoying his banner year on the PGA Tour,

Tigermania was launched that autumn when Woods won two of his first seven starts as a pro.

The parrying continued into 1997. Woods won the season opener at La Costa, and then Mickelson struck back with a victory at Bay Hill just three weeks before the Masters. Augusta National, always the sport's grandest stage, was where these two leading men were supposed to trod the boards. The expectations for Woods had been monumental going back to the previous year's Masters, when, after he played a practice round with Jack Nicklaus and Arnold Palmer, the Golden Bear said, "Arnold and I both agree that you could take his Masters [four victories] and my Masters [six] and add them together and this kid should win more than that." Mickelson was now battling a war on two fronts when it came to his reputation: Woods was challenging his hegemony as the game's best young player and there were growing doubts as to whether his freewheeling style of play could succeed in the more exacting conditions of the major championships. Mickelson had been only one shot off the lead going into the final round of the 1995 U.S. Open, but kicked away a chance at victory with a series of ghastly shots and questionable decisions en route to a double bogey on the par-5 sixteenth hole. He opened with a sizzling 65 at the '96 Masters, but sputtered from there, finishing third. "There was some frustration, for sure," says Dean Reinmuth. "Phil already knew the major championships were a key to his legacy. He didn't talk about it the way Tiger did, but he had the same ambitions."

And then, at the 61st Masters, the ground shifted beneath Mickelson's feet. He played like a guy trying way too hard, shooting 76-74 to miss the cut by a mile. At twenty-one, Tiger produced a performance for the ages, winning his first green jacket and instantly reshaping the sport in his image. The banner headline across the front page of the *Augusta Chronicle* said it all: "WOODS LAUNCHES NEW ERA."

Mickelson wasted no time in trying to reinvent himself. Even as he was winning four times in '96, he began to feel he needed a fresh perspective on his game; at that point he had been working with Reinmuth for nearly half his life. By year's end, they had parted ways and Mickelson had hired Rick Smith as a new swing coach. After Woods's demolition of Augusta National, Smith felt a difference in his pupil. "It was pretty clear the bar had been raised," says Smith. "Higher than anyone imagined possible, really."

The rest of '97 was nightmare fuel for Mickelson. Ernie Els, his old rival from the Junior Worlds, won his second U.S. Open. Justin Leonard, two years younger than Phil, took the Open Championship. When Davis Love prevailed at the PGA Championship, there was no longer any question that Mickelson now owned the dreaded title of BPNTHWAM (Best Player Never to Have Won a Major). He kept scooping up regular PGA Tour wins—an International here, a Crosby Clambake there—but that began to feel superfluous as he looked increasingly overmatched at the majors. Across the '97 and '98 seasons, Mickelson had only one top ten at the game's most important championships, and just barely: a tie for tenth at the 1998 U.S. Open.

At least there was some happy news off the course. He and Amy had married in November 1996, on Maui. Now she was pregnant with their first child. The baby was due June 30, 1999, two weeks after the U.S. Open at Pinehurst was to conclude.

In the post-Watson era, there was no American golfer more compelling than Payne Stewart. He had the face of a movie star, dressed like Old Tom Morris, and his swing was so delicious that it was often described in culinary terms, *syrupy* and *buttery* being the most common. But Stewart was a spicy personality who often rubbed people the wrong way. He could be churlish with the press and caustic with his colleagues. Known for his gamesmanship, Stewart refused to shake Tom Kite's hand after losing in a playoff at the 1989 Tour Championship. At that year's PGA Championship, Stewart scorched the final nine in 31 and prevailed when Mike Reid collapsed on the closing holes, but the victor rankled many when he admitted, "I said a prayer in the [scoring] tent: How about some good stuff for Payne Stewart one time?"

But Stewart was also a loving friend and enthusiastic host, a celebrated margarita mixologist who was always the life of the party. He inspired fierce loyalty among a generation of U.S. players as the heart and soul of the Ryder

Cup teams during the blood feuds of the late 1980s and early '90s. Stewart was thirty-four when he won his second major championship, the '91 U.S. Open. A couple of years later, he cashed in with a blockbuster deal with Spalding that compelled him to play game-improvement clubs ill-suited to his swing. He developed a series of compensating moves that sabotaged him under pressure, and over the next four seasons he racked up twenty-eight top tens but only one win. "We started calling him Avis," says Peter Jacobsen, who was the lead singer to Stewart's blues harmonica in the faux-rock band Jake Trout and the Flounders.

Stewart's on-course struggles led to a period of deep introspection. He devoted more time to his children, Aaron and Chelsea. When his best friend, Paul Azinger, battled cancer throughout 1994, Stewart confronted his own mortality for the first time. His religious faith deepened, and he helped to popularize the WWJD bracelet on Tour. Stewart broke a four-year victory drought in February 1999 at the Pebble Beach Pro-Am and immediately turned his attention to the U.S. Open. The national championship had extra meaning for this adoptive Southerner because it was to be the first Open played at Pinehurst No. 2, Donald Ross's masterwork in the Sandhills of North Carolina. With its distinctive turtleback greens, Pinehurst puts a premium on shotmaking, and the USGA offered an imaginative setup with less rough, allowing for more artistic expression. A vast canvas of land, Pinehurst accommodated some of the biggest crowds ever at a U.S. Open.

The thunderous cheers were a fitting soundtrack to a sport that was going big time. The 1999 season was the first played under monster TV deals that had been negotiated in the wake of Woods's game-changing victory at the '97 Masters. But always the iconoclast, Tiger decided after that triumph to rebuild his swing into a tighter, more repeatable action. He needed two years to master the changes. A month before the '99 U.S. Open, he called his swing guru, Butch Harmon, from the range at the Byron Nelson Classic and uttered three iconic words: "I got it." Woods, twenty-three, would win his next two starts, in Germany and at the Memorial, but even then he arrived at Pinehurst as only the co-headliner.

Mickelson was the talk of the Open because of Amy's precarious condition at home in Scottsdale. She had been on bed rest since her fifth month of pregnancy. It was deeply important to Phil to be there for the birth, but ultimately he couldn't resist the siren song of a course with which he had fallen in love while attending a golf school there at thirteen. "I didn't decide I was going to go to Pinehurst until after we went to the doctor on Tuesday morning [of U.S. Open week]," Phil says. "He said it looked like there was at least another week to go, maybe two. Even though I got in only one practice round, I had been working on my game at home, so I was sharp."

"When Phil left, it was the most emotional goodbye we've had," Amy says. "But he was so determined. He said, 'I am going to win the U.S. Open, I'm going to come home, we're going to have the baby, and it's going to be the best week of our lives.'"

"I had no doubt in my mind I was going to win the tournament," Phil adds.

His caddie, Jim Mackay, carried a beeper in his pocket, and Phil vowed to walk off the course if summoned by Amy, even if he was leading the United States Open. "Oh, gawd, that beeper," says Bones. "I was stressed about it the whole time. If I would have lost that thing, I'd have been filing for unemployment. I heard plenty of people say after the fact, 'Oh, he wouldn't have left, this and that.' When he showed up in Pinehurst, he got in my grill and said, 'I don't care where I am, I want to know ten seconds after this thing goes off.' He was dead serious."

On the Wednesday of Open week, Amy went to see her doctor. She says, "He checks me out and he goes, 'Wow, things have changed. If you had looked like this yesterday, I wouldn't have told your husband he should go.' My heart just sank."

Paired with David Duval—the red-hot world number one who had inexplicably burned the fingers on his right hand in a mishap with a scalding kettle the week before the Open—Mickelson shot a three-under 67 to share the first-round lead with his playing partner on a rain-softened course. Woods and Stewart were a stroke back. In the second round, Mickelson and Duval posted matching 70s, while Stewart fired a 69 to join them in a three-way tie for the lead. With a 71, Woods was tied for fourth, two back.

"Amy saw the doctor today," Mickelson said after his round. "It looks like it's still going to be another week and a half. I'm really not overly concerned."

"On Friday, I started to have contractions," Amy says. "Phil and I are talking all the time on the phone, but I'm not saying what is going on, which was really stressful because we share everything. So we'd have these conversations, and as soon as he hung up I'd burst into tears."

For moving day, Stewart and Duval were in the final group, immediately behind the dream pairing of Woods and Mickelson. There was an electricity in the air and even the players were feeling frisky. "Before the third round, Tiger and Payne were on the putting green," says Chuck Cook, Stewart's swing coach, "and Tiger says to him, 'When I start designing golf courses, I'm going to make them nine thousand yards long, and then you old guys won't stand a chance.' Payne comes right back at him, 'Well, if it's the U.S. Open, you'll still have to drive it in the fairway.' Tiger didn't have an answer for that one."

After two days of baking in the sun, Pinehurst turned into a firm, fiery test for the third round. Afterward, Lee Janzen said, "I've been asked many times what's the hardest golf course I've ever played. Now I have the answer." Duval bogeyed four of the first eight holes. Woods started double bogey–bogey. When Stewart bogeyed three straight holes beginning on number eight, Mickelson suddenly had a three-shot lead. But Phil bogeyed eleven, fifteen, sixteen, and seventeen, to fall one stroke off Stewart's lead. "Phil's cut shot wasn't working that week," says Mackay. "He could only hit draws. So he drove it in eighteen fairway, and the pin was way left, and he hadn't hit a cut shot in fifty-three holes, but he says, 'I want to birdie this hole and get in the last group, so I'm going to have to try and cut an 8-iron.' And he cut an 8-iron to five feet, made it, and got in the last group for Sunday." Standing in the eighteenth fairway, Stewart waited for Mickelson's extended standing ovation to subside and then stuffed a 7-iron to twelve feet and made a birdie of his own to retake sole possession of the lead.

"Big brass ones," says Azinger.

Despite putting problems, Stewart ground out a 72, and at one under was the only player in the field below par. Mickelson's 73 left him alone in second. With a 72, Woods was two behind, tied for third with Tim Herron. Back in

Scottsdale, things were getting dicey. "Saturday night my contractions started coming really fast," Amy says, "so we decided to go to the hospital. Phil happened to call right about then, but I didn't say anything. At the hospital they put me on a monitor and gave me terbutaline to slow the contractions. Eventually Dr. Webb comes and stays with me. I'm asking him every five minutes, 'Should I call Phil?' He keeps saying not yet. This went on for a few hours. Finally the contractions slowed enough to where he felt comfortable sending me home."

Following custom, the final round of the Open fell on Father's Day. Stewart was ironing his clothes at his rental house while watching the early finishers when NBC played a tribute to Payne and his father, Bill, an accomplished amateur competitor. Bill signed up his son for his first Open qualifier when Payne was fifteen and even played alongside him. "Payne had tears in his eyes watching that feature," says Tracey Stewart of her husband. "He was an emotional person, an emotional player, and I believe that thinking of his father [who died of cancer in 1985] gave him that extra motivation to go out and win the tournament."

The Mickelsons shared their own emotional moment. "On Sunday morning, Phil calls and I don't tell him a thing about the night before," says Amy. "My lip is quivering. That was probably the most difficult moment of the whole thing."

For the final round, Woods and Herron were in the second-to-last pairing, ahead of Stewart and Mickelson. It was an unseasonably cool and damp day. Stewart, wearing a navy rain jacket, took a pair of scissors to the sleeves to free up his swing, unwittingly creating a new fashion trend.

"The biggest bleachers I have ever seen at a tournament in the U.S. were at that event, to the left of eighteen green, and when you left the range to go to the first tee, you had to walk across eighteen fairway pretty close to the green," says Mackay. "To this day, one of the coolest memories of my caddying life came when Phil and Payne were walking to the tee. The whole grandstand stood up and cheered. It was almost like two gladiators going into the Colosseum."

Woods set the tone for the day with a birdie on the first hole, but Stewart answered with one of his own, pushing his lead to two. Mickelson cut the deficit in half with a curling twenty-five-footer on the seventh hole, which would be his only birdie of the day. When Stewart bogeyed ten and twelve, Mickelson stood alone at the top of the leaderboard.

At number fourteen, Woods drained a big-breaking thirty-footer for birdie. He dropped to one knee and pumped his fist, sending the gallery into a frenzy. "You could feel the energy building," Mickelson says. "You knew Tiger was going to keep coming."

Stewart rallied on the thirteenth hole to bury a fifteen-footer for birdie to reclaim a share of the lead. "I wasn't going to just hand the trophy over to [Mickelson]," he says after the round.

At 489 yards, the sixteenth hole was, to that point, the longest par-4 in U.S. Open history, and for the final round it played into the wind. From 210 yards out, Woods reached the green with a laser-like 4-iron and then made a twelve-foot birdie putt, uncorking a vintage uppercut. He was a stroke off the lead. "It was football-game loud," says Herron. "It would give you chills up and down your arms to hear it."

Back at the par-3 fifteenth hole, Stewart pulled a 4-iron left of the green and missed an eight-footer for par, falling into a tie for second with Woods. "I felt like I was in control of the tournament," Mickelson says. "I was leading, and it's a very difficult course to make birdies on. All I needed was three pars."

At sixteen, Mickelson tugged his approach from 226 yards into the rough, short and right of the green. Stewart mis-hit his 2-iron, and his ball died ten yards short of the green. He ran the next shot thirty feet past the hole. "When he bladed his chip shot, I didn't really consider him the number one threat," says Mickelson. "I thought Tiger was."

On the downhill 196-yard par-3 seventeenth, the pin was back-left. Woods overcooked a drawing 7-iron into the greenside bunker. A decent recovery shot left him a crucial five-footer to save par. "He had played an incredible back nine, and he had all the momentum from the crowd," says Herron. "I was thinking there's no way he misses the putt."

He misses the putt.

"That's the last important putt Tiger missed for a decade," says Azinger.

Back at sixteen, Mickelson had what he calls a "very easy" chip, but he left it eight feet short. His one-of-a-kind Yonex wedges had a razor-sharp leading edge, and Mickelson would later confide that in certain conditions he could not be certain how the club would interact with the turf. It had been bugging him for a long while, but by the next year he had walked away from Yonex, largely because of that one shot.

Stewart followed Mickelson's chip by ramming in his thirty-footer for an unlikely par. "If that ball doesn't go in, it runs fifteen to twenty feet by," Mickelson says. "It had the potential to go off the green."

As the leaders played toward twilight, the conditions became dark and misty, highly unusual for a tournament that always heralds the start of summer. "There was an almost eerie feeling," says Rick Smith. "And you know, there's this church across the street from Pinehurst. Seconds after Payne made that putt on sixteen, the bells started ringing, and that beautiful sound went out across the course. It felt like some kind of a sign."

Back at sixteen, Mickelson faced a do-or-die eight-footer. "That's when I realized, *If I don't make this putt, we're tied.* I thought I was going to have a two-stroke lead with two to go."

On the NBC telecast, Johnny Miller intoned gravely, "Biggest putt of his life."

Mickelson pulled it, his first bogey of the round. With honors at the par-3 seventeenth hole, Stewart played a gorgeous drawing 6-iron to four feet. Mickelson answered with a high fade to six feet. "When Phil's ball hit and got close to the hole, that was a smell-the-roses moment for me," says Mackay. "The place went crazy."

Now Mickelson faced another defining putt, but was uncertain about the break. He called in his caddie for a second look. "I thought it was pretty straight," Bones says. "But [the putt] certainly turned a little right, and it missed. In hindsight it was probably left edge. In my [twenty-five] years as a caddie, if I could have one do-over, it would be reading that putt, by a million miles."

Stewart brushed in his birdie putt, and in the span of twenty minutes, went from one down to one up. He hit a pretty good drive down the right side of the eighteenth fairway, but his ball kicked into the rough by one foot. "Worst lie of the week," Cook says. "There was no way he could get to the green." Stewart hacked out, leaving himself seventy-seven yards from the flag. Mickelson split the fairway—for the round he missed only two—and from 178 yards followed with what he called an "average" 7-iron that stopped thirty feet right of the hole. Stewart knocked a lob wedge eighteen feet below the cup. Putting first, Mickelson played a tad too much break and missed by an inch or two. The situation facing Stewart was now breathtaking in its simplicity: Make the putt and he's the United States Open champion. Miss it and he's headed to an eighteen-hole Monday playoff.

"I kept my head still on that putt," Stewart said afterward. "And when I looked up, it was about two feet from the hole and it was breaking right in the center and I couldn't believe it. I couldn't believe that I'd accomplished another dream of mine."

Says Cook, "I don't know if there is an outside force directing all of it, but the environment created in situations like that tournament pushes a certain outcome. It was such a great moment, the only outcome that made sense was for Payne to make that putt."

Stewart loosed a guttural scream and two lusty fist pumps, and his caddie, Mike Hicks, jumped into his arms and wrapped his legs around his boss. Stewart then walked to Mickelson, cupped Phil's face in his hands, and said, "Good luck with the baby. There's nothing like being a father!"

Says Azinger, "When you talk about the greatest showings of sportsmanship in golf history, you have to say number one is Nicklaus's concession to Tony Jacklin at the Ryder Cup. But that right there is probably second. Payne could immediately empathize with Mickelson. Payne knows the agony of defeat. Who knew it more than him?"

Mickelson bolted for the airport and arrived home at midnight. Amy went into labor the next morning, about the time Phil would have been warming up for a playoff. Amanda was born that evening.

"Here we are fifteen years later," Phil told me in 2014, "and I can tell her with all sincerity that her birth is the most emotional moment of our lives. It's something I would never want to miss, and I'm so glad I was able to be there, because it really is one of the greatest experiences in the world. I loved her even before I knew her."

Two months later, Woods won the PGA Championship, touching off a historic run. "What happened at Pinehurst hardened Tiger," says Jacobsen. "It proved to him that just showing up wasn't enough—if he wanted to win more majors, he would have to find another gear. And he found a gear no one else had. Payne showed him the way."

The anguish/exhilaration of losing the Open but welcoming a daughter also had a profound effect on Mickelson. "I believe one of the greatest influences Payne had was in how he helped change Phil as a man," says Azinger. "Payne was a great example of a guy who had found perfect balance in life. Phil had always done the right thing, he'd always been a good guy, but golf was everything to him. What happened at Pinehurst bonded them forever, and it set priorities for Phil."

Four months after Pinehurst, at the contentious Brookline Ryder Cup, Stewart was the team leader on the golf course and at the victory party after the U.S. regained the Cup. "Payne gave those teams so much fire," says Amy. "He loved playing for his country. I remember him one time at the team hotel running down the hall in these red, white, and blue pants, carrying a boom box that was playing 'Born in the U.S.A.' At Brookline he was the last one standing at the party. I still have this image of him on top of a piano drinking out of a champagne bottle."

Four weeks later Stewart, forty-two, was flying from Orlando to Houston for the Tour Championship when the Learjet he was traveling on depressurized, incapacitating the pilots and passengers and sending the plane on a ghostly four-hour flight across the U.S. When it ran out of fuel it crashed into a field in South Dakota, killing all six aboard. "To lose Payne so soon after Pinehurst, it gave that tournament a kind of mythical quality," says Jacobsen. "I don't think there's any question it's the greatest U.S. Open of all time. All the elements came together: an iconic venue, two generations of stars battling on Sunday, a historic putt on the last hole. That alone would make it a classic. But Payne's death guaranteed that what happened there would live on forever."

CHAPTER SEVEN

Heading into the 1999 PGA Championship, Phil Mickelson spied a newspaper headline that rankled so much he talked about it for years afterward: "Last Chance for Phil Mickelson to Win a Major Tournament Before the Millennium Ends." His inability to win the big one was already a thing, clearly, but it was about to get much worse: Tiger Woods took the '99 PGA and then in 2000 had the greatest season in golf history, winning the U.S. and British Opens by a combined twenty-three shots and then prevailing at the PGA Championship in a thrilling playoff versus Bob May. The 2000 campaign was Mickelson's finest to date, with four wins, twelve top-ten finishes, and a career-best $4.7 million in earnings to finish second on the money list (a mere $4.5 million from the top spot). Amid Tiger's dominance, Mickelson's career year barely registered, but he had put in place important building blocks. "What Tiger was doing lit a fire under Phil," says Rick Smith. "Of course it did. He always worked harder than people gave him credit for, but he definitely kicked it up a couple of notches. He wasn't just going to give in to Tiger. He wanted to challenge him."

Mickelson's game was razor-sharp in the run-up to the 2001 Masters: another victory at Torrey Pines, runner-up at Bay Hill, third place in Atlanta. Per the new norm, Woods was simply better, with back-to-back wins at Bay Hill and the Players Championship. Tiger arrived in Augusta chasing the tantalizing, once-in-a-lifetime opportunity to hold all four major championship trophies at the same time. Since this feat would bleed across two seasons, it was not a traditional Grand Slam, and thus demanded a new moniker: the Tiger Slam.

Inevitably, Woods and Mickelson collided at the Masters. Standing in the fourteenth fairway during the third round, Phil was one shot off Ángel Cabrera's lead and one stroke ahead of Tiger. Mickelson's approach shot came up short to a back flag and trickled down the vertiginous slope to just off the front of the green. Every other golfer in the field would have putted the next shot or played a bump and run. Not sexy, but either play would eliminate the monumental screwup. Mickelson, ever the adrenaline junkie, couldn't resist pulling out his 60-degree wedge and trying to fly his ball all the way to the flag. He was dancing on a knife's edge. With the Masters hanging in the balance, it was the kind of shot that could make him a folk hero, but he caught it heavy and his ball expired well short of the target and then slowly, agonizingly, rolled back down the green. It took Mickelson three putts from there, a galling double bogey that allowed Woods to race past him and take the lead. They would play together in the final pairing on Sunday, surely the most important round of Mickelson's career, and maybe Woods's, too. Saturday night in the press tent, Mickelson didn't shrink from the magnitude of the moment. "I desperately want this," he said.

And what made him think he could somehow beat the great Woods despite a one-stroke deficit, after years of having fallen short? "I'm a different player," he said. "Not only mentally but physically. You could attribute it to mental toughness or you could attribute it to improved ball-striking, improved putting. I think I would attribute it to the latter. I feel very confident tomorrow, because I've been playing well this last year and a half, and the swing changes that I have made, I feel like a much more consistent ball striker day in and day out and I feel like I have become a more consistent putter as well. So the anxiety that I would have between rounds on whether or not [my game] would be there tomorrow, is really no longer there. I feel very comfortable that when I get on the tee tomorrow, it will be there."

When Tiger bogeyed the first hole on Sunday, they were tied for the lead. It stayed that way until Phil clanked a three-footer for par on the sixth hole and then Woods birdied the next two. He was still one stroke ahead of Mickelson when they reached the brutal par-4 eleventh hole. Trying to play a big slinging hook around the corner, Mickelson overcooked it and nailed a tree. He fought hard to leave himself an eight-foot putt for par, but missed it on the low side.

Woods birdied the hole, thanks to a pinpoint approach, a two-shot swing that dropped Mickelson to third place, a stroke behind a streaking David Duval, who had birdied seven of the first ten holes. To have any chance at victory, Mickelson needed to light up the back nine par-5s. On thirteen, with his driver, he smoked a hard fade around the corner. Woods stepped up and, with his 3-wood, ripped a towering draw twenty yards past his would-be rival.

"I could sort of sense that Mickelson was feeling a bit dejected," says Steve Williams, Woods's caddie at the time. "He's just hit the best drive that he can, and then Tiger's hit a 3-wood and whipped it by him. And then Phil says to Tiger, 'Do you always hit your 3-wood that long?' And Tiger says, 'Normally further than that.' It's amazing the little games within the game Tiger would play. That shot just deflated Phil's ego, and he couldn't bounce back."

That's not entirely true: Mickelson birdied the thirteenth hole and then hit a daring slicing long iron from behind the trees on fifteen to set up another birdie and pull within one of Woods. If you were a golf fan, you could barely breathe.

At the par-3 sixteenth hole, the pin was in its traditional Sunday spot, back-left, seducing players into feeding their tee shots off the sloping green toward the hole. Mickelson had honors and a chance to send the crowd to the moon, but he hooked his 7-iron well right of the flag and his ball died up on the slope, leaving a nearly impossible putt down the hill. The best he could do was trickle it to five feet past the hole. He pushed the must-make par putt and his bid was over. In victory, Woods was so overwhelmed he covered his face with his cap so the world wouldn't see his tears. He owned the Tiger Slam, while Mickelson was once again left to dissect where it all went wrong.

"I feel as though my game is to a point where I feel like I can finally win these tournaments and contend in them regularly," Mickelson said, following the final round. "I really do have that confidence. When I look back on this week, though, if I'm going to win with Tiger in the field, I cannot make the mistakes that I have been making. I've got to eliminate those somehow. I may be able to make one or two, but I can't make as many as I've made all the week, from double bogeys on twelve and fourteen earlier in the week, to four bogeys today that were really not tough pars. So, I just can't afford to keep throwing away shot after shot. But all in all, I don't feel as though I'm that far off. I just think that mentally, I'm not there for all seventy-two holes. I feel like I'm just slacking off on two or three holes and just kind of letting momentum take over and not really thinking through each shot, and it's cost me some vital strokes."

More tests awaited. At the ensuing U.S. Open, Mickelson was only two strokes back heading into the final round, but he self-immolated with a 75. "I don't know exactly what I learned today," he said dejectedly afterward. "I think that it was a difficult day for me, in that I did not play the way I would have liked, obviously. I'm not going to beat myself up over today's round. It's certainly not the finish I would have liked, but out of playing forty-five majors or so now, and not winning any, I'm tired of beating myself up time after time."

But Mickelson has always been able to take a punch; two months later he came back for more at the PGA Championship. He opened with three straight 66s at Atlanta Athletic Club, but the golf gods were not on his side, as late in the third round, moments after Mickelson claimed a two-stroke lead, David Toms made an ace to close the gap. Phil's game was clearly tighter and he'd proven he could contend at any given major, but questions remained about his mental toughness. That turned into a low roar after the events on the sixteenth hole on Sunday. Mickelson was tied for the lead when he played a mediocre approach shot to forty-five feet. At every golf tournament there are always a few hardos who camp out by a particular green and, after watching putt after putt, feel like they know the break better than the pros. As the crowd hushed for Mickelson to survey his birdie, a couple of these well-lubricated fans shouted advice. "They're telling me how slow it is and I tried to block it out of my mind, but it hit my subconscious," Mickelson said. "I just gave [my putt] a little bit extra, and it's disappointing that I was not able to block that out, because I've been focusing very well all week. I've been able to not let distractions interfere with my train of thought, and on that putt, what was said kind of crept in and I just gave it a little extra, and sure enough ran it eight feet by and now I've got a downhill breaking putt that was pretty quick that I didn't have the chance to be aggressive with." It was a shocking (but human) admission. Mickelson missed the comebacker to tumble out of the lead. On the seventy-second hole, he had a twenty-five-footer for birdie that could have altered the outcome, but he committed the cardinal sin of leaving it six inches short, dead on-line. Toms, having driven into the rough and laid up short of the watery green, pulled a Payne Stewart and gutted a ten-footer to break Mickelson's heart yet again. Phil shot a four-round total of 266, what would have been the lowest in major championship history if Toms wasn't one stroke better.

The notion that Woods and Mickelson might be buddies died at the 1998 Los Angeles Open, when Phil goaded the young master into a practice round. A money game ensued, of course, and Mickelson hustled Woods—a notorious tightwad—for $500, which Tiger paid off with five crisp hundred-dollar bills, each emblazoned with the dour mugshot of Ben Franklin. Phil being Phil, he made photocopies of one of the greenbacks and taped it in Woods's locker along with a note: *Just wanted you to know Benji and his friends are very happy in their new home.* Woods was not amused; it would be two decades before he deigned to play another practice round with Mickelson.

The relationship only grew frostier as Woods serially crushed Mickelson's spirit, including beating him again at the 2002 Masters, Tiger's third green jacket in the space of six years. A month after Augusta, at the Byron Nelson, John Hawkins of *Golf World* magazine wangled a lunchtime interview with Woods in the player dining area. They had just settled into a corner booth when Mickelson padded up, carrying an overstuffed tray of food.

"Mind if I join you guys?"

Says Hawkins, "I look at Tiger, he looks at me, and his expression is like, *Are you fucking kidding me?*"

Oblivious, Mickelson sat down and turned off Hawkins's tape recorder and proceeded to dominate the conversation. He is an extrovert while Woods is an introvert, and a lot of their awkwardness with each other flowed from there. The Lakers and underdog Nets had just secured their spots in the NBA Finals, so Mickelson, while wolfing down his lunch, said to Woods, "I know you love the Lakers, so I'll take the Nets for a hundred dollars."

Says Hawkins, "Phil gets up and leaves and the first thing out of Tiger's mouth is 'Can you fucking believe that guy?' It was so obvious to both of us that Phil was willing to pay a hundred dollars just to earn a little love from Tiger."

Mickelson had never been in a worse headspace than the spring of 2002. At Bay Hill, he led Woods by a shot with six holes to play on Sunday, but gave away the tournament on the par-5 sixteenth hole, which has a green protected by water. Mickelson hooked his drive into the trees, but instead of punching out and giving himself a solid birdie chance from the fairway, he tried to play a crazy-ass low slice under branches, over a pond, and between three deep bunkers. As he stood over the ball, Johnny Miller on the NBC telecast called it a "one in a hundred" shot, and when Mickelson inevitably plunked his ball in the water, a baffled Dan Hicks said on the telecast, "It's almost like he's addicted to high stakes and he just can't help himself." Mickelson bogeyed the final three holes to hand the trophy to Tiger. (The *Orlando Sentinel* headline said it all: "Mickelson Gambles and Woods Collects.")

"The difference between them is that Phil wants to hit an amazing shot, but all Tiger wants to do is hit the right shot," says Golf Channel analyst Brandel Chamblee. "Phil is a gambler. Tiger is the house, and he knows the house always wins. Phil thinks he knows more than the house."

The next time Mickelson showed his face on Tour, at the Players Championship, the press room bards were all over him, and he launched into what sounded like a well-rehearsed manifesto. "I won't ever change my style of play," Mickelson said. "I get criticized for it, but the fact is that I play my best when I play aggressive, when I attack, when I create shots. That's what I enjoy about the game, that challenge. And if I were to change my style of play, I won't perform at the same level, nor would I enjoy the game as much. So to win twenty tournaments the way I have, I have had to do it the way that brings out my best golf, and my best golf comes out when I play aggressive and play with creativity. Now, I may never win a major playing that way. I don't know, I believe that if I'm patient, I will. But the fact is that if I change the way I play golf, one, I won't enjoy the game as much and, two, I won't play to the level I have been playing. So I won't ever change. Not tomorrow, Sunday, or at Augusta or the U.S. Open, or any tournament."

Mickelson was reminded that, for all of his power, Jack Nicklaus—maybe the greatest winner in all of sports, ever—was a plodding tactician at heart. "I enjoy watching Jack Nicklaus play, I just don't enjoy playing that way myself," Mickelson snorted.

A month later, the U.S. Open arrived at Bethpage, a retrofitted muni outside of New York City. It was a beastly test, and in practice rounds, players were widely forecasting carnage. Then Woods opened with rounds of 67-68, and only one player, Padraig Harrington, was within seven strokes of him. It was déjà vu all over again, but the teeming gallery of Noo Yawkers were bored by Woods's relentless excellence and perhaps put off by his imperious manner. They turned their lonely eyes to the only player who didn't seem cowed by Tiger's very presence: a flashy lifelong Californian with a stiff perma-grin. It wasn't a natural kinship, but Mickelson would have to do for the Bethpage crazies. On Saturday he channeled the energy of the crowd into a 67, the second-lowest round of the day, moving into a tie for third. Hunter Mahan would play with Mickelson at the ensuing Bethpage Open, and he says of the lovefest with the fans, "You never know about people and what they're gonna like. In a weird way, Phil kind of looks like the Bethpage fans. He doesn't have Tiger's physique, he definitely doesn't have his intensity or tunnel vision. [Mickelson] works with the fans and interacts with them and enjoys them. Not many golfers do—we tend to be more internal. But he gives them a lot of himself and they enjoy and appreciate it."

Heading into the final round, Mickelson was five shots back of Woods, who had already proven to be a ruthless closer. It seemed like an impossible ask. But Mickelson made an admirable charge in the final round, eagling the ninth hole and then birdying eleven and twelve to move within two strokes of Woods's lead. Bethpage was bonkers. But Tiger birdied thirteen, Phil bogeyed fourteen, and the dream was dead. Woods had won his seventh of the last eleven majors; only Ben Hogan from 1948 to '53 had ever enjoyed a stretch as dominant.

Mickelson was again left to ponder what might have been. Forty-two years earlier, as Arnold Palmer was relaxing in the locker room at Cherry Hills between rounds of the thirty-six-hole finale to the U.S. Open, he mused to a nearby newspaperman, "A 65 would give me 280. Doesn't 280 always win the Open?"

Not anymore. Across four days at Bethpage, Mickelson had taken exactly 280 strokes, even par. But Woods was three shots better.

"Heading in, I thought even par would be an incredible score for four rounds," Mickelson said Sunday night at Bethpage. "I was able to accomplish that. I have to lower that number if I'm going to win tournaments with Tiger in the field. I'm starting to realize that, and I've got to continue to work harder in all areas of my game to compete at the highest level."

Along with reconfiguring the record books, Woods was reshaping popular opinion: turns out golfers could look like athletes, too. With his obsessive workouts, Tiger's upper body was increasingly the shape of a martini glass. Mickelson, meanwhile, was doughier than ever. He had put on a lot of weight in 2001, when Amy was pregnant with their daughter Sophia. His explanation? "You know how it is—she would eat, I would eat."

In fact, he had always been a legendary chowhound. In the player dining tent at a long-ago PGA Championship, Mickelson hit the dessert buffet with such a vengeance that one fellow competitor reported, "He appears to be trying to commit suicide by chocolate éclair." Gary McCord loves to tell the story of a young Mickelson, while en route to the course for a casual game, calling to offer to pick up Taco Bell for the rest of the foursome. They instructed him to order a dozen tacos. When Mickelson arrived at the course, the huge bag was full of discarded wrappers. McCord dug around and found three remaining tacos at the bottom; Mickelson had eaten the other nine. "It was maybe a ten-minute drive," McCord says. "He averaged a taco a minute."

In the Woods-Mickelson polarity, Phil's pudge was a metaphor for his lack of discipline, on and off the course. Tida Woods took to referring to him as "the fat boy" and "Hefty," a play on the Lefty nickname. Her son could be even more brutal. "One time in the Bay Hill locker room," says Hawkins, "Tiger summoned me over. His manner was very serious. I got this feeling like he was pissed off, and I was wracking my brain trying to think of what I had written that would have set him off. He was tying his shoes and then he stood up slowly and leaned into me, to the point where he was violating my personal space. And he says, 'Hey, Hawk, do you think Phil lactates?'"

In February 2003, Mickelson finally clapped back, telling one of the golf magazines, "In my mind, Tiger and I don't have issues between us. Well, maybe one. He hates that I can fly it past him now [off the tee]. He has a faster swing speed than I do, but he has inferior equipment."

Strictly speaking, Mickelson wasn't wrong: Woods had chosen not to max out the latest space-age technology, using a ball that spun more (and thus didn't carry as far) and a 43.5-inch, steel-shafted driver when most of his peers had embraced longer, lighter graphite shafts. This setup cost Woods distance but gave him more control and allowed him to shape the ball more effectively, a good trade in his eyes. "What Phil said was funny because it was true," says Nick Faldo. "That Nike driver Tiger was using was horrendous." But that's nuance. Mickelson got barbecued in the press and the locker room for being so uppity, given that at the time Woods led him 8–0 in career major championship victories. Tiger relished every second of the backlash. "That was just Phil being Phil," he said, and he didn't mean it as a compliment. "He was trying to be a smart aleck, and in this case it didn't work."

On March 26, 2003, Evan Mickelson was born. It was a harrowing delivery. Before being swept into the hallway by the nurses, Phil stood over his son and pleaded, "Breathe, Evan, breathe." The little boy went seven minutes before taking his first breath, and only the quick work of the nurses and modern technology prevented catastrophe. Meanwhile, Amy was fighting for her life. She had sustained a six-inch tear in a major artery and was bleeding profusely, necessitating emergency surgery. "We were two or three minutes away from losing her," Phil says.

Two weeks later he blew into the Masters and somehow finished third, two shots out of the Mike Weir–Len Mattiace playoff. But in the months that followed, Mickelson was understandably focused on caring for his family and he suffered only the second winless season of his career.

And yet, near the end of that summer, strange rumors began to waft out of Toledo: not unlike Michael Jordan a decade earlier, Mickelson had decided to chase his boyhood baseball dreams. The Mud Hens, a AAA affiliate of the Detroit Tigers, were granting him a tryout as a pitcher. There was loose talk that if Mickelson excelled, he might get a one-day call-up in the season's final week as a publicity stunt with the woebegone Tigers, who were on their way to losing 119 games. It seemed like fantasy camp for dilettantes, but Mickelson was quite serious, hiring renowned pitching coach Tom House to guide him. They spent months working in secret, sometimes on a mound Mickelson had built in his backyard. Hefty also began working with a functional fitness trainer named Sean Cochran to get in better shape. "He busted his hump," says House. "His work ethic is off the charts."

According to House, Mickelson was occasionally touching eighty-four miles per hour with his fastball. Asked whose delivery Mickelson's evoked, House cites Justin Verlander, but quickly adds, "By no stretch of the imagination was he Justin Verlander. But same action, same basic delivery. He had a decent breaking ball and he was really proud of his split finger. He kept saying that was his money pitch he'd use to get guys out in the big leagues. Typical Phil, after two days he knew everything there is to know about pitching. He didn't lack for confidence, that's for sure."

Mickelson's tryout with the Mud Hens came in late August, the day after the World Series of Golf ended in Akron. Paul Azinger, Fred Couples, Justin Leonard, and Jay Haas were among the golfers who came along to lend support and/or talk trash. Mud Hens manager Larry Parrish didn't want Mickelson to get killed by a line drive so he didn't let him throw to any position players, just the pitchers, among them Fernando Rodney and Steve Avery. Mickelson wedged three Benjis to the batting cage and said the first player to hit a home run off of him could claim the money. He loosened up and then fired his best fastball. Mickelson asked what it registered on the speed gun.

68.

Incredulous, he reared back and uncorked another heater.

68.

His splitter was clocked in the 50s. No wonder none of the hitters could take him deep. Says Azinger, "A reporter later asked me how he did and I said they couldn't touch him because those guys ain't seen 68 since Little League. He printed it and Phil got mad at me."

House attributes Mickelson's embarrassing lack of velocity to a golfer's mentality. "He told me that when he was working on swing changes he might hit five hundred balls in a day," says House. "That's not how it works with a pitcher. Leading up to the tryout he was throwing a hundred pitches a day in his backyard. There isn't a big leaguer alive who can throw seven hundred pitches a week. When he went back [to Toledo] he was at a deficit. His arm was dead."

After pitching batting practice, Mickelson stuck around for the game that followed, sitting in the dugout with the Mud Hens. "He was way into it," says A. J. Hinch, the future Tigers manager who was then rehabbing an injury at the end of his playing career. "He asked a ton of good questions. A bunch of us were serious golfers, so we were peppering him with questions, too. It was fun. I give him credit for trying. You could tell he was coached, that he had put in the work. It wasn't a gimmick. The effort was sincere."

From what he saw, could Mickelson have been even a single-A prospect?

"No, not even close," says Hinch, who carries a 6.6 handicap index. "That's like asking if someone who hits their driver two hundred yards can compete on the Korn Ferry Tour. There's just no way."

Mickelson's baseball cameo may have been a swing and a miss but there was an unexpected benefit: he hired Cochran full-time and got into the best shape of his life, aided by a no-fun diet that included a ban on sugar and six small, healthy meals a day (and no buns for his cheat days at In-N-Out). The off-season of 2003 was a time of reinvention for Mickelson. He gathered his intimates and took stock of where he was in his life and career. Earlier that year, while Evan and Amy had been battling to live, he sat in a lonely hospital hallway and made a covenant to lead a more impactful life. Now he and his wife founded the Phil and Amy Mickelson Foundation and they pledged to use their growing fortune for large-scale philanthropy. Looking ahead to the coming season, Mickelson instructed his swing coach, Rick Smith, and short-game specialist, Dave Pelz, to come up with detailed game plans for improvement and then put in man-hours implementing their suggestions. With

Smith, who ministered to the long game, Mickelson focused on quieting his lower body during the swing and committing to mastering a fade with his driver, which would help rein in the big miss. With Pelz, Mickelson focused on controlling the spin and carry distances with his short irons and wedges. He began putting towels on his practice areas at five-yard increments so he could more precisely dial in his carry distances.

This period of personal growth was bittersweet for one reason: Nunu's health was failing. Every year, a couple days after Christmas, Grandchildren's Day was held at the Santos home. Al and Jennie would host their seven grandkids to share a big meal, tell stories, and dispense old-world advice. It was a treasured tradition for all of them. By Christmas 2003, Nunu was ninety-seven and his kitchen was festooned with twenty-one flags, one for each of his grandson's Tour victories. Knowing this would be their last such gathering with Al, each of the grandkids went around the room and offered heartfelt words about their relationship. Phil broke down in tears reminiscing about their fishing trips and many rounds of golf together. As the evening was ending, Nunu motioned for Mickelson to come over to him. "Philip, this is your year," he whispered. "You're going to win the Masters." Al Santos died ten days later. Those were the last words he ever spoke to his grandson.

CHAPTER EIGHT

Late on Easter Sunday, Phil Mickelson stood over a birdie putt on the eighteenth hole to win the 2004 Masters, and it was as quiet as church. Thousands of fans had encircled the green, glowing from sweat and the most exciting Masters finish since forty-six-year-old Jack Nicklaus turned back the clock in 1986. Ernie Els, the game's gentle giant, was in the clubhouse after a dazzling 67, having rushed to the lead of the tournament with two eagles in a span of six holes midway through the round. Mickelson chased him down with a back-nine charge for the ages, and now, having endured countless heartbreaks in his decade-plus pursuit of a first major championship, Mickelson was facing the most important putt of his career, eighteen feet that meant so much to so many.

Behind the green, Amy Mickelson had been blinking back tears since the fifteenth hole, so overwhelming was the emotion of the day. Nearby, two sets of grandparents were passing around Phil and Amy's three young children, including Evan, who had just turned a year old and showed no aftereffects of his fraught arrival into the world. Standing sentry behind Amy was Steve Loy, Mickelson's college coach turned consigliere. On the edge of the green, fidgeting nervously, was Jim Mackay. He is part of what Amy calls "our gang." She said that week, "We joke that Phil is the only player in golf history to have the same wife, caddie, agent, and nanny his whole career." Shades of Pinehurst, Bones had a beeper in his pocket, but this time it was for his wife, Jennifer, a college friend to Amy, who served as matchmaker. Jen was about to burst and had spent much of Masters Sunday on a raft in their backyard pool in Scottsdale. "The doctors said the weightlessness makes the baby not want to come out," Bones explained. This Masters would be defined by life and death:

on the morning of the first round, Bruce Edwards lost his long battle with Lou Gehrig's disease. Known as the "Arnold Palmer of caddies," Edwards had long been a mentor to Bones. As his boss eyed his birdie putt, Mackay's mind wandered to Edwards. "I had a strong feeling he was looking down on us and smiling," he said.

Back in San Diego, Mickelson's ninety-two-year-old grandmother, Jennie Santos, rested comfortably in front of the TV. Nunu's widow had been getting ready to leave for Augusta when she suffered a mild stroke.

All of this feeling and personal history was distilled into one downhill right-to-lefter. Making a putt like this has very little to do with technical proficiency. It is an X-ray of the soul, revealing the unseen parts of a golfer that cannot be measured on a launch monitor: heart, guts, balls. At last, Mickelson nudged his golf ball toward the cup. Moments earlier he had studied playing partner Chris DiMarco's unsuccessful effort from virtually the same spot. "Chris's ball was hanging on that left lip, and when it got to the hole, it just fell off," Mickelson said. "And my putt was almost on the identical line. Instead of falling off, it caught that lip and circled around and went in. I can't help but think [Nunu] may have had a little something to do with that."

The crowd exploded, a release of emotion years in the making. Mickelson did a low-flying jumping jack and screamed, "I did it!" He hugged Bones and then kissed his golf ball and threw it into the crowd. (It would later be returned by the fan who caught it and then mounted next to the eighteenth-hole flag and displayed in the Santos kitchen.) Behind the green, Mickelson scooped up Sophia and planted a kiss on her cheek. "Daddy won! Can you believe it?" he shouted. He wrapped Amy in a long, tearful hug. The eighteenth green at the Masters has seen some of golf's most memorable displays of emotion. Phil and Amy were in almost the same spot where Eldrick Woods and his father, Earl, embraced after Tiger's victory in 1997. The final green is where Ben Crenshaw was doubled over in agony and ecstasy after having been guided to victory in '95 by the unseen hand of his teacher Harvey Penick, who died two days before the tournament began. Now Mickelson had joined the pantheon of Masters winners. After seventeen career top tens in the majors, including three straight third-place finishes at Augusta, he had proved himself in the most audacious fashion imaginable. On a course that is far tougher than it was in '86, when Nicklaus shot a back-nine 30 to surge to victory, Mickelson birdied five of the last seven holes to finish with a 31 on the final nine on Sunday. He became only the sixth player to snatch the Masters with a birdie on the seventy-second hole, a list that includes Palmer, who had a birdie-birdie finish in 1960.

"Now we can finally stamp him APPROVED," said Davis Love III, a friend of Mickelson's. "It's like a . . . what's the right word? . . . It's like a coronation."

You can't have a coronation without the King, and over the first two rounds Mickelson and every other competitor had to take a backseat to Palmer, who was saying goodbye to Augusta after fifty years of mythmaking. Palmer was the first player to win four green jackets, between 1958 and '64; the Masters is where his Army first marched. As he said goodbye on Friday, the pines echoed with the roars from the standing ovations he received on every hole. At eighteen, in a golden twilight, Palmer tapped in for a final bogey. Behind the green, he kissed a pretty girl—his then fiancée, Kit Gawthrop—and then he was gone. At that moment, on the seventeenth hole, Mickelson was charging. Something in his strut looked familiar during a week in which so much footage of the vintage Palmer was unreeled. As Mickelson walked toward the green, where a frighteningly fast thirty-footer for birdie awaited, his swing coach, Rick Smith, whispered to Amy, "Look how fast he's going. He knows he's going to make this putt. He's dying to hit it!" Sure enough, Mickelson poured in the putt, the exclamation point on a solid 69 that vaulted him into a tie for fourth place, three shots back of Justin Rose, the young Englishman.

Phil the Thrill had put himself in contention with admirable restraint. In the previous three Masters, Mickelson had made sixty birdies, while the respective champions combined for fifty-eight; to win he would have to make fewer big numbers. Augusta National's dangerous par-5s were the battlefield where the war played out between the old and new Phil. When, instead of boldly firing at the flag on thirteen during the first round, he conservatively aimed thirty-five feet left, it was clear that Mickelson was playing a different game than in years past. And when you don't tempt the golf gods, you are rewarded. At thirteen on Friday, Mickelson pulled his approach, and it rolled off the green toward Rae's Creek before stopping inches above the hazard, the most momentous Velcro job since Fred Couples's ball stayed up on the twelfth hole in 1992. Mickelson turned a would-be 6 into a 4, the key break of the tournament.

For this Masters, Mickelson throttled back in another way, abandoning his trademark flop shot on Augusta National's tight lies and using his putter from off the greens. This wasn't glamorous, but it got the job done. At the eighteenth on Saturday, he got up and down from behind the green with a deft putt off a mound, preserving a bogeyless 69 that gave him his first fifty-four-hole lead in a major. Relying on his new fade off the tee over the first three rounds, Mickelson played the most controlled, disciplined golf of his career, hitting 73.6 percent of his fairways and leading the tournament in greens in regulation. In fact, on Saturday, after Mickelson had spent the day hitting all but four fairways, Amy greeted him by saying, "Honey, I miss you lately. You never hit it over by the ropes anymore."

Still, Sunday loomed as the ultimate test. That Woods, his nemesis, was in twentieth place at three over par, surely helped. "Well, it doesn't suck," Mickelson said, breaking up a loosey-goosey press conference. However relaxed Mickelson seemed, you just knew he wouldn't make it easy on Sunday. Early on, he came down with a case of the yips (missing a three-and-a-half-footer for par on three) and then the fluffs (leaving a sand shot in a bunker on five for another bogey). Mickelson was three down to a relentless Els when he reached the heart of Amen Corner. He might have played Nicklaus's brand of percentage golf to get this far, but now it was time to get after it like Arnie. On the par-3 twelfth, the scariest little hole in golf, Mickelson attacked the flag, sticking an 8-iron to twelve feet for the birdie that began his comeback. At thirteen, he ripped a high fade around the corner and then rifled a 7-iron to twenty feet, setting up a two-putt birdie. He was one back, but only for a moment, as Els played a superb chip at the par-5 fifteenth, capping a run in which he went six under in a nine-hole stretch. On the CBS telecast, David Feherty enthused, "He's got the green jacket by the collar!"

Els finished with three pars, including a bailout tee shot on the par-3 six-teenth and then a drive on eighteen that bounded into a bunker. Looking back now he says, "What an unbelievable Sunday. The frustrating thing for me is I felt I had more to give [on the last three holes], but I played it too safe. I didn't want to make a mistake coming in, knowing Phil's record in the majors to that point and that seventeen and eighteen are tough driving holes. I thought I'd be okay."

Mickelson was still one down when he arrived at sixteen, the hole that had cost him dearly in 2001, when his hooked 7-iron put him above the hole, resulting in the three-putt that killed his chances. On Thursday of this Masters, he had double-bogeyed the hole, but Mickelson is nothing if not fearless: he played another draw, but this time started it out over the water, leaving himself eighteen feet below the hole. Off-air, Feherty had this reaction when seeing Mickelson's hyperaggressive start line: "Holy shit!" Phil buried the birdie putt to finally draw even with Els. "Oh, baby," he shouted. "Wow." Walking off the green, he nudged Bones and said, "Let's get one more." A par at seventeen set up the drama of the seventy-second hole.

Mickelson's breakthrough brilliance made it clear this Masters would be not the culmination of a career but the beginning of a wondrous second act. One of the game's greats, Ben Hogan, didn't win his first major championship until he was thirty-four. By the time he was forty-one, he had eight more. Mickelson was only thirty-three. For years, golf fans had been pining for someone to play Palmer to Woods's Nicklaus. Now Mickelson had arrived. The King was gone. Long live the new king.

When you win the Masters, the green jacket ceremony is the beginning of the festivities, not the end. Long-standing tradition compels the new champ to have dinner with the entire Augusta National membership, in a ballroom that is constructed annually just for that purpose. "It's amazing when you walk in the room and see all those green jackets," says Patrick Reed, the 2018 champ. "Mine, I get to go out and play for it and try to earn it on the golf course, and for them to be invited and be the very few select around the world that have the opportunity to be a member here and to come to such a coveted place and to play such an amazing golf course and be a part of such a small group and to get them all together is really special." This is part of the reflexive awe so many players have for Augusta National: it is rare for them to be the poorest person in a room.

Unlike the Tuesday night Champions Dinner, the club handles the menu—lobster macaroni and cheese is a perennial favorite—and covers the cost. But after his life-altering victory, Mickelson pulled aside then-chairman Hootie Johnson. "He was so overjoyed to have won, he really wanted to celebrate," says Amy, "so he tells Hootie, 'Go deep in the wine cellar and pull out your best stuff.'" Augusta National's cellar is legendary and has been widely described as among the best in the world. A particular favorite among certain green jackets is Château Lafite Rothschild, a Bordeaux of which some vintages can retail for up to $15,000 a bottle. Says Amy, "Phil got pulled away, and after he was gone I heard Hootie say to another club official, 'Do be sure that Mr. Mickelson is presented the bill for the wine.'"

Cell phones are verboten even in this private setting, so just as the Mickelson coterie was arriving for dinner, he was summoned to an old-fashioned landline within the clubhouse. "Now I know why you play golf instead of basketball," President George W. Bush told the new champ. "You can't dunk!"

Later that night—much later—the party moved to a private house the Mickelsons had rented for the week. A phone kept ringing, but nobody answered it. "Tell them we went to the moon," Amy said dreamily.

Her husband was strutting around in black shorts, black T-shirt, white socks, an Arizona State cap . . . and his new green jacket. "I don't mean to be disrespectful," Phil said with a rakish grin, "but I just can't take it off!" No kidding. Guess what he slept in that night?

CHAPTER NINE

The hangover from the Masters win, emotional or otherwise, was short-lived. After two weeks of goofing off—Leno, Letterman, and ringing the opening bell at the New York Stock Exchange, all while wearing a spiffy new green sports coat—Phil Mickelson turned up at the Tour event in New Orleans and finished tied for second. He just kept riding that momentum all the way to the U.S. Open at Shinnecock Hills. Windblown, with 164 ball-gobbling bunkers and small, terrifying greens, Shinnecock is one of golf's great tests. The USGA offered a new-school setup with wide fairways and shaved areas around the greens, requiring talent and imagination to play the recovery shots. Mickelson fell in love with the course presentation when, in a new tradition, he went to Shinnecock a couple of weeks before the Open to perfect a game plan with his swing coach, Rick Smith, and short-game specialist, Dave Pelz. Aided by a similar scouting mission to Augusta, Mickelson had won an epic Masters with the most calculating golf of his career. The big question now was whether or not New Phil could stay on script.

Much of his pretournament preparation involved the sixteenth hole, a short (537 yards), tricky par-5 that rewards precision, not pyrotechnics. On his way to a fourth-place finish at the 1995 Open at Shinnecock, the callow, gung ho Mickelson had played the hole double bogey–bogey–bogey–double bogey. In the first round of this Open, Mickelson pulled his drive into the right rough, 247 yards from the hole. Trying to reach the green in two with a violent rip of his 4-wood, he missed in the worst place possible—long and right. Now Mickelson faced a third shot over a gaping bunker to a pin tucked on a downslope just a few paces beyond the sand. After hurrying to a vantage point near the green, an edgy Smith sized up the play: "This is the shot of the tournament," he said. "This is the most dangerous shot he may face all week." In years past, Mickelson would have attempted to stuff the ball next to the flag with his trademark high-risk flop shot, inviting bogey or worse. (A flop from a similar spot during the final round in '95 came up inches short of the green and trickled back into the bunker.) Mickelson went through a series of practice swings as Smith described each: "That was the high flop. . . . That was a low controlled spinner that he would play to the middle of the green. . . . That was the flop." You could imagine an angel on one of Mickelson's shoulders and the devil on the other. Finally, he settled into the shot. Mickelson took a short, tight backswing and the ball shot out low and hard, landing well past the flag and leaving a twenty-five-footer. He had conceded birdie, but was rewarded with a tap-in par. "He did the right thing," Smith said with a weary smile. "That was his first big test, and now he's off and running."

Indeed, Mickelson followed his opening 68 with a bogeyless 66 to surge into the lead. He was still atop the leaderboard late in the third round, but Retief Goosen reeled him in, birdieing the fifteenth and sixteenth holes while a tired-looking Mickelson staggered home bogey-bogey. Goosen's rock-solid 69 was largely lost in the howls of protest engulfing Shinnecock Hills. The blue blazers at the USGA may have gotten the pretournament setup right, but they forgot one thing: just add water. Overcast, windless conditions and a Thursday-evening shower made Shinnecock playable for the first two rounds, but on a sunny, windy Saturday, the USGA began to lose the greens. By the time the last group teed off at 2:50 p.m., the crusty, baked putting surfaces "looked like someone took a Bunsen burner to them," according to Smith. The shrillest criticism was reserved for the seventh hole, a 189-yard par-3 with a Redan green that slopes severely from front to back. On Saturday, only eighteen of the sixty-six competitors would be able to hold the putting surface with their tee shots, and so many players had chips roll back to their feet it looked like a Skee-Ball competition. Mickelson's double bogey began with an 8-iron that scooted off the back of the green. After a delicate chip, his ten-foot par putt trickled by the hole, wavered, wiggled, just about stopped, started up again, and then meandered twenty feet past. He missed the comebacker. Asked afterward by a reporter if the hole is fair, Mickelson shot back, "What do you think?" This is the beginning of his cold war with the USGA, which will finally bubble over fourteen years later amid another setup screwup at Shinnecock Hills.

Whining about the course is the soundtrack to most U.S. Opens, but when Sunday arrived with a bright blue sky and the strongest winds of the tournament, Shinnecock's burned-out greens crossed the line from extremely difficult to patently unfair. The bloodbath began with the early starters. Billy Mayfair, a five-time winner on the PGA Tour, shot a 47 on the front nine and finished at 89. Hall of Famer Tom Kite parred the last six holes . . . to shoot 84. Asked to describe the fried greens, Goosen offered one word: "Dead." In the early afternoon, the USGA finally decided to intermittently water the putting surfaces. This meant that different players faced different speeds. On the seventh tee, Mickelson watched the maintenance crew water the green for the twosome in front, but not for him and Fred Funk. "Total crap," Mickelson recalls thinking. He intentionally hit his tee shot into a greenside bunker to leave himself an uphill shot to the flag. Mickelson stuck it to three feet to save a crafty par.

Amid this tempest, Goosen was unflappable. Struck by lightning when he was seventeen, he still plays as if he doesn't have a pulse. He led by three strokes with seven holes to play, but Mickelson put together a back-nine surge that was fast becoming his trademark. Goosen bogeyed fourteen, while Mickelson birdied thirteen and fifteen, and suddenly they were tied. At the sixteenth hole, Mickelson played a gorgeous third shot, feeding his pitch off a slope toward the flag. Around New York he had been the people's choice since finishing second to Tiger Woods in "The People's Open" at Bethpage in 2002, and Long Island shook as Mickelson's ball inched to within eight feet of the cup. As he was approaching the green, some grim-faced state troopers cleared a path for Rudy Giuliani to worm his way behind the putting surface. Mickelson rolled in the birdie putt to take his first lead of the day, at four-under par, and amid the roars I asked Giuliani to explain Phil's appeal in the Empire State. "New Yorkers love a winner," said Giuliani, panting heavily with his oxford shirt drenched with sweat. "They especially love someone who wins with class. Phil reminds me, and I think he reminds a lot of us, of the Captain, Derek Jeter. There is no higher praise."

Goosen watched Mickelson's birdie from the fairway, then coolly stuffed a wedge fifteen feet below the hole and brushed in the putt as if it were a practice-round gimme. Tied again. The crescendo came at seventeen, a 179-yard par-3. Mickelson lost a 6-iron into the left bunker, but was left with what should have been a straightforward bunker shot—uphill and into the wind. Funk later estimated that, absent U.S. Open pressure, Mickelson would get it up-and-down nine times out of ten. But there was one itty-bitty problem: a small rock sitting just behind Phil's ball. "I tried to go behind the rock and underneath it, and it took all the spin off it," Mickelson said years later. "It had over-spin on it. It shot past the hole in the one spot I couldn't go: downhill, downwind. It was not a hard shot. Couldn't have been easier. But that one thing changed everything. All because of that fricking rock."

Funk confirms Mickelson's account: "I saw him a few weeks later and I had read all of the post-round comments and the things he said after that. And not once did he mention the rock. I knew what had happened. The sound of the shot was weird, and the ball came out with no spin. So I asked him about it, and all he said to me was 'I never should have been in the bunker in the first place.'"

Still, Mickelson had only four feet to save his par. But he played too much borrow and missed on the high side, his ball racing four feet by the hole. He yanked the comeback for a crushing double bogey. Goosen followed by getting up-and-down from nearly the identical spot in the front bunker. "It was like a morgue going up eighteen," Funk says. "We went from this incredible theater with the possibility of a playoff or Phil winning outright to now he is two behind and there's nothing. That was a screw job on that seventeenth hole. And he never mentioned it to anyone. It was probably one of the worst breaks I ever saw."

There is plenty more heartbreak to come in the U.S. Open, but Mickelson still stews about Shinnecock. "That is the one I should have won more than any other," he says. "I played phenomenal that last day. Given the difficulty of the course, I would say that I have not played better in a U.S. Open in my life."

Mickelson had only one top twenty in his first ten Open Championships, back in 2000, when he finished eleventh, twelve strokes behind Tiger Woods.

But a month after Shinnecock, he blew into Royal Troon with entirely different expectations. Mickelson had played the Scottish Open the week before to acclimate, and Dave Pelz made the journey across the pond to help him prepare for Royal Troon, site of the Open Championship. Mickelson's diligent work on his game in the preceding few years finally allowed him to control the spin and trajectory of his shots, which is crucial on a windy, firm, quirky links course. Troon's front nine plays downwind and the backside is a brutal slog home straight into the prevailing gale. Mickelson cooked up a game plan that featured a variety of different shots, including a newly acquired sawed-off swing with a fairway wood that, into the wind, never got above head high and rolled for miles. "I was taught growing up to hit the ball low, you scoot the ball back in your stance, which delofts the club and that's how you do it," he said. "The problem is you come in steeper and create a lot more spin. And even though the ball is flying low, it's spinning. That's what you don't want. You're changing ball position, you're changing angle of attack, you're changing the golf swing. So now the only difference for me is I keep everything the same, ball position, swing, so forth. I just shorten the backswing a little bit, accelerate through. It doesn't have enough speed to create the same spin, comes in from a shallower angle of attack, and gets the ball launching lower without the speed, without the spin."

An opening 73 felt like more of the same ol', but Mickelson rallied with rounds of 66 and 68, going bogey-free both days to roar into third place, just one stroke off the lead shared by Ernie Els and Todd Hamilton. In the cold, blustery final round, Mickelson chipped in for eagle on the fourth hole and birdied number seven to storm into a tie for the lead. But once Mickelson turned into the wind, he repeatedly found himself fighting to save par; when he failed to get up-and-down on thirteen it was, incredibly, his first bogey in the span of fifty holes. Els and Hamilton pushed deeper into red numbers. A birdie on the sixteenth hole gave Mickelson a glimmer, but he finished one shot out of the Els-Hamilton playoff.

Phil just kept coming, making another spirited run at the PGA Championship at Whistling Straits. A third-round 67 (tied for the lowest score of the day) propelled him into a tie for third, four strokes behind Vijay Singh.

The Straits played brutally hard on Sunday. Mickelson doubled the par-3 third hole after skulling a bunker shot and followed with bogeys on five and nine. But after steadying himself on the back nine, he arrived at the seventy-second hole needing a birdie to tie for the lead. After a perfect drive, he blocked his approach shot into a greenside bunker, ultimately making a bogey that dropped him into a tie for sixth, two strokes out of the Singh–Justin Leonard–Chris DiMarco playoff. Across 2004's final three majors, he was, theoretically, only eight total shots from winning them all. Rather than rue the ones that got away, Mickelson was buoyant in the aftermath of the PGA. "Win, lose, or draw, I just love having a chance on Sunday," he said.

Over the first dozen years of his career, Mickelson had created a solid-gold brand: prolific winner, gracious loser, loving husband, doting father. The people closest to him only added to his appeal, whether it was his dutiful caddie, Bones, who seemed like a brother as much as a looper, or Amy, who could always be found flashing a megawatt smile in the gallery and chatting with random fans or positioning herself between green and tee to steal kisses with Phil. "I would say she is the heir to Barbara Nicklaus's throne," says Kimberly (Mrs. Brian) Gay, referencing Jack's bride, who always set a gold standard for graciousness. "I don't know how she does it, but Amy is always warm and lovely to everyone she meets. She is always open and accessible, even with all the lights shining on her. And she treats you the same no matter where your husband is on the money list, which isn't always the case. She's just always been a ray of sunshine."

With all of this accumulated goodwill to go along with a thrilling Masters victory and the run of excellence in the ensuing majors, the time had arrived for Mickelson to cash in. His advocate continued to be Coach Loy, who had already managed to land endorsement deals with blue-chip companies like Ford, despite his rough edges; when an associate first mentioned a possible pact with KPMG, the vast Big Four accounting and financial services firm, Loy was baffled. In a line that is oft repeated by his ex-colleagues, Loy responded, "Phil Mickelson is not going to sign with a fucking radio station."

Mickelson had long enjoyed an endorsement deal to play Titleist golf balls, and throughout 2000—the year he left Yonex—he pushed hard for the release of the prototype Pro V1, in a doomed attempt to keep pace with Tiger Woods, who had begun playing Nike's solid-core ball that May. When the Pro V1 finally dropped in October 2000, Mickelson proved to be its most hyperbolic honk, claiming the ball was golf's biggest technological revolution since steel shafts replaced hickory. At the end of 2000, Mickelson extended his relationship with Titleist to include playing its irons and woods in a five-year deal worth a reported $4 million annually. Titleist makes top-notch gear. In fact, it's so good, the company wants the product to be the star, not an individual endorser. In the late nineties, both Woods and David Duval had been Titleist ambassadors, but as their careers took off they were released from their contracts early to chase megadeals that reshaped the equipment endorsement landscape. Mickelson was looking to renegotiate his deal even before he won the Masters.

Those who consider him Machiavellian often point to the voicemail Mickelson left Mike Galeski, Callaway's head of PGA Tour relations, in the fall of 2003, in which he lavished praise on Callaway's new HX Tour ball and ERC Fusion driver. Mickelson had to know his words would create a huge stir within the halls of a putative competitor. Sure enough, Galeski played the voicemail to a room full of Callaway sales reps at a national meeting. When word of that inevitably wafted back to Wally Uihlein, the persnickety CEO of Titleist's parent company, he threatened both Mickelson and Callaway with legal action, the beginning of the Phil-Titleist divorce. It took a year for the blockbuster deal to be consummated, but in September 2004, Mickelson became the face of Callaway Golf, whose biggest endorser at that moment was Charles Howell III, with one career victory. The timing was problematic for only one reason: Mickelson's first start after signing the contract would be the Ryder Cup, golf's most overhyped, overheated event.

After his undefeated debut in '95, Mickelson had mixed results in subsequent Cups. He went 1-1-2 in the U.S. loss in '97 and then got skunked in two matches on the opening day in '99, helping Europe to build a big lead. But Mickelson delivered a crucial point in Saturday afternoon better ball, and then, sent out third in singles, he blitzed Jarmo Sandelin 5 & 3 to help fuel the Americans' rousing comeback. In 2002, he brought home 2.5 points across four partner matches, but in singles got beat by someone named Phillip Price, a monumental upset that was instrumental in Europe stealing the Cup.

This was an era of parity for the Ryder Cup. The generational talents that had made Europe a superpower in the 1980s—Seve Ballesteros, Nick Faldo, Bernhard Langer, Sandy Lyle, Ian Woosnam—had all exited stage right. The U.S. was also searching for a new identity without its previous emotional leaders, Paul Azinger and the late Payne Stewart. Woods should have been the American alpha, but he didn't want the job. He spent the 103 weeks between Ryder Cups trying to intimidate every other top player, and even in the sanctum of the team room Woods was disinclined to reveal anything from the well-guarded fortress of his inner self. Mickelson tried to fill the vacuum. "Tiger held everything close to the vest," says Stewart Cink, who played on five Ryder Cup teams in the Woods-Mickelson era. "He never understood how Phil got any juice out of showing his hand. But that's just Phil's nature, to tell everyone what he's thinking and feeling, and to explain what's next and how to prepare for it. In a team environment, you'd definitely choose Phil's way. He was very much into team-building and he thrived in that environment. He wanted to win, badly, and it was infectious. You could feel it. Tiger wanted to win, too, because he wants to win at everything he does, but his was a much more mechanical and solitary approach. He was like, 'I'm going to go out there and try to win five points and that's all I can do.' He tried to break his job down into its simplest form and not get too wrapped up in the team thing."

But at the 2004 Ryder Cup, Mickelson's commitment to his team, to say nothing of his country, was thrown into question when he showed up with a bag full of shiny new Callaway clubs and a new ball that he had never before tested in competition. He claimed Callaway was not forcing him to use the gear, but no one quite believed him. The Ryder Cup preamble is interminable; with the event not beginning until Friday, the army of bored sportswriters needs to generate plotlines, and Mickelson potentially putting his pocketbook above his flag was red meat for the typists. "I have to disabuse the notion of the contract clause that allegedly existed," says Larry Dorman, who was then senior vice president of global public relations at Callaway. "There was a lot of speculation about it in the press that week, but I read every word of Phil Mickelson's contract and there was no obligation to play any Callaway equipment at that Ryder Cup."

Mickelson's preparations grew more chaotic when, two days before the competition was to begin, U.S. captain Hal Sutton informed him he would be playing with Tiger Woods in alternate shot. The blockbuster pairing was two decades in the making, but Mickelson was pissed at the late notice. Back then, teammates had to play the exact same model of golf ball throughout the round. (Now they can switch out balls on each tee.) One problem: Woods played a rock that spins a ton, while Mickelson favored a low-spin model. In deference to the king, Phil volunteered to play Tiger's ball. He spent that Wednesday on his own testing Woods's Nike and took some shrapnel in the press for going rogue and separating himself from his teammates.

Of course, Mickelson used his own—albeit still somewhat foreign—Callaway ball in the better-ball format, when he and Woods were sent out in the Ryder Cup's very first match against European stalwarts Padraig Harrington and Colin Montgomerie. The superstar pairing had Detroit fans in a tizzy around the first tee. Captain Sutton added to the high noon atmosphere by showing up in a cowboy hat. But it was Harrington and Montgomerie who came out shooting, birdieing the first four holes with precise iron shots and a couple of long putts. Mickelson/Woods looked tight and had an abject absence of chemistry. They went down meekly, 2 & 1, setting the tone for a disastrous session during which the U.S. eked out only half a point across four matches. "It would be foolish to say the Ryder Cup was over after one match," says Paul McGinley, a member of Team Europe, "but you can't overstate the importance of us beating Tiger and Phil. It took the crowd right out of it and just applied that much more pressure to the other [American] guys, while sending a huge charge through our team. You could feel the whole atmosphere change."

Ol' Hal doubled down by sending Woods/Mickelson out that afternoon in alternate shot. Harrington and Montgomerie had put ten birdies on the board and, in Sutton's mind, they would have beaten any U.S. duo. After the fact, he even tried to couch his motives as altruistic: "I said, you know what, let's just suppose that they play great. I never left a Ryder Cup match, where I played with someone that I went to war with, I didn't leave there a better friend with him. Win or lose, I was a better friend with him. Because we had tried to accomplish something together. And I said, if they leave better friends, golf is the winner." Playing the inexperienced team of Lee Westwood and Darren Clarke, the Americans took an early lead but had frittered it away by the time they reached the eighteenth hole. Mickelson had the tee. Given the controversy over his equipment change, his complicated relationship with Woods, and a scoreboard that at that moment was bleeding European blue, it was one of the most pressure-packed swings of his career. Alas, he uncorked a block slice that sailed miles left. Woods's withering look of disdain became instantly iconic. They lost the hole and the match. By nightfall, the U.S. trailed 6.5–1.5, en route to a historically lopsided 18.5–9.5 loss.

So much ill will lingered that a dozen years later, Mickelson didn't miss the opportunity to have another go at Sutton. At a Ryder Cup press conference at Hazeltine, Mickelson relived the surprise of being told at the last minute he would be playing with Woods in alternate shot, saying, "I grabbed a couple dozen of his balls, I went off to the side, and tried to learn his golf ball in a four- or five-hour session on one of the other holes, trying to find out how far the ball goes. It forced me to stop my preparation for the tournament, to stop chipping and putting and sharpening my game in an effort to crash-course learn a whole different golf ball that we were going to be playing. And in the history of my career, I have never ball-tested two days prior to a major [event]. I've never done it. Had we known a month in advance, we might have been able to make it work. I think we probably would have made it work. But we didn't know until two days prior. Now, I'm not trying to knock anybody here, because I actually loved how decisive Captain Sutton was. I feel like that's a sign of great leadership. But that's an example, starting with the captain, that put us in a position to fail and we failed monumentally, absolutely. To say, well, you just need to play better, that is so misinformed, because you play how you prepare. I've had to be accountable for that decision twelve years ago. Even a month ago, I hear there's an analyst on the Golf Channel that accuses me of being a non–team player for having to go out and work on an isolated hole away from the team, away from my preparation." Sutton let it be known how wounded he was by these remarks, and Mickelson apologized the next day, admitting his belated criticism was "in bad taste."

Sutton found the U.S.'s uninspired, fractious effort so disenchanting he walked away from the game at age forty-six. "I was bitter," he said years later, adding, "I took the blame for everybody. Nobody played good that week. It's tough on a captain when people don't play well. It's hard to beat anybody. If I still need to shoulder the blame for Phil's poor play, then I'll do that."

If 2004 was supposed to be the moment that Team USA became Mickelson's squad, it was an unmitigated disaster. Something curdled that week for the U.S. side, touching off a series of embarrassing losses. All the frustration would finally lead to a rebellion led by Mickelson a decade after Oakland Hills.

After a long off-season to experiment and dial in his new equipment, Mickelson got off to a rip-roaring start in 2005. In back-to-back wins at Phoenix and Pebble Beach, he dropped a 60 on TPC Scottsdale and then torched venerable Spyglass Hill for a bogeyless 62. As always, Woods loomed. His 2003 and '04 campaigns had been fallow by his incomparable standards, as he divorced himself from swing guru Butch Harmon and toiled to absorb the teachings of Hank Haney. (He was also distracted by his October 2004 wedding to Elin Nordegren, a onetime bikini model; in the unofficial competition to romance blond babes, Tiger and Phil were now all square.) When Woods won his 2005 season debut at Torrey Pines, it seemed inevitable that he and Mickelson would tangle soon, and it happened in early March, at Doral. Phil opened 64-66 to sprint to the lead. On Saturday, Tiger dropped a 63 to close within two strokes of Mickelson, who had shot another 66. Ever since the 2001 Masters, the golf world had been craving another showdown between the game's leading men. Mickelson had clearly closed the gap since then, but how much?

On Sunday, Woods announced his intentions by birdieing four of the first ten holes to tie for the lead. The Miami crowd was in a frenzy. "It was electric," Woods said. "It was definitely bipartisan out there. You could hear Phil fans, you could hear Tiger fans. They were yelling at the top of their lungs. When we got to the tee boxes, my ears were ringing." At the par-5 twelfth hole, Woods mashed a 291-yard 3-wood and then gutted the twenty-five-foot eagle putt, loosing a vintage uppercut in celebration. It felt like a knockout punch, but Mickelson staggered off the ropes to birdie the next two holes and reclaim a share of the lead. "What a day," Woods said. "If you're not nervous on a day like this, you're not alive."

Still tied on the seventeenth green, Woods buried a twenty-footer for birdie to wrest back the lead. At eighteen, Mickelson's last-gasp birdie chip burned the edge of the cup. He had tied the tournament record at 23 under, but was vanquished by one stroke in a titanic battle that elevated both players. "After what he did in 2004, Phil's name was always the first one we looked for on the leaderboard," says Haney. "Whatever was going on with them personally, Tiger had the utmost respect for Phil's game. He felt he was a great closer because he knew he wasn't afraid. Tiger had more respect for Phil's short game than any other part of any other player's game. And he always marveled at Phil's mental strength. Tiger used to say, 'I can't believe how he hits one off the map and then stiffs the next one.' Most players, Tiger included, hit a couple of foul balls and then they start worrying, *Where the fuck is the next one going?* Phil had an amazingly short memory, which might be his greatest trait. All that said, Tiger wasn't really worried about Phil. He knew in his heart he was better, but he liked to send messages. Doral was a message."

Perhaps chastened by Woods's power advantage at the Blue Monster, Mickelson spent the rest of 2005 chasing distance, enabled by the Callaway engineers who, unlike the buttoned-down Poindexters at Titleist, were happy to indulge Phil's mad scientist bent. (Still to come was the one-of-a-kind "Phrankenwood," which had a driver shaft and loft, but a head the size of a 3-wood.) Mickelson's play in the majors suffered accordingly, as he was a nonfactor at the first three of the year. Meanwhile, Woods won his fourth Masters—as defending champ, Mickelson had to slip the green jacket on him—and second Open Championship to reassert his hegemony.

A reinvigorated Tiger was not the only pall on Phil's seemingly perfect life; his gambling issues were becoming an open secret on Tour. Steve Flesch was paired with Mickelson on a Sunday at the Hyundai Team Matches around the turn of the century. "Every hole, he was checking like a beeper or something," says Flesch with a laugh. "He could not have cared any less about what we were doing on the golf course. He was definitely more concerned about who was winning the football games and who was covering the spread." Tom Lehman had a similar experience with Mickelson at the 2000 Presidents Cup, when he was paired with Mickelson for a Saturday afternoon better ball versus Mike Weir and Steve Elkington. "Phil is hitting it everywhere—he's barely finished a hole through the first eight holes," says Lehman. "He keeps saying, 'Don't worry, I'll show up eventually.' On the ninth hole he buries it in the front bunker and is out of the hole again. He walks way back into the trees and is sitting on a stump with his back to everybody and his head down. I think he's giving himself a pep talk, so I go over there to try to make him feel better and he's got his phone out and he's checking the football scores."

In February 2001, Mickelson's gambling spilled into public view when he made headlines for cashing a $560,000 Super Bowl ticket, as months earlier he plunked down $20,000 on the Baltimore Ravens at 28-1. (As the Ravens wreaked havoc throughout the regular season, Mickelson let friends and family buy into the bet, spreading the wealth.) Mickelson was so invested in the Ravens' run that when the AFC Championship game fell on Saturday of the Tournament of Champions in Kapalua, Mickelson surreptitiously listened to the game during his round with an earpiece and a radio hidden in his clothes. Later in 2001, when the Tour visited Firestone, Mickelson was lounging in the locker room watching a Woods–Jim Furyk playoff. On the first extra hole, Furyk left himself in a greenside bunker and Mickelson barked out that he would bet $20 on Furyk holing the shot, at 25-1. Mike Weir took the wager and then had to pay Mickelson $500 when Furyk did, in fact, jar it. When *Golf World* reported what had happened, Mickelson earned a talking-to by PGA Tour commissioner Tim Finchem for potentially violating Section VI-B in the *PGA Tour Player Handbook*, which states, "A player shall not have any financial interest, either direct or indirect, in the performance or the winnings of another player."

Mickelson's need for action carried over into actual Tour events. "When

I was in the tower," says former CBS announcer Gary McCord, "every time Phil got to my hole, Bones would look up at me and I would flash the odds. If Phil had a fifteen-footer, I'd flash three fingers, which meant the odds were three-to-one. If he was sixty feet, I'd give him two-to-one on a two-putt. Bones would go down and whisper in his ear and Phil would look up at me and shake his head yes or no. I can't tell you how many wadded-up twenties I threw out of the tower, until the Tour found about it and I got word through CBS I was no longer allowed to gamble with Phil while up in the tower."

There was enough chatter about Mickelson's betting that his manager began to fret about his public image. "Steve Loy was really on Gary [McCord] and me because we affectionately called him Lefty on the [CBS telecasts]," says Peter Kostis. "He thought that Lefty was a derogatory reference to gambling and other things. He didn't want us to call him Lefty anymore." Ironically, this became the centerpiece of a wager when Kostis and McCord took on Mickelson in a friendly eighteen-hole match. "If we lost, we wouldn't call him Lefty on the air ever again," says Kostis. "But if we won, we could keep calling him Lefty. So in our match we had this great Mongolian reversal on the last hole where Phil hit it in the shit and Gary and I made birdie. We went from down eight hundred dollars to up, I don't know, eight hundred dollars or so. And Phil is so angry that he lost that he just keeps walking once we get to the cart area. And he goes to his car and doesn't pay. Doesn't do anything. And as he's getting in his car, Gary and I are going, 'Hey, Lefty, don't be so upset, Lefty. Come on, Lefty. You haven't even paid us yet, Lefty.' So we used Lefty about forty-seven times in three minutes. That was fun." And yet the nickname vanished from the airwaves. "Scottsdale's a very small town," Kostis says with a sigh. "We didn't want to rock the boat too much. So we didn't refer to him as Lefty anymore, regardless of the bet."

Continued whispers that Mickelson was dropping a lot of coin in Vegas sports books compelled *Golf World* to launch an investigation. Veteran scribe Ron Sirak haunted Las Vegas alongside a local reporter who was well-connected in the gambling industry. "We found Phil had a lot of big losses, but casinos only keep track of losses, not winnings," says Sirak. "He may have won big the next day—we didn't know that. We talked to the casino guys who handle the whales. When they lose big [using a line of credit], the casino gives them forty-five days to pay off the losses. Most people would wait until the forty-fourth day. Phil paid on day one." *Golf World* never published an article about Mickelson's gambling. "That was my recommendation," Sirak says. "The only story I had was a rich guy who liked to gamble, and we already knew that. I saw no indication that Phil owed anybody money or had done anything that would make people uncomfortable."

Amid the low roar about Mickelson's gambling, even more insidious rumors were also being spread in Tour circles.

"Ah yes, the Black Baby," says John Garrity, the veteran *Sports Illustrated* writer. "That was an urban legend that refused to die."

"Oh gawd, the Black Baby—that story had more legs than a spider," says longtime *Golfweek* senior writer Jeff Rude. "That rumor boomeranged on me over a period of at least five years. Different people came up to me and said, 'I heard a story about Phil and a Black Baby. Is it true?' Well, I never heard it substantiated."

The Black Baby was a rumored love child Mickelson had purportedly sired during a dalliance at Jack Nicklaus's Memorial Tournament, in Columbus, Ohio. The tale was oddly specific: the mother supposedly worked at the local First Tee chapter. This being golf, she was said to be Black, which made the whole affair that much more taboo. "It wasn't hard to figure out who the woman was," says Farrell Evans, then a young reporter at *Sports Illustrated*. "There aren't a lot of Black people in golf. Phil would not have been remiss getting with her. She was fine." Evans, who happens to be Black, picked up the phone and called the woman in question: "I told her what I heard. She said, 'Yes, I know Phil, we met once at the Memorial. But I've never slept with him and there is no baby.'"

And yet the rumor was so persistent the Mickelsons eventually hired a private investigator to ferret out its origins. Their sleuth couldn't offer a definitive answer, but the collected evidence pointed strongly to a journeyman who was said to be jealous of Phil's success. (*Golf Digest* reported his 2004 income at $40 million, 85 percent of it through endorsements.) The Black Baby chatter sucked in the mainstream golf press. "After months of cajoling me, my editor at *Golf World* said, 'You gotta ask Phil about the Black Baby,' " says John Hawkins. "It was at Palm Springs, after his round. We're walking and talking, we get to the parking lot and he's throwing shit in the car. I don't know how I got the question out. I said something like 'There have been rumors about you and your personal life and stuff that might jeopardize your marriage and . . .' Phil wheels around and gets in my face and says, 'If you ever write anything like that I will sue you and your fucking magazine and then I'll own your magazine and the first thing I'll do after I sign the papers is fire your fucking ass.' "

This explosion hints at how much stress the rumors were causing. Amy, as always, had a lighter touch. At a Tour stop in 2006, Evans encountered her sitting alone near the clubhouse. "We were just chitchatting," he says, "and the feeling was right, so I just said, 'Do you know Phil has a Black love child?' She laughed and laughed and finally said, 'I've heard a lot of good ones, but not that one.' I said, 'If it means anything to you, I talked to the alleged baby mama and she refuted the story.' "

Another persistent rumor had Amy enjoying a fling with Michael Jordan, who had become a regular presence at the Ryder Cup as a fan/groupie/motivational speaker. It had so much traction in the nether regions of the internet that for a long time if you typed *Amy Mickelson* into the Google search box, the first words that auto-filled were *Michael Jordan*. It became such a thing that Deadspin.com wrote a long story under the headline "How Did That False Amy Mickelson–Michael Jordan Rumor Start Anyway?" Amy, in her indefatigable way, started greeting her favorite reporters by asking, "Have you heard about me and Michael?!" The rumors were so inexhaustible that in 2012 the Mickelsons finally sued the internet service provider Vidéotron S.E.N.C. in Quebec Superior Court, seeking the identity of a troll who, according to the complaint, posted "several highly defamatory statements posted by one or more individuals on the Internet, in particular on a Yahoo! Website, under the pseudonyms of 'Fogroller' and 'Longitude.' . . . The postings suggest that plaintiff has an illegitimate child, that his wife has affairs and other similar vexatious statements that are absolutely untrue and, simply put, vicious." Says Mickelson's lawyer Glenn Cohen, "The really sad thing is it turned out to be a sixteen-year-old autistic kid in Toronto. We talked to his parents and they took away his computer. We did that several more times, where people were lying about Phil and Amy on the internet and we put a stop to it." He recalled one occasion of Phil being impersonated "on Twitter or one of those other stupid [social media] things." Cohen claims it took $75,000 worth of sleuthing until they found their man. "It turned out to be a high school golfer in Dallas," says Cohen. "This one had a funny ending: the father had the audacity to write to me saying him and his son were going to be at the Masters and they wanted to meet Phil and get their picture taken with him. I said, 'Are you out of your fucking mind?' If I was there I would have knocked the kid's face off."

Why were the Mickelsons the targets of such whisper campaigns? "Maybe because they seemed too perfect," says Evans. "Or maybe they weren't perfect after all. I guess you have to give them credit because despite all the shit swirling around them they just kept living their lives."

Nothing changes the narrative like winning. The 2005 PGA Championship, at venerable Baltusrol, in New Jersey, was Mickelson's last shot that season at everlasting glory. The story of his breakthrough victory at the 2004 Masters had been his newfound restraint, as he employed exclusively a high, soft cut off the tee, which cost him distance but effectively kept him out of trouble. With his souped-up new Callaway gear, he had returned to a hot draw that brought the big miss back into play. Mickelson is such a know-it-all that the other players had tagged him with two sardonic nicknames: Genius and FIGJAM (Fuck I'm Good Just Ask Me). But he clearly outsmarted himself by abandoning the cut shot that won him the Masters. During a practice round at Baltusrol—a traditional U.S. Open venue that for this PGA featured skinny fairways and tangly rough—Mickelson had the *Eureka!* moment to go back to hitting nothing but cuts off the tee, even on dogleg rights that would normally favor a draw for a left-hander. The strategy was validated by an opening 67 that tied him for the lead and fired up the Jersey boys. Mickelson had first emerged as the tristate sweetheart at the 2002 U.S. Open at Bethpage. Baltusrol is a quick ride in a town car from Gotham, and during this PGA, the *New York Times* anointed Mickelson "New York's pro." At Baltusrol he played shamelessly to the Jersey faithful, summoning the same kind of love he got at Bethpage. On the sixth hole of his first round, Mickelson's drive clipped a tree, forcing him to play his second shot down the adjacent seventeenth fairway. That left him a wedge into the green that he hit directly over the heads of the swollen gallery. After sticking the shot to five feet, Mickelson pulled a Hale Irwin and knuckle-bumped his way to the green, drawing deafening roars. "I love the feel that the people here provide," he said afterward. "It's just an amazing feeling from a player's point of view to have that kind of support." Mickelson surged to a three-stroke lead on Friday with a 65 that featured seven birdies and an eagle. This sent the throng into such hysterics that Steve Elkington described it as "probably the loudest I've ever heard at a golf tournament."

Of course, even a throttled-back Mickelson can't help but produce drama. If Woods had a three-stroke lead midway through a major, it was time to call the engraver. On Saturday at Baltusrol, it took Mickelson all of six holes to fritter away his lead as he made three bogeys. By day's end, Davis Love III, suddenly resurgent at age forty-one, had caught him at six under after a third straight 68. One shot back was Thomas Bjørn, a Hamlet in spikes who was emerging as the brooding prince of Danish golf; during the third round he shot a stunning 63. Two back of Mickelson and Love were Vijay Singh, the defending champ, and Elkington, forty-two, the oft-injured 1995 PGA Championship winner who still had the prettiest swing in golf.

On Sunday, Mickelson looked as though he was going to end all the suspense early. The first seven holes are the meat of the Baltusrol layout, and they played especially stout because the final round brought by far the toughest conditions of the week—a stiff breeze and firmer, faster greens. After opening with four pars and a birdie, Mickelson had a three-stroke lead as the other would-be contenders fell away. But Mickelson can make a thirty-yard-wide fairway seem like a tightrope. Beginning on number six, he bogeyed four out of five holes, once again letting everyone else back in the ball game. Mickelson regained the lead with a fifteen-foot birdie putt on the thirteenth hole. With par-5s looming at seventeen and eighteen, the 87th PGA Championship was speeding toward a thrilling finish, but a lightning storm suspended play until the next morning, forcing Mickelson to sleep on a lead for the fourth straight night.

When play restarted on Monday, all the contenders shrank from the moment. All but Phil. Standing on the eighteenth tee, he was tied with Bjørn and Elkington, and he split the fairway with what Bones called "the single best full swing I've ever seen him make at the ball." The drive settled near a plaque commemorating Jack Nicklaus's famous 1-iron to twenty-two feet that clinched the 1967 U.S. Open. Ever the showman, Mickelson tapped the plaque for good luck. But Mickelson's approach, a full-blooded 3-wood from 247 yards, wasn't quite as artful, finishing in thick rough four paces short and right of the green. One more up-and-down in a career full of them and the Wanamaker Trophy would be his. Sizing up his chip, Phil was struck by déjà vu. "We had some pretty thick rough in our backyard, and that's exactly what I was thinking on eighteen, that this is no different from what I've done in my backyard since I was a kid," he said. He made an aggressive, fearless swing, and an instantly famous chip cozied to two feet. Happiness is a tap-in to win the PGA Championship.

Mickelson's victory validated his green jacket; at that moment there were 113 players with one career major championship victory, but a second win put Mickelson in the august company of Hall of Famers like Greg Norman, Johnny Miller, Bernhard Langer, and Ben Crenshaw. He was halfway to his stated goal of winning the career Grand Slam.

During the brutal years when Mickelson wore the burdensome title Best Player Never to Have Won a Major, he kept insisting his goal was not to win just one major championship, but a bunch of them. He was well on his way now.

CHAPTER TEN

Phil Mickelson's second major championship victory elevated him to super-duperstardom. The spoils were extravagant—his very own Gulfstream V, a hilltop mansion in tony Rancho Santa Fe, California—but so was the scrutiny. In January 2006, *GQ* named Mickelson number eight on its list of the ten most hated athletes in the world, alongside douche canoes like Barry Bonds and Terrell Owens. The corresponding write-up used *fraud*, *preening*, and *insincere* to describe Mickelson. This was, and remains, a common critique. "I remember when I came on Tour, guys told me he's a phony or a fake or whatever," says Hunter Mahan. Tour veteran Bo Van Pelt tells an illustrative story about the time he was paired with Mickelson at the 2004 Colonial. A fan following them kept yelling, "Phil! I went to ASU! Go Sun Devils!" Mickelson smiled at the guy, waved to him, gave him the patented thumbs-up . . . and this only further encouraged the yahoo. "He shouted the same thing for five straight holes," says Van Pelt. "Finally, he gives one more 'Phil, I went to ASU!' and Phil mutters under his breath, 'Yeah, you and fifty thousand other fucking people out here.'" It was an understandable reaction—who wouldn't be annoyed? But Van Pelt remembers being impressed by Mickelson's ventriloquism: "Even as he said that, he was still smiling and waving. The fans had no idea."

One Aussie PGA Tour veteran recalls a long-ago BellSouth Classic when weather delays forced a thirty-six-hole Sunday. In the locker room that morning, all the players were grumpy because such a slog was suboptimal preparation for the ensuing Masters week. Mickelson was particularly agitated, tossing around f-bombs. At the end of the long day, the locker room was crowded with players drying off and packing up. Mickelson appeared on the TV screen and waxed poetic about how much he enjoyed the challenge, saying that it had been a refreshing throwback to the old days of the Tour. The assembled players burst out laughing.

Among Mickelson's colleagues there is much eye rolling about his marathon autograph sessions at tournaments. The underlying feeling is that it is just a shameless brand-building exercise. This is not wrong. By the time Mickelson won the 2005 PGA Championship, he had hired a former San Diego newspaperman named T. R. Reinman to serve as a press liaison and to shepherd him during tournament weeks. "I remember one time after a round, he had been signing autographs for forty-five minutes or so and the crowd was getting bigger, not smaller," says Reinman. "It started to rain, so I went out there to run interference. I tried to say something about him coming inside and Phil cut me off: 'Hey, I'm working here.'"

Brandel Chamblee recalls a Crosby Clambake in the mid-1990s when he and Mickelson arrived in their cars at Poppy Hills just after dawn for an early tee time. A little kid was waiting in the otherwise empty parking lot to ask Mickelson for his autograph. "Phil just kept walking and said, 'I'll get you afterward,' and this little boy was crestfallen," says Chamblee. "He wasn't gonna wait around for six hours to ask again and they both knew it. Of course, I signed for the kid—it took five seconds. I'm not saying this to denigrate Phil, just to illustrate that it was strategic when he decided to start signing all those autographs. Because early in his career he didn't sign a lot. I'm ninety-nine percent sure it was strategic because Tiger hated signing and pretty much refused to do it. Phil saw there was a void and decided he would be the superstar who signs for everyone. And that elevated the narrative surrounding Phil."

Of course, the fans don't care *why* Mickelson gives so much of himself, they're just thrilled and grateful that he does, especially since so many Tour players blow by them with a thousand-yard stare. (Chamblee calls professional golfers "likely the biggest prima donnas in all of sports.") Phil likes to tell the story of early in his career observing Arnold Palmer interact with people and that he has always tried to emulate that generosity of spirit. "He's not phony, he's just kind of goofy," Mahan concludes. "I've never seen any kind of fake side to him. And I've never seen him be rude to any person."

Mickelson is famously generous with folks in the service industry, dispensing Benjis as if they're business cards. Years ago, when *Golf Digest* asked various players how much cash they were carrying, Mickelson's number was $8,100: sixty-five Ben Franklins, eighty Andrew Jacksons. "I want to take care of people," Mickelson said, not acknowledging that a fat stack of greenbacks might also be useful for paying off gambling debts. "If someone does something for you, you should take care of them." Some players also see this as contrived, with one major champion saying, "It feels like he's trying to buy goodwill." Again, regardless of the motive, isn't taking care of people preferable to stiffing them? (As a young pro, Tiger Woods routinely left nothing for the locker room attendants, so his pal Mark O'Meara would tip them $100 on his behalf . . . and then have to get paid back later.) If the worst critique people can come up with is that a person is trying too hard to be nice, they must be doing something right. "When I came out on Tour in the eighties," says Mike Donald, "we were supposed to leave a ten-dollar tip for the locker room guys. In 1991, when I was on the policy board, it was suggested we go up to twenty dollars, and there was upheaval in the room. Some guys wouldn't use the locker room at all because they didn't want to pay the money!" Fast-forward to a Honda Classic in the mid-nineties on a Sunday afternoon, when Donald is alone in the locker room with Mickelson, who has just completed the final round, having finished in the middle of the pack. "I saw him hand the locker room guy a wad of cash, thank him, and then he left," Donald says. "I wandered over and asked, 'How'd we do?' It was eight hundred dollars. I thought that was so classy. From that point on, I tried to be more generous with my tipping and be more appreciative of people. I think other guys did, too, because of Phil. He changed the culture a little bit, and the only beneficiaries were the guys cleaning the shoes."

On Masters Sunday in 2004, Mackay hung around Augusta National deep into the night, waiting for his boss to finish his dinner with the club membership. Finally, he saw some stirring in the player parking lot. "It's pitch-black dark out there," says Mackay, "and there's two or three other people around Phil, so I walk over there to help out with packing the bags. As I walk up, I see these guys are hugging Phil. And they're not just hugging him, it's like an emotional hug. And as I get closer, I realize that I have no clue who these guys are. Well, it turns out, these are the guys who work in the lower locker room at Augusta National who Phil's been tipping all these years and taking such good care of. And now that Phil's won the Masters, he's going to the champions locker room. And these guys are losing him forever, and they are just devastated." When one of the longtime waiters in the Augusta National clubhouse was up for a promotion, Mickelson provided him a letter of recommendation.

The Callaway Performance Center in Carlsbad, California, is a quick drive from his home, and when Mickelson rolls in he often has bags full of In-N-Out for the staff. "He doesn't get any publicity for that," says Larry Dorman, the former Callaway executive. "Phil Mickelson does not have to care whatsoever about the guy operating the robot at the test center, but he still makes the effort. That's not a phony to me."

John Hawkins recalls an occasion at Colonial when Mickelson lit him up for a full thirty seconds in front of a large group of fans about something he had typed in *Golf World*. "I felt about four inches tall," Hawkins says. "A couple minutes later he circles back and says, 'Hey, I've got an exclusive for you.' It wasn't a big deal, just a new ball Callaway was debuting, but he was throwing me a bone. He went from an asshole to my best friend in two minutes. The best players are always the meanest dogs in the lot. Tiger set the standard." (Indeed, Woods once counseled Sean O'Hair, a gifted but soft Tour player, "You need more prick juice.") Continues Hawkins, "Phil could be a motherfucker, too. But he was smart enough and composed enough to be able to morph back into the guy he's supposed to be. Yes, he's a phony, but he's a sincere phony."

No wonder Steve Elling, the former golf writer at the *Orlando Sentinel*, calls Mickelson "Captain Mindfuck."

Reinman's presence in the press room every week was a manifestation of Mickelson's sophistication; no other player had their very own flack just to deal with reporters. (Woods later stole the idea.) A schmoozer and a raconteur, Reinman would dispense little nuggets to scribes, gently offer potential story lines, and always promise to do his very best to deliver an exclusive interview with Mickelson. Even though these pretty much never materialized, Reinman's human touch was a stark contrast to Woods's agent, Mark Steinberg, who seemed to derive so much pleasure big-timing reporters he earned the nickname Dr. No. If other players, including Woods, resented the mostly adoring press Mickelson received, a lot of that had to do with the agreeable people around Phil. Bones eventually became more comfortable in his own skin and began giving thoughtful interviews, a vivid contrast to Woods's surly caddie, Steve Williams, who once tossed a photographer's camera in a pond. Amy Mickelson was always chatty and helpful to reporters, whereas Elin Woods was a cipher who never, ever acknowledged the press's existence. Rick Smith exuded warmth and gregariousness; Hank Haney had a lot to say, but was always mindful that his predecessor, Butch Harmon, had been canned partly because Woods resented his high profile in the media. When Mickelson played poorly he was not above stomping away like a petulant child, ignoring the hardworking reporters who were just trying to do their job. But no one made a big deal of it because he had so many proxies to tell his story. Woods accepted the responsibilities of stardom and spoke to the press after 99.99 percent of his rounds, good or bad. Yet any transgressions in his dealings with the media were widely commented upon.

Mickelson always has his antenna up around reporters. At a Bob Hope Classic, Jerry Foltz was serving as the on-course commentator for Mickelson's group on the Golf Channel telecast. "He wanders over and wants to ask me a question about another player," says Foltz. "Phil asks, 'Is that mic off?' I said yes. Then he says, 'Unplug it.' That's how savvy he is." Writer John Feinstein was interviewing Mickelson at a clubhouse table in front of a large picture window at the Memorial years ago on a sultry Ohio afternoon. "A lot of women were dressed fairly scantily," says Feinstein. "Every once in a while he would crane his neck and watch one walk by. One particularly attractive woman in shorts and a halter top strolled by and Phil watched her go and blurted out, 'She's pretty hot.' Then he says, 'That's off the record, right?' Yes, Phil, all leering is off the record."

Mickelson can be nakedly transactional in his dealings with the press. When Karen Crouse was new to the golf beat for the *New York Times*, in 2012, she asked Mickelson a pointed question about Augusta National's all-male membership practices early in Masters week. Mickelson offered a carefully worded response that didn't really answer the question. The next day, in the press room, Crouse was passed a note with an 858 area code. She rang Mickelson. Says Crouse, "He said, 'Well, Karen, I just want you to know this is obviously a very delicate, hot-button issue, and how you use my quotes will determine what kind of relationship we have moving forward.'" Crouse wrote a nuanced story, and a few days later Mickelson was brought into the press room as he surged into contention at the Masters. He flashed Crouse a thumbs-up, signaling his approval of her story. They embarked on such a cozy working relationship that Mickelson wound up Zooming in as a guest speaker to a sportswriting class that Crouse was teaching at Arizona State. "He was so good," she says, "and my students thought I walked on water for the rest of the semester."

Deep into the writing of this book, I received a phone call from one of Mickelson's lawyers—he has a bunch of them—with whom I hadn't had any contact in at least a decade. Glenn Cohen woke me up at seven a.m. on a Saturday, saying he had spoken to Mickelson and they wanted to make me a paid consultant in an attempt to wrest control of Phil's media rights from the PGA Tour. Cohen referenced a story I wrote on the topic way back in 2015. "It's a brilliant piece of work," he said, unctuousness oozing out of the phone. "It's so good it could have been written by a graduate of Harvard Law." The job offer felt like a bribe to me and I declined it, citing the glaringly obvious conflict of interest that I was working on an f-ing book about his client. "Well, you wouldn't be getting paid by him, you'd be getting paid by me," Cohen said. No dice. Naturally, we segued into a conversation about this book. "Phil is scared to death about it," he said, but added, "I swear to Christ that's not why I called." A series of questions about the content of the book inevitably ensued, with Mickelson's fixer admitting he was on a "fishing expedition." Cohen would repeat the job offer at least a half dozen more times in the ensuing months, despite my demurrals; his numerous phone calls often came at odd hours, like 12:34 a.m. on New Year's Day. The ham-handedness evoked Deep Throat's summary of the bungled Watergate cover-up: "The truth is, these are not very bright guys, and things got out of hand."

Then there was the occasion when Rick Reilly of *Sports Illustrated* was speaking with Mickelson as he signed autographs. They encountered what in

Tour parlance is known as a "rope-hoper": a young woman on the rope line who is overly flirtatious with the players. Mickelson deflected her advances by saying, "Have you met Rick Reilly, America's greatest sportswriter?" Reilly began chatting with the toothsome lass as Mickelson slipped away. Moments later, Reilly's cell phone rang. "Hey, it's Pimp Daddy," said Mickelson. "You owe me one."

Perhaps as a thank-you for all the In-N-Out burgers, the Callaway technicians cooked up a new toy for Mickelson in the spring of 2006: a heel-weighted driver with a longer shaft that helped him hit towering draws and gave him what he claimed was an extra twenty-five yards off the tee. Rick Smith immediately dubbed it "the bomb driver." But Mickelson still wanted to employ his regular driver for the more reliable butter cuts so, for the Tour stop in Atlanta the week before the Masters, Mickelson dropped one of his wedges and kept both drivers in the bag. All he did was finish 28 under par to win by thirteen strokes in the most dominant performance of his career, averaging 309.1 yards per drive and hitting 80.4 percent of fairways along the way. (He had been averaging 297.2 yards and 57.5 percent coming in.) For the first time since Tiger Woods was an undergrad, he was not the clear-cut Masters favorite.

The intrigue surrounding Mickelson's twin drivers stoked the larger story of how the revamped Augusta National would play. Following the 2005 tournament, the course underwent another round of retrofitting, being stretched by 145 yards to 7,445 in its continuing evolution from a wide-open shotmaker's delight to a longer, tighter, more penal test that demands precision as much as power. Mickelson opened with a 70, three shots back of Vijay Singh's lead. During the second round, a swirling breeze gave Augusta National more teeth; Chad Campbell's 67 propelled him to a three-stroke lead. Mickelson was four back after a 72, during which he hit nine fairways and birdied all the par-5s.

He had ground it out over the first two rounds without his biggest fan, Amy. She had been by his side during the early part of Masters week, but on Wednesday flew from Augusta to San Diego to watch eldest daughter Amanda's school play. Dressed as a rainbow, Amanda, six, had only one line. "But it was a compelling line," Amy would say later, with utter sincerity. Phil was so bummed to miss the performance he tried to persuade a friend to set up a live feed, but it didn't pan out. Mother and daughter jetted back to Augusta on Friday, with Amy arriving just in time to make a six p.m. cocktail party. On Saturday, she didn't get to see her hubby strike his first shot until suppertime. At 1:02 p.m., rain and lightning forced a delay of four hours and eighteen minutes. Mickelson squeezed in five holes before darkness halted the round. He didn't make a par, following three straight birdies with two bogeys. On Sunday morning, Mickelson played the remaining thirteen holes of his third round in one under, taking the lead at –4. During the break between rounds, he predicted the rest of Sunday would be "an eighteen-hole shootout." Indeed, as he played the seventh hole, he was in a five-way tie for first and fifteen players were within three strokes of the lead, including three of his primary rivals: Woods, Singh, and Retief Goosen. What had the makings of a classic back-nine dogfight instead turned into a suspense-free coronation. Mickelson made textbook birdies at the seventh and eighth holes to regain the outright lead, and then produced the kind of methodical, indomitable, airtight golf that has been the hallmark of Woods's biggest victories. Mickelson simply refused to make a bogey while patiently allowing everyone else to beat themselves. By the time he reached the sixteenth hole, Mickelson was four strokes ahead and cruising. "This is the best round I've ever seen him play," Smith said from behind the sixteenth green. "He has incredible control out there." Only a meaningless bogey on the eighteenth hole prevented Mickelson from becoming the fifth Masters champion to play the final round without a blemish. "The back nine I drove it as good as I probably ever have," Mickelson said.

The sunset was throwing off gorgeous light as the defending champ, Woods, placed the green jacket on Mickelson. It was the third straight year one of them had starred in this quaint tradition, harkening back to the glory days when Arnie and Jack passed the jacket back and forth for five straight years, beginning in 1962. Taking the microphone to address the throng, Mickelson called Sunday "a day that is going to be one of the most memorable of my life, after the birth of my kids and my wedding." Even in his finest hour he took the time to nod at Woods and ask the crowd to say a prayer for Tiger's gravely ill father, Earl. "We all know how important parents are in life," Mickelson said.

Now halfway to the Mickelslam, having won three of the past nine major championships, he was beginning to transcend comparisons with his contemporaries and stir the ghosts of the game's all-time greats. It was a mind-bending change from the lost years, during which Mickelson was measured not against other golfers but against Dan Marino and Charles Barkley and other megatalents who never won the big one. Any chance Mickelson would get complacent after his latest triumph? He offered a resounding answer in the champion's press conference: "Tomorrow we'll start preparing for Winged Foot."

Johnny Miller won the 1973 U.S. Open by torching fearsome Oakmont with a final-round 63. The USGA exacted its revenge the following year, when it took seven over par for Hale Irwin to win the Open, the highest score in the postwar years. That tournament was dubbed "The Massacre at Winged Foot" and cemented the course's reputation as the sport's ultimate examination, a fearsome combination of booby-trapped greens, carnivorous bunkers, maneating rough, and other horrors. Mickelson was determined to crack the code. In the two months between the Masters and the U.S. Open, he made three separate scouting trips to Winged Foot, spending a total of ten days on the property, many of them nine- or ten-hour grindfests. After his first trip, he rang up Roger Cleveland, the wedge maestro at Callaway, and requested a special 64-degree weapon to use in the cavernous bunkers and for touch shots around the greens. Asked what inspired the 64-degree wedge, Mickelson, ever the smart-ass, said, "Well, I wanted one less than 65 degrees and one more than 63, and it just worked out perfect." When tournament week arrived, he had four different drivers in tow, giving him varied options depending on the course setup and meteorological conditions. He also dropped his sand wedge and 3-wood, opting instead for a 4-wood and 3-iron.

It was left to Jim Mackay to help sort through all the options. His profile had risen along with Mickleson's; at tournaments, Bones was now getting more attention from the gallery than many (most?) of the actual players. His dedication to Mickelson was absolute. Mackay was once rooming with fellow caddie John Wood at the Las Vegas tournament when a freak earthquake shook their room on the fifteenth floor of the Golden Nugget. Wood is a California native so, unimpressed, he rolled over to keep sleeping. Mackay, meanwhile, bolted out of bed toward Mickelson's golf bag, which was standing in the corner. Gently, lovingly, he laid the bag on the ground, lest it topple over and the clubs sustain a little scratch. Says Wood, "I think it tells you something about the guy that his first instinct wasn't his own safety, it was protecting Phil's clubs."

A perfectionist and worrywart, Bones could not have been more different than his freewheeling boss, which added to the fun and frisson of watching them work together. Each year, Mickelson granted his looper one—and only one—veto. "I say something like 'I am officially submitting my veto to the committee,'" says Mackay. "But technically he is the committee when it comes to the veto. So, I have to deal with that, too, when it happens. Apparently, Phil can filibuster the veto."

The first-ever veto came at the Tour stop in New Orleans, on the par-4 ninth hole at English Turn. Mickelson drove it into the right rough, under some trees. A lake was directly between him and the green. He says, "I thought I'd take a little 3-iron and I'm just gonna shoot a little skipper and it's gonna skip off the water and hop up the bank and onto the green. And [Bones] goes, 'Hell, no. You're layin' this up. You're gonna hit a 9-iron out to the left. You're going to hit a wedge up there close and make par.' I go, 'I really think three's not out of play here. If I double skip it, it'll hit in the bank just perfectly.' And I was actually serious. I'm laughing now, but I was serious at the time. I thought I could do it. He said no and I had to go with it because I gave him his veto. I hit a 9-iron out there. I wedged up to four feet. I made par. Probably the right play."

Did he consider missing the putt on purpose just to spite Mackay?

"I think that subconsciously I wanted to, but I just couldn't bring myself to do it."

At the 2002 British Open, at Muirfield, there was another veto dustup. On the par-4 fourteenth hole, Mickelson drove it into a bunker down the left side of the fairway. "Those bunkers, you really just have to wedge it out," he says. "The ball was up against the right edge. I got down on my knees and I thought, *I have a swing. If I get on my knees with a 6-iron, I think I can do it.* So Bones says, 'Hell no, I'm using my veto.' And I go, 'That's only good in the continental United States, so you don't get your veto.' So I try to hit this 6-iron. And to make a long story short, I had to make about an eighteen-footer for a double [bogey 6]. Had I just wedged out, I would've made five, it wouldn't have been an issue, it would've been no big deal. That was one of the dumbest shots I've tried to play."

Early in the week at Winged Foot, Mickelson was asked what role Bones plays between the ropes at the big events. "Well, we don't really talk too much about course management and stuff," he said. "That game plan is set up well before we show up on Thursday. He is awesome at club selection, and he's awesome at green reading. So, I have found over the years that he is right more often than I am on club selection and certain reads for greens. However, I still seem to go with my decision, and as I tell him, I say, 'Look, if you like a 6 and I think it's a 7, I can live with me hitting a 7 and coming up short. It's hard for me to hit a 6 and go long.' So I can live with my own mistakes if I'm wrong, and as it's turned out, I'm wrong more often than not." This is known as foreshadowing.

In the first round of the U.S. Open, Mickelson hit only eight greens in regulation but finagled an even-par 70, putting himself in a tie for second, one back of Colin Montgomerie. He credited his 64-degree wedge and all the homework he had done for a great escape. On Friday, he missed short par putts on each of the first two holes. Mickelson fought hard from there to piece together a 74 that left him tied for seventh, four back of Steve Stricker's lead. Mickelson bogeyed the last hole after a big block off the tee, but he felt strangely buoyant because the wild drive was followed by further misadventures in the trees, yet he pulled off a semi-miraculous up-and-down to escape with a 5. "I know I can't go left, and I still did like an idiot, and I barely made bogey," Mickelson said. "Even though I walked off with a bogey, I walked off on a high note because it could have been a big number. Bogeys are okay. I just had to prevent the double, the big mistake." (More foreshadowing.)

On the front nine of the third round, Mickelson was, in his words, "all over the place" off the tee. It is a vexing question that has always followed him: Why is it so hard for such a great player to hit a goddamn fairway?

"Phil has gone through various instructors, but his swing has never really changed," says Peter Kostis, who served as an unofficial swing adviser to Mickelson early in his pro career. "The lead hand is your power hand, and because Phil is naturally right-handed, he's pulling the hell out of that club with his right side. And because he has weak right-hand grip, he has an extraordinary amount of face rotation through impact. The straighter players have less rotation through impact. But they tend to have less speed as well. And Phil's pursuit of speed, I think, has been addictive. The more you can get the toe to close over the heel, the farther you can hit the ball, but you never know where it's going."

"Phil has the laziest legs I've ever seen in a great player," says Brandel Chamblee. "He has a very steep angle of attack but, partly because his legs aren't powering through the swing, he doesn't hold the angle, so the release coming down is inconsistent."

"He has a lot of wrist action at the bottom, a little bit of a flip," says Johnny Miller. "Right after impact, the toe turns over. He does not keep the face square very long at all through the ball. That is the opposite of the really great drivers of the golf ball: Trevino, Calvin Peete, Moe Norman, Dustin Johnson. Their face is so stable. His club flops around. One thing about Phil, timing is everything for him. He's such a gifted feel player that if he's feeling good and timing his swing just right, he can have hot stretches, but it's a dicey move under pressure. It's amazing, really, that he's won what he's won, given the fundamental flaws in his swing." This is part of Mickelson's obsession with equipment: instead of changing his swing, he'd rather engineer a quick fix, which might actually be a defensible position, given all of his success.

On the back nine on Saturday at Winged Foot, Mickelson's swing clicked; he hit five fairways in a row and came home in thirty-three. His 69 was one of only two scores under par on the day, and at +2 overall, he moved into a tie for the lead with Kenneth Ferrie, a little-known Englishman. The gifted but callow Aussie Geoff Ogilvy lurked one shot back. Montgomerie was among those tied for fourth, three strokes off the lead. Flying high after his stellar back nine, Mickelson enthused after the round, "Every year, one time a year, we get tested like this, and I love it. I love being tested at the highest level of the most difficult and sometimes ridiculous golf course setups we'll ever see. I love it because I get to find out where my game is at, where my head is at, and it really challenges me as a player."

The final round presented Mickelson with a defining test, but he was battling his swing from the jump. A long putt on number four brought him a precious birdie, but on the very next hole there was cause to wonder about his head: after a wild drive he tried to play a 4-wood out of the gnarly rough. He foozled the shot about ten feet, leading to a bogey on one of Winged Foot's two par-5s. That Bones couldn't talk him out of such a capricious play did not portend well. Mickelson bogeyed the seventh hole to fall two strokes behind Ogilvy, but this final round was destined to be a war of attrition.

As Mickelson played the eleventh hole, he was in a four-way tie for the lead with Ogilvy, Montgomerie, and Jim Furyk, all at +4. Singh and Padraig Harrington were a shot back. (All but Ogilvy are in the World Golf Hall of Fame, or will be.) On eleven, Phil played a gorgeous ¾ punch wedge that landed fifteen paces short of the green and trickled to ten feet. He buried the putt and uncorked a lusty fist pump. The lead was his alone, but the rest of the back nine featured more melodramatic twists than a telenovela. Ogilvy clanged a bunker shot off the pin on thirteen to save par. On the fourteenth tee, Mickelson overcooked a draw one foot into the rough; from a nasty lie he took a violent swing and somehow muscled his ball to five feet. The ensuing birdie gave him a two-stroke lead. The well-lubricated crowd was off the rails.

At the par-4 seventeenth, Ogilvy got hung up in the rough and, laying three, was still chipping. His caddie, Alistair "Squirrel" Matheson, pulled a Bruce Edwards, and his boss was all too happy to play the part of Tom Watson. "He said, 'Just chip it in,'" Ogilvy recalled afterward. "'Why don't you just chip it in?'" So he did, to save a highly unlikely par. At sixteen, Mickelson hooked his drive into deep rough, then his approach expired twenty yards short of the green, into a fried-egg lie in the bunker. He took a bogey to fall back to +4, slicing his lead in half. Harrington, riding a flawless round, gave himself a chance to win from the clubhouse, but bogeyed the final three holes to post +7. Furyk tugged his approach at eighteen into a greenside bunker and then missed a five-foot par putt, posting +6. On the seventeenth hole, Mickelson's drive was trash. Literally. He blocked his ball so far left it sailed over the gallery's head and hopped into a garbage can. (On the day he will hit only two of fourteen fairways.) After taking a free drop, he played a crafty slice under a tree branch and his ball bended perfectly·into the middle of the green. The roar could be heard clear across Westchester County. Mickelson saved his par, and he was so close to finally nabbing his U.S. Open you could almost taste it.

Up ahead, Ogilvy's approach to eighteen came up just short and trickled backward off the false front, leaving him a thirty-yard pitch up and over the mound. Having grown up in Australia's Sandbelt, he knew exactly how to play the shot and zipped it to five feet and then wiggled in the putt to take the clubhouse lead at +5. "I thought that might be for a playoff," said the twenty-nine-year-old Ogilvy, who to that point in his career had only two PGA Tour wins. Montgomerie, having inherited Mickelson's title as the dreaded Best Player Never to Have Won a Major, was next to arrive at the exacting finishing hole. He hit a perfect drive. At +4, Monty was tied for the lead with Mickelson and flooded with the confidence of having just made a forty-foot birdie bomb on the seventeenth hole. One more good swing by one of the game's preeminent iron players and the trophy could be his. But Monty uncorked a shot so bad it called to mind Dan Jenkins's description of Watson's errant approach on the Road Hole that cost him the 1984 Open Championship: "a semishank, half-flier, out-of-control fade-slice." Montgomerie's ball buried in the rough short of the green. He blasted a pitch forty feet past. Looking more and more like Mrs. Doubtfire with every flailing moment, Monty three-putted to make a tragic double bogey. This would be the last good shot to win a major for the kind of guy Fleet Street likes to call a "nearly man." "I had a very bad flight home that night," Montgomerie will later write in his autobiography. "I remember sitting there in a daze, not knowing what to say or do. I wasn't crying.

I had gone beyond that. I was incapable of any analysis. The same three words kept going through my head: *What just happened?*"

After all this craziness, Mickelson arrived at the seventy-second tee with the clearest of mandates: make a par, win the U.S. Open, at last. Two days earlier, Tiger Woods, still mourning the recent death of his father, missed his first cut at a major championship since turning pro. With one more par, Mickelson would be three-quarters of the way to Woods's grandest achievement, the Tiger Slam. For all of his spectacular success, Mickelson had never been player of the year or reached number one in the world ranking; he was one more par from securing both honors. There was a frenzied feeling in the air, fed by the final-hole crack-ups and the fact that for the preceding seventy-one holes, Mickelson had been juggling chain saws on a high wire while wearing Rollerblades. "He had no business being anywhere near the lead," says Miller. "He had literally no control of his golf ball. What Phil did at Winged Foot might be the greatest four days of scrambling in golf history. Well, three days and seventeen holes."

Now Phil and Bones had to decide which club to pull on the tee of a 450-yard dogleg left. "You can't hit driver there," says Jack Nicklaus, a four-time U.S. Open champion. "How many fairways did he hit that day? Two! Driver is just inviting trouble. You have to keep the ball in front of you." Bones will go to his grave defending driver. "There was never even a consideration about hitting anything but driver," he said the day after the tournament. "Phil hits his 4-wood no more than about 240 yards. A 4-wood into a ten- to fifteen-mile-per-hour wind uphill is going to go about 225 yards. There was no possible way to hit 4-wood long enough to reach the dogleg if he missed the fairway." That was the calculus: given the two-way miss that haunted Mickelson throughout the round, it seemed likely he would uncork another wild drive, and in that case it would be better to wind up closer to the green, allowing for more recovery options. Two-time U.S. Open champ Andy North disagrees with that thinking. "It's the dumbest fifteen minutes in golf history," he says. "You hit 3-iron then 5-iron and win the U.S. Open. Hello?! Even if he comes up a little short of the green, the way Phil was chipping and putting that week, you have to bank on him getting it up-and-down, like Ogilvy did." On Sunday's fourteenth hole—which played only eight yards shorter than eighteen—Mickelson had employed his 4-iron off tee; he made a mediocre swing but the ball stopped a couple paces from the edge of the fairway, in the intermediate rough, allowing for a straightforward approach shot to the heart of the green. "I know what Bones is saying," says Miller, "but what makes Phil so shaky with his driver—that steepness in the downswing—is what makes him such a good iron player. All he has to do is get a 3- or 4-iron in play off the tee and he is still in control of the tournament. It doesn't seem that hard."

As Mickelson settled over the ball, holding lumber, Miller intoned on the telecast, "This better be the 4-wood."

It ain't.

"I tell you what, Ben Hogan is officially rolling over in his grave," Miller added in an instantly famous quip.

With his driver, Mickelson took a mighty lash at the ball. "Phil has had the same miss his whole life," says his boyhood teacher Dean Reinmuth. "His left knee and foot pop out toward the ball on the way down, not forward to the ball and up into his toe like on a normal swing. His left hip drops, his pelvis thrusts toward the ball, and it's like a baseball player with an inside pitch—he gets jammed. The club is blocked by his body on that way down, so he misses left. Add in adrenaline and pressure, and slight flaws get amped up." This is the swing Mickelson made on the eighteenth hole at the 2004 Ryder Cup, leading to Woods's icy glare. It's the swing he made fifteen minutes earlier on the seventeenth tee at Winged Foot. He did it again on eighteen, and his ball flew so far left, it hit the roof of a hospitality tent seventy or eighty or a hundred yards off-line. Given the stakes, and the result, it could quite possibly be the worst drive in golf history. But Mickelson got the break of a lifetime when his ball ricocheted in the direction he was aiming and drew a clean lie in rough that had been trampled down by the fans. Still, a towering Norway maple tree was directly between him and the green. Now he faced another decision. "It's a crazy game, *innit?*" says Nick Faldo, a celebrated tactician in his day. "If you need a three there, it's easy—all the decisions are made for you. If you need a four, there are so many ways you can make that score. People talk about choking under pressure, but just as often that is mental, not physical. When

Phil knocks it in the trees, his thinking has to change. It's no longer about making a four. He's got to make a five no matter what. Not losing the tournament becomes more important than winning it outright. Because if there is [an eighteen-hole Monday] playoff, he's going to beat Geoff Ogilvy."

"You're talking about one of the best wedge players of all time," says three-time U.S. Open champion Hale Irwin. "He can hit a little shot back into the fairway to his favorite yardage. Then you knock that up to ten or fifteen feet, and you have that putt to win the championship. Worst case, you tap in for bogey and take your chances in the playoff. I have a hard time understanding any other play, but maybe I'm old-fashioned." Mickelson knows how ruthlessly effective this kind of thinking man's golf can be: he lost major championships to both Payne Stewart and David Toms when they laid up on the seventy-second hole par-fours after errant drives and then saved par with full-swing wedges.

Mickelson and Bones quick-walked to the ball, propelled by the unseen forces of fate. They were moving fast, but the ensuing discussion was brief; Mickelson unsheathed his 3-iron. He was going to attempt to reach the green with a banana slice around the tree, more or less the exact same shot he had played on the previous hole.

"I was trying to make a four," Mickelson said.

After a lifetime of swashbuckling and being celebrated for his derring-do, he couldn't see any other way out of the trees. Says Miller, "He got seduced into trying the hero shot. He wanted to win in dashing style. I guess Phil thought winning with a layup would somehow be less manly. He wanted the thrill of hitting a high-risk shot on the last hole of the Open."

For those who know Mickelson's game intimately, the slicing 3-iron did not seem like a risky play. "When I saw he had a good lie, I raised my arms because I knew he was going to win," says Rob Mangini, Mickelson's college teammate and still close friend. "That's just a bread-and-butter cut for a guy who can curve the ball more than any human on the planet. I've seen him do that a thousand times. Phil can play that shot in his sleep." Ogilvy agrees, saying, "His handicap is how good he is at that shot. Most players don't have that shot, so they don't see it and don't even consider that it's an option. They just wedge it out. They're forced into the right decision because they don't have the skills. Unfortunately, Phil has the skills to hit it from anywhere. He thought he had the shot, so you can't second-guess that because he can pull off the impossible."

For 71.5 holes, Mickelson had been tempting the golf gods with unlikely and occasionally miraculous recoveries. Now, finally, at the worst possible moment, his luck ran out. For his approach shot to the green, the strike was clean but the start line ten yards too far left. His ball headed inexorably for the trunk of the elm. I was standing right there with Rick Smith and will never forget the sound of the ball hitting the tree: as loud as a judge pounding the gavel with a guilty verdict. Smith went ashen—he knew his life has just changed. Mike Lupica, the in-your-face New York newspaper columnist, panted up to Smith and shouted, "He might not make five from there!" Smith somehow didn't punch him.

Mickelson's ball ricocheted into the rough, maybe twenty-five yards ahead of where he had been standing. "You rarely see a great player hit two bad shots in a row," says Paul Azinger. "Ever rarer is for them to make two bad decisions in a row. Somehow Phil did both."

The situation was grim, as Mickelson still had tree trouble and now a worse angle to a well-fortified green. This time he played too much cut and his ball expired short and left of the green, burrowing into the fluffy sand. With the green sloping away from him, it would be impossible to get the ball close to the hole and everyone knew it. The swollen crowd around the eighteenth green whistled and buzzed with disbelief. The enormity of the unfolding disaster visited Mickelson as he trudged up the fairway. There was a blank look in his eyes and his face went sallow. He blasted out of the bunker and his ball skittered across the green and into the rough. Now he had to make the bogey chip to force a playoff. He missed the hole, and his last chance at salvation. For the fourth time in the last eight years, he had blown the United States Open.

Mickelson hid out in the scorers' area for a long time, trying to collect himself; Amy draped an arm around his shoulders and whispered in his ear. When Phil finally emerged, his eyes were red and watery. "I still am in shock that I did that," he says. "I just can't believe I did that. I am such an idiot. I can't believe I couldn't par the last hole. It really stings."

"For the most part, the best players are the best because they're the best up here," Ogilvy said in the champion's press conference, tapping his melon. "Tiger Woods is the best golfer in the world because he's got the best brain. He hits the ball well, but there are plenty of guys that hit the ball well. He's got the best head."

Conspicuously absent from the discussion was the star-crossed Mickelson. He had retreated to the privacy of the second floor of the clubhouse and was sitting at his locker, motionless, staring into space with his head resting wearily in his hands. Amy came by to give him a kiss, but Phil didn't seem to notice. "I've never seen him like this," she whispered. "I think he's in shock."

Finally, Phil stirred, packed up his belongings, and began the slow trudge home. As he snaked through the locker room, he passed numerous mementos of Winged Foot's glorious U.S. Open history and the legends who have enjoyed starring roles. There was a reproduction of a 1929 newspaper trumpeting Bobby Jones's victory. A 1959 clipping celebrated Billy Casper's heroics. A photograph from 1984 showed a beaming Fuzzy Zoeller holding the winner's trophy aloft, and there was also a picture of Irwin, signed by the man himself: *To Winged Foot G.C. Where my dreams were fulfilled*. Mickelson walked past all of this history without even noticing, leaving the locker room deserted but for its ghosts.

CHAPTER ELEVEN

A couple of days after the final round of the 2006 U.S. Open, Rob Mangini called up his old friend, expecting to have to talk him off the ledge. Instead, Phil Mickelson answered the phone from the happiest place on earth. "He was like, 'I'm in line with the kids at A Small World, wearing a hat and big ol' Prada sunglasses, and no one knows who the fuck I am—it's great,'" says Mangini. A day later, they met for lunch. Mickelson got a huge sandwich with a side of self-loathing. "I was on pins and needles, not really sure what to say about Winged Foot," says Mangini. "Phil just sits down, and right off the bat he blurts out, 'Can you believe I almost won that fucking golf tournament playing like that? This is bullshit. I have to get better.'" Mickelson was not yet aware of Johnny Miller's lacerating commentary during his final hole meltdown, but when Mangini mentioned it, his lunch date demanded a replay be cued up by phone. "He was cracking up," says Mangini. "He said, 'It's totally true. What a debacle.'"

Things were only going to get worse for Mickelson. Three weeks after Winged Foot, Tiger Woods summoned the most precise and disciplined golf of his career, picking apart Hoylake to win the Open Championship. He dissolved into sobs on the final green, which had more to do with missing his late father, Earl, than the catharsis of winning his eleventh major championship. This was the beginning of an almighty tear, as Woods would win his next five starts, including the PGA Championship. Two months earlier, as Phil arrived on the seventy-second tee at Winged Foot, it had been possible to delude ourselves into thinking he was nearly Tiger's equal. Now there was once again a yawning chasm between the game's two best players. A month after the PGA, Mickelson laid another egg at the Ryder Cup, going 0-4-1, as the U.S. got blown out for the third straight time.

All of this strife finally culminated in Rick Smith's firing in April 2007, which had become inevitable even before the ball came to rest after doinking the tree on the final hole at Winged Foot. The stunner was the announced successor: Butch Harmon. Gruff, profane, old-school in the extreme, Harmon brought a very different personality than anybody else in Mickelson's inner circle. "Apart from Amy, I don't think Phil has ever been told in his life to do something and done it," says Peter Kostis. "If you want to be hypercritical, he's surrounded himself with yes-people." Harmon had the credibility and the self-belief to tell Mickelson what he needed to hear.

Their immediate focus was improving Mickelson's driving accuracy. "If we can get him to play out of the fairway, he can rival Tiger," woofed Harmon. He shortened his pupil's backswing, while moving his hands farther from his head at the top of the swing, creating more width. Harmon also wanted to, in his words, "clean up the lower body and footwork and legwork, which was all over the place—he almost looked like Elvis Presley trying to hit a golf shot sometimes." Working with Smith, Mickelson had become much more efficient from 150 yards and in, but his default shot with his wedges and short irons remained a big, hard swing that sent the ball sky-high with loads of spin. Harmon preached more ¾ shots and knockdowns, which would allow Mickelson better access to pins tucked on the very back or very front of greens. It was like teaching a changeup to Nolan Ryan. This shotgun marriage brought together two of the game's biggest personalities, and Mickelson quickly fell under Harmon's spell. "I have been entertained quite a bit with some great stories," he said a month into the relationship. "There's always a point to the stories; you know, whether they're about his dad"—Claude Harmon, the 1948 Masters champion—"or other players, they always have a point. I find that very interesting. It's a fun way to learn."

The third tournament of the Harmon era was the 2007 Players Championship, on the Stadium Course at TPC Sawgrass, a tight, claustrophobic, penal house of horrors so ill-suited to Mickelson's game he had contended only once (barely) in thirteen previous tries. But in the first round he shot 67 in a stiff breeze to take the lead. "I was able to keep the ball in control, and my misses were very small and that allowed me to take a lot of the big trouble out of play that I had found in the past," Mickelson said after the round. "I'm not curving the ball as much right-to-left or left-to-right. The ball is not having as much sidespin. It seems to be a much straighter flight."

Mickelson wasn't quite as sharp during the second round, but on Saturday he hit nine fairways and two other drives found the very playable first cut of rough. He had fought his way into the final pairing, one stroke back of leader Sean O'Hair. Mickelson's putter overslept on Sunday, but he enjoyed his best ball-striking performance since the 2006 Masters, hitting sixteen greens in regulation to keep the pressure on O'Hair, who, despite Woods's counsel, had never imbibed the prick juice. O'Hair led by two strokes heading to the dangerous seventeenth hole, but he drowned two tee shots in the water and Mickelson had a leisurely walk up eighteen, three strokes clear of the field. Owing to his suddenly reliable long game, he described the win in the most unlikely term imaginable: "stress-free." That it came on such a fiddly finesse course only made the performance that much more satisfying. (Years later, he would say, "I was thinking to myself as I was walking around, *I can't believe I've actually won here.*") During a very jaunty champion's press conference, I asked Mickelson how good he thought he could become under Harmon's tutelage. "You are a cute little man, aren't you?" he replied. "That's such a good question from a brilliant individual. I don't know."

The answer would have to wait, as Mickelson's ascent was slowed when he tweaked his wrist in the tangly rough at Oakmont during a U.S. Open scouting trip. He struggled throughout the summer as his practice time was curtailed by the balky wrist. He got healthy just in time for the season-ending FedEx Cup playoffs, and a showdown with Woods at the Deutsche Bank Championship. What added juice to the Harmon hiring was that he had been Tiger's teacher and confidant for the better part of a decade. Now, after their bitchy split, Harmon was more than happy to share with Mickelson some of his rival's secrets. Harmon explained that Tiger had employed four little bits of gamesmanship to try to unnerve Phil:

1. Woods always tried to putt-out first so the crowd would be moving to the next tee while Mickelson was putting.

2. He would linger behind the green and let Phil walk up to the tee box first, so when Tiger arrived, his playing partner would have to listen to the roar.

3. On holes when he was between 3-wood or driver, Woods would choose less club so he could fart around in the fairway and make Mickelson watch him hit what would inevitably be a laser-like approach.

4. If Phil was amped up and moving fast, Tiger would slow his walk and pace of play; if Mickelson had a more leisurely vibe, Woods sped up his gait and routine. Either way, the goal was to try to upset his adversary's rhythm.

"He's been doing it to you his whole career and you don't even know it," Harmon told Mickelson. With this as the backdrop, the Deutsche Bank Championship became fascinating theater as Woods and Mickelson played together in the penultimate pairing. This was their sixth final-round showdown in the same group, and Mickelson was oh-fer-five, while Woods had won three times. Phil started with a one-stroke advantage and came out flying, birdieing half of the first ten holes. He was strutting around as if *he* had the psychological advantage, and, indeed, Mickelson and Bones Mackay were stealing knowing glances at each other over Tiger's theatrics, which they finally could recognize. With eight holes to play, Mickelson had seized the tournament lead and was up five strokes on his nemesis. But a wayward approach on the twelfth hole cost Phil a double bogey, and then Tiger birdied fourteen, slicing the lead to two strokes. At the par-3 sixteenth, they produced one of the most memorable sequences of their long would-be rivalry. Hitting first, Woods stuffed his tee shot to eight feet, and the Boston yahoos went a little crazy. (Perhaps as a rebuke to the Phil-loving New Yorkers, the Beantown brethren seemed to be pulling harder for Tiger.) Then Mickelson stepped up and hit a bullet that settled a couple feet inside of Woods's ball. *Check.* Both made their birdie putts, and Mickelson iced the win with a nifty chip on the eighteenth hole for a closing birdie. *Checkmate.* "It does mean more to win against Tiger because I knew he was going to make a late charge and he did," Mickelson said. "So, to stand there on sixteen after he knocked it close and follow it up with my own close shot and then put birdie on top of birdie, it feels terrific.

"Look, for ten years I struggled against Tiger in some of those settings. So, it means more to win this one and I value Butch's insight."

Of course, Mickelson managed to sully what should have been one of the most triumphant moments of his career. Standing on the edge of the eighteenth green for the victor's TV interview, Mickelson was asked by Jimmy Roberts, who had been tipped off to the gathering storm, if he would skip the ensuing playoff event in Chicago even though it hurt his chances to scoop up the $10 million FedEx Cup bonanza. "I'm really torn, because I feel like there's an obligation for me to play," Mickelson said. "I'd be paired with Tiger again. I think it would be really great for the game and the Tour and the FedEx Cup. Another part of me is really frustrated because for the past year, I've been asking the commissioner to do a couple of things, and I told him I would play the last four [playoff] events [if he consented], and he has not done that. So I'm kind of torn."

It was a bizarre moment and a wildly inappropriate way to air what turned out to be a minor grievance: after the Labor Day finish in Boston, Mickelson objected to the idea of having to play in a Wednesday pro-am in Chicago. For years he had been lobbying Tim Finchem to drop pro-ams from the playoff events, to give the players more downtime and the events more of a big-time feel. Mickelson flew into Chicago to host a corporate outing and then headed home, blowing off the tournament and leading to much hand-wringing. "It's hard for me to interpret some of his thoughts," said the Chicago tournament director John Kaczkowski, choosing his words carefully.

But Mickelson has always been strident about Tour politics. Brandel Chamblee recalls a B.C. Open at which he and Mickelson were paired together for all four rounds. "Knowing that I was on the Player Advisory Council," says Chamblee, "he spent the whole time in my ear saying the PGA Tour should be reduced to only thirty players—nothing but the stars. He was totally oblivious to the fact that would eliminate my job." Mickelson is a vocal opponent of "opposite events," the tournaments conducted for the Tour's middle class during the same weeks when the big names gather at the limited-field World Golf Championships. "I despise conflicting events," he says. "I don't think they're right because I think they detract from the product that we're presenting." When his colleagues whisper snarky things about Mickelson it is not really because of jealousy, as is often cited as the reason; tournament golf is the ultimate meritocracy and other players respect that he has earned the crown and the jewels. What bothers the average Tour player is they know Mickelson thinks they are untalented, unpopular leeches. As one journeyman says, "Tiger might be a dick, but at least he knows who I am. Phil doesn't know and doesn't care."

When paired with a rookie or marginal player for the first time, Mickelson has a favorite practical joke: in the scorer's tent he will say, "I made a couple of mistakes on your card—let's see if you can find them." He thinks it's hilarious, but for the other player it can be stressful and/or embarrassing. Mickelson is a dispenser of biting nicknames. He tabbed former Tour player Colt Knost "The Hammer," explaining, "In poker, that's the worst hand you can be dealt. That's Colt. He got dealt the worst hand. He's short, he's fat, and he hits it short off the tee." Mickelson's reputation among certain peers has never fully recovered from an incident at the 1999 Las Vegas Invitational, when he big-timed the other players and decided to hit balls from the back of the range at TPC Summerlin, even though signage expressly forbade using that tee. After working his way through his bag, Mickelson launched a driver, and his ball carried over the heads of the players at the other end of the range and pegged in the knee Dave Renwick, Vijay Singh's caddie. Renwick went down like he had been shot and ultimately needed medical attention. He was unable to caddie for Singh that week. This was the beginning of the feud between the big Fijian and Mickelson, which ultimately boiled over when they went nose to nose in a heated confrontation in the champions locker room at Augusta National in 2005; Singh had complained to Masters officials about the spike marks Mickelson was leaving on the greens from his ornate pre-putting routine.

Of course, Phil can be as magnanimous as he is petty. In 2007, it became public that he had been paying the college expenses of Holli Dobler, a young woman he had never met. She is the daughter of Conrad Dobler, who was left disabled after a brutal ten-year NFL career. In 2001, his wife, Joy, became a quadriplegic after a freak fall from a hammock. Mickelson was a fan of Dobler's from his playing days, and when he saw a TV report about the family's misfortune he was moved to help, leading Joy to call him "an angel without wings."

Mickelson has been the source of many other random acts of kindness. At the 2005 PGA Championship, a young fan named David Finn was sitting in his wheelchair behind the fourteenth green during a Tuesday practice round. David suffers from a mitochondrial disorder that has left his limbs withered and has robbed him of his ability to speak. But a broken body can't suppress the powerful spirit within. David's bright blue eyes convey intelligence and an eagerness to connect. Mickelson sensed this and, after putting out on Baltusrol's fourteenth hole, he walked over to David and said, "Hi, buddy, thanks for coming. Here's a souvenir for you." He laid an autographed glove in the kid's lap. Says David's father, John, "So many people don't know how to act around the severely disabled. Pity is the worst possible emotion. The glove was a wonderful gesture, but what made that moment so meaningful was that Phil treated Dave like a normal kid, which is all he wants." The Finns followed Mickelson throughout the week, with Phil often acknowledging David with a smile or gesture. Mickelson, of course, won the tournament, but even in one of the headiest moments of his career, he thought of his biggest fan, so as the trophy ceremony was beginning, Bones Mackay hustled over to say his boss was wondering if David would like to have a picture taken with the Wanamaker Trophy. The moment was recorded for posterity by the Newark Star-Ledger: Phil has the trophy in one hand and the other is placed tenderly on the left shoulder of David, whose head is thrown back in ecstasy. The glove is now enshrined in glass in David's room, and he has a thick scrapbook of his PGA Tour adventures, which his three older sisters call The Book of Phil. Asked about his affection for Mickelson, David spelled out on a touchscreen monitor, "Phil is the Arnold Palmer of today." His father gently chided him for parroting something they had heard on Golf Channel. David thought a bit longer. With great determination, he tapped, "Phil was the first person to make me feel special."

Back in San Diego, the Mickelson kids moved in the same circles as the Northbrook family—Sophia had dance classes with Sydney Northbrook, while Sydney's brother played on the same coed peewee soccer team as Amanda Mickelson. Eric Northbrook would see Phil at games and dance recitals and get a friendly nod, dad to dad, but their relationship didn't go much deeper than that. When his son was four and his daughter six, Northbrook crashed his motorcycle and was paralyzed from the chest down. He spent five months in a specialized hospital in Denver, recovering and learning to adapt to his new reality. When his family returned to San Diego, the Mickelsons had retrofitted the Northbrook home with ramps, an interior elevator, hardwood floors instead of carpet, and wheelchair-accessible bathrooms, a project that cost roughly a quarter-million dollars. "It was a game changer," says Eric. Determined to live a purposeful life, Northbrook started his own foundation, HeadNorth, which has now raised over $3 million to help nearly six hundred families in San Diego County affected by catastrophic spinal cord injuries. "It's my legacy," Northbrook says. "Phil inspired me to pay it forward."

True to his word after almost losing Amy and Evan in the delivery room, Mickelson has used his influence to better the lives of others through large-scale philanthropy. In the days after Hurricane Katrina, he donated $250,000 to relief efforts and added the New Orleans Classic to his schedule, pledging to charity all of his winnings for the 2006 tournament, which inspired a number of players to do the same. Mickelson was disappointed to finish fifteenth and earn "only" $81,720, so he rounded up his donation to a quarter mil, then matched that same number the next year. When your annual income is north of $40 million, it's easy to just write a check, but Phil and Amy wanted to experience firsthand Katrina's impact and meet folks who had been affected. The day after the '06 tournament, they spent nine hours exploring the city and chatting with residents. "They were deeply moved," says Tommy Fonseca, the tournament staffer who spent the day driving the Mickelsons across New Orleans. "I remember Amy breaking down three or four times."

As a tribute to his dad, the old Navy pilot, Mickelson became so involved with military charities that in 2004 the PGA Tour took his idea and formed Birdies for the Brave to support a variety of home-front charities. Mickelson remains a financial supporter and spokesman for the Wounded Warrior Project, dedicated to providing college scholarships for the children of fallen special ops soldiers, and Homes for Our Troops, which purchases and adapts houses for seriously injured soldiers. Staff Sergeant Jake Keeslar is a beneficiary of one of these homes. In the Al Anbar province of Iraq, Keeslar was manning a .50-caliber machine gun from the gunner's hatch of a Stryker, an eight-wheeled armored fighting vehicle, when it rolled over an IED buried in the sand. The explosion tore a three-foot hole in the metal floor of the Stryker. Jake was standing directly above the blast. His back was broken in five places, his pelvis shattered, his liver lacerated, and his legs were, in his words, "pulverized." Jake awakened four days later in Walter Reed Army Medical Center and had stumps for legs, as each had been amputated at the knee. Homes for Our Troops purchased for Jake and his wife, Vanessa, a three-bedroom house in Fallbrook, California. Among the special adaptations are ramps, wider doorways, lower countertops, cutouts beneath the sink and stove to allow Jake to roll right up, a huge wheelchair-accessible shower, and one heckuva fancy toilet. Says Jake, "It's pretty cool that, one way or another, my dad's favorite golfer helped build my house."

Every summer, the Mickelson ExxonMobil Teachers Academy selects six hundred educators from around the country for a week of cutting-edge math and science instruction. The academy has outposts in Houston, New Orleans, and Jersey City, and the trips are all-expenses paid, which is how Mirandi Squires, from the two-stoplight town of Johnsonville, South Carolina, wound up on an airplane for the first time at the age of forty-two. She calls her week at the academy "life-altering"; after incorporating all that she learned into her classroom, Squires won a presidential teaching award. In a state that routinely sees squabbles about adding creationism to the school curriculum, Squires became an elected officer of the South Carolina Science Council and joined a review panel of the statewide science standards. A good deal of her inspiration came from mingling with the host of the academy. "When we got to meet Phil, it was obvious how passionate he is about education," says Squires. "People like to say that children are our future, but Phil and his wife are actually making a real investment in them."

That investment is even more direct when the Mickelsons host their annual Start Smart event at a Target in east San Diego at the end of the summer. Bus after bus disgorges two thousand elementary school kids from the region's economically depressed school districts. Each child can pick out a backpack, clothes, shoes, and school supplies. The Mickelsons are always on hand to help supervise the controlled chaos. At the Start Smart I attended (uninvited), Amy spent the whole time helping young girls try on shoes. One little pixie kept shaking her head no every time Amy presented an option. "I totally understand because I'm picky about my shoes, too," she said with a laugh. Finally, Amy found a pair of hot-pink, glittery sneakers and the girl didn't need to say a word—her huge smile was the answer. Acting as a chaperone at a different Start Smart was a gent named Donte Locke. His daughter, Kailea, a third-grader, and son, Donte Jr., a first-grader, were getting much-needed provisions. Life was a paycheck-to-paycheck struggle for this single dad. He called Start Smart "a tremendous blessing," adding, "I had wanted to take them school shopping, but, honestly, the finances were not there. It was great for their self-esteem. It made me feel good, too, because I want my kids to have nice, new things. They deserve that." Donte had never heard of Mickelson, but came away impressed. "Just watching Phil interact with the kids and parents, you can see he's genuine," he said. "You can see it's from the heart. Because he doesn't have to help people like us."

Mickelson is a giver and a taker. He is always canny about mixing business and friendship. "Phil is the only guy on Tour who actually likes pro-ams because he can pick the brain of a surgeon or pilot and then for the rest of his life he will reuse the information in conversation as if he's an expert," says Davis Love with a smirk. If paired with a CEO or investment guru, Mickelson has been known to pump them for usable intel and then buy stocks accordingly. Whereas Woods and Rory McIlroy leveraged their superstardom to get their fathers as pro-am partners at the Crosby Clambake, Mickelson has always used the tournament as a networking event, insisting on playing with a top executive from one of his endorsement partners. In 2007, when he was in the final year of a lucrative deal with BearingPoint (a management and technology consulting firm), he arranged to play with Harry You, the company's CEO, who carried a handicap index of 18. Ahead of the tournament, he sent You to the Callaway Performance Center to be custom-fit with the latest technology, and once the tournament began Mickelson worked his tail off to help his partner succeed (and possibly earn a contract extension for himself). On the fifth hole at Spyglass Hill, You knocked his tee shot onto the windswept green. As he waited to try a long birdie putt, Mickelson whispered in You's ear, "The wind can actually affect the roll of the ball. With a putt like this, I sometimes put a little saliva on my cheek as I'm addressing the ball and that helps me gauge at the last minute how much break to play." You replied, "Phil, I'm not good enough to deal with that—my brain would short-circuit." Mickelson won the tournament on his own ball and led his partner to victory in the pro-am portion, what You calls one of the highlights of his life, golfing or otherwise.

"We paid Phil eight to ten million bucks a year and people were startled by that number, but he's worth ten times more," says You. The logo on the front of Mickelson's hat is prime real estate, but the company was really buying Mickelson's time: a half dozen private outings a year, in which he would play and dine with BearingPoint's most important clients. Prior to these events, Mickelson would be presented with index cards containing biographical information about the key attendees. Mickelson likes to claim he has a photographic memory, and it certainly seemed like it at these outings. "We'd introduce him to someone and Phil would say, 'Hey, I heard you and your dad just won the member-guest at such-and-such club,' and you should see how their faces light up," says You. "He makes people feel happy and feel special, and in the context of entertaining and building relationships, that's invaluable." Mickelson provided other services. You recalls BearingPoint bidding on a fat contract with the state of California when a company insider heard that one of the key decision-makers in Sacramento happened to be a big golf fan. Mickelson gladly called this fellow up to chat and make a little sales pitch for his favorite consulting firm. BearingPoint won the $70 million contract. "No one else on Tour would do something like that," says You. "I can't say if that was a factor in the decision. I can say it certainly didn't hurt."

After his disappointing showing in 2007's major championships, Mickelson came out guns blazing in '08, winning on two of the best courses on Tour, Riviera and Colonial, sandwiched around a tie for fifth at Augusta. This just ramped up the anticipation for the U.S. Open in his hometown at Torrey Pines, where he had won three times in his first decade on Tour. But in the days after that third win, the bulldozers rolled in, reshaping Torrey from a beloved muni to a penal championship test. Mickelson hated the changes, which might account for his weird headspace when the '08 Open rolled around. On a 7,643-yard course, playing in foggy coastal air, the man who won a Masters with two drivers in his bag elected not to carry even one big stick. Over the first two rounds, Mickelson was paired with Woods, who was as baffled as the rest of us. Says Hank Haney, "Tiger was like, 'How does he come up with this shit? It makes no sense.' He got a kick out of it." Mickelson couldn't hit a fairway even with his 3-wood. On the thirteenth hole on Saturday, he had three straight chips roll back to his feet and took a nine, helping to send him to a dispiriting eighteenth-place finish. Meanwhile, Woods summoned his most mythologized performance, winning on a broken leg for his fourteenth major championship victory.

The always complex relationship between Tiger and Phil had another flare-up at season's end, stoked by Woods's caddie, Steve Williams. Speaking at a boozy charity dinner in his native New Zealand, Williams told the crowd, "I wouldn't call Mickelson a great player, 'cause I hate the prick." Those fighting words were inevitably leaked to the press, creating quite a kerfuffle. Woods issued a bland statement saying, "I was disappointed to read the comments attributed to Steve Williams about Phil Mickelson, a player that I respect. It was inappropriate. The matter has been discussed and dealt with." Mickelson went with something spicier: "After seeing Steve Williams's comments all I could think of was how lucky I am to have a class act like Bones on my bag and representing me."

Proving the golf gods have a sense of humor, Mickelson and Woods were paired together for the final round of the 2009 Masters, their first Sunday head-to-head at a major since the 2002 U.S. Open at Bethpage. Even though they were seven strokes off the lead shared by Ángel Cabrera and Kenny Perry, both players were feeling frisky as they retreated to the champions locker room for lunch ahead of their afternoon tee time. "It's a small locker room, if you've ever been in it," says Butch Harmon. "There's only three tables in it. Phil's at the middle table and there was somebody's sandwich on the first table. So we sit down and Phil's taking his pants off and Tiger walks in. That's Tiger's sandwich. Tiger doesn't sit with us. About this time, Phil's standing there in his underwear and he's folding his pants over this chair. Tiger goes, 'Dude, what are you doing?' Phil goes, 'Look, I don't wear the cheap Nike shit like you do. Tom Ford makes my pants. I don't want them wrinkled when I'm kicking your ass this afternoon when we play.' And Tiger Woods, without missing a beat, says, 'I don't care who makes your pants, cover your shit up so I can eat my sandwich.'"

Once the round began, Mickelson wasted no time eating Woods's lunch, birdieing five of the first seven holes. Struggling with his swing, Woods finally showed some fight on the 570-yard eighth with two mighty blows to set up an eagle, but Mickelson answered with yet another birdie. After parring nine from out of the trees—where else?—Mickelson was within one of the lead, having tied the front-nine record with a six-under 30. (Woods will say he "Band-Aided" his way around in 33.) "I would say it was the most fun I've ever had on a golf course caddying," says Bones.

But Mickelson made a killer mistake on the twelfth hole, pulling his tee shot into Rae's Creek, which led to a double bogey. He was rattled enough to blow two ensuing golden opportunities: a ten-footer for birdie on fourteen and a four-footer for eagle at fifteen that would have tied him for the lead. Of the latter, he said, "I didn't trust my read, I didn't commit to it, I just made a terrible stroke." In a Masters parable of the tortoise and the hare, Woods patiently chased down Mickelson, and when Tiger stuffed his tee shot at the sixteenth and made birdie, the two were ten under and tied for second, setting Augusta National on its ear. The fun didn't last much longer, as both players' bids petered out at seventeen, when Tiger made bogey after an errant tee shot and Phil missed another short birdie putt. The only solace for Mickelson was that he clipped Woods again, 67–68. "It was a very emotional day because it's up and down, up and down, a lot of highs and lows," Mickelson said. "The crowd made the highs even higher and the moans made the lows even lower, and it was just an emotional day."

Shortly after the Masters, I asked Mickelson for an interview for a story I was writing about PGA Tour commissioner Tim Finchem. He waved me off, saying, "I promised my wife I wouldn't create any controversy this year. There's been too much of that the last year, year and a half. We just want things to settle down."

A couple of weeks later, Amy detected a lump in her breast.

CHAPTER TWELVE

The third round of the 2009 Colonial Invitational brought the most unexpected and touching sight: PGA Tour players wearing pink polos, pink trousers, pink shoes, pink belts, pink hats, and pink visors. The PGA Tour Wives Association had organized the "pink-out" to honor Amy Mickelson nine days after her breast cancer diagnosis. Back home in Rancho Santa Fe, Amy and her husband were ugly-crying as images of the tribute were beamed into their living room. The outpouring of support and affection for the Mickelsons was a reflection of Amy's unique place in the game: a combination of den mother, big sister, and head cheerleader. "I can't think of any other person who would bring the whole Tour together like that," says Amanda (Mrs. Justin) Leonard, a close friend of Amy's.

Phil took nearly a month off after the diagnosis, but in early June resurfaced at the Tour stop in Memphis, striving for what he called "a little normalcy." Amy was not going to have surgery until July 1, so he was squeezing in a little golf ahead of that: Memphis was a tune-up for the following week's U.S. Open. (En route to Memphis, he had flown overnight to work in a practice round at Bethpage.) In a wrenching press conference, Mickelson said, "Well, I mean, we're scared, yeah. These last three weeks have been kind of an interesting thing—I've never felt this emotional. I've never been this emotional where if I'm driving alone or what have you and I'll just start crying. It's kind of a weird thing. I'm looking forward to having a four- or five-hour mental break [on the golf course] where I force myself to focus on something else."

At the time of the diagnosis, Amanda was nine; Sophia, seven; and Evan, six. "We're going to go through this together," their dad said. "She's always been there for me. She's always been there for her friends and family. It's our turn to be there for her." Mickelson spoke with great emotion about the woman he has always called his soul mate: "I think she's the most charismatic person I've ever met. She touches people in a way that people don't get touched. It's just right to the heart."

Amanda Leonard recalls reaching a nadir at a long-ago FedEx Cup event; she was traveling with three kids under three when her husband fired their nanny midweek. Amy happened upon her in the clubhouse and, reading Amanda's body language, asked how she was doing. "The way she looked at me, with such real care and concern, I just burst into tears," says Amanda. They talked for a while, and then Phil appeared, antsy to leave after his round. Amy shooed him away to go the hotel on his own and stayed behind to console Amanda and help her work out childcare logistics. Julie (Mrs. Ben) Crenshaw says she has seen Amy befriend kids in the crowd at countless Tour events and, mid-round, snag a ball or glove from her hubby or Bones to impart as a gift. Every year on their wedding anniversary, Phil and Amy take a big trip, just the two of them, and they alternate years in which each does all the planning and surprises the other. "I think every wife on Tour is jealous of that," says Julie with a sigh. "It's so romantic."

Amy began the tradition of the American players and wives exchanging gifts at every Ryder and Presidents Cup. Hers are noted not for being extravagant but for the thought and detail that goes into them. One year Amy gifted bracelets with different colored stones, each said to have its own intrinsic healing property. During a practice round, Patrick Reed's bracelet busted mid-swing, scattering the stones into the rough. "We had six or eight guys crawling around trying to find them," says Davis Love, who wore his bracelet for years afterward. "Someone was shouting, 'Just find the blue ones, they bring peacefulness!'" Phil is also a beneficiary of Amy's gift-giving; for his birthday in 2008, this science nerd received from his bride an intact T. rex skull, valued into the low seven figures, and for that Christmas she got him a three-hundred-pound meteorite.

Now it was Phil's turn to deliver something special. "[Amy] has left me a number of little notes, texts, cards, hints, that she would like to have a silver trophy in her hospital room," he said arriving at Bethpage. "I'm going to try to accommodate that." He insisted he was not as rusty as his ragged play at Memphis the week before had indicated: "When Amy's going through tests and I'm sitting in a hospital for ten hours, I was thinking about a lot of things, but I would take a break and think about my golf swing. I would talk to Butch."

So, Mickelson was not surprised to fire a 69 in the opening round of the U.S. Open, though it was only good for a tie for seventh on the rain-softened course. Mike Weir led with a 64. On Friday, Mickelson double-bogeyed the second hole and had to fight hard for a 70 that left him in thirteenth place, eight shots off the lead of Ricky Barnes, whose two-round total of 132 was a record low. On Saturday, Mickelson birdied four of the final six holes for another 69 that moved him into a tie for fifth, six back of Barnes. Among the players in front of him, the only major champion was David Duval, a surprise contender who had been suffering through a brutal multiyear slump. The crowd was always going to be on Mickelson's side but, given the situation back home, something felt different. "They were incredibly loud, but it wasn't just cheering, it was like encouragement," says Hunter Mahan, who was paired with Mickelson. "It felt like the crowd wasn't just there to watch, they were trying to will him to victory."

After three days of weather delays scrambled the schedule, the final round was halted by darkness on Sunday evening with Mickelson on the third hole. It had been a long, grinding, emotional week, and he looked flat once the Monday morning restart commenced, bogeying the sixth and seventh holes to fall off the leaderboard. But dastardly pin positions, juicy rough, and the greens drying out a bit had finally given Bethpage some teeth, and one by one the contenders began going backward. Mickelson birdied the ninth hole, rousting the fans. At twelve, he poured in a forty-footer and celebrated with a big fist pump. Suddenly he was only two strokes off Lucas Glover's lead. At the par-5 thirteenth, Mickelson smashed a 325-yard drive and played a precise long iron that never left the flag. Eagle, and a share of the lead. "It was electric," says Mahan. "There's no one else you'd want to be with in that arena other than Phil. He was having fun, the crowd was going crazy, it was just an incredible atmosphere." The air was tinged with disbelief. Could Mickelson really win the U.S. Open at last for his cancer-stricken wife? You can't make this stuff up.

Alas, the arc of the U.S. Open bends toward cruelty, not sentiment. On the brutal par-4 fifteenth hole, Mickelson played a stellar hybrid out of the rough, but his ball skittered to the back fringe, leaving a big-breaking downhill putt. It expired three feet short. He made a tentative stroke on the par putt, missing on the low side to fall one off the lead. But Glover bogeyed fifteen, so as Mickelson stood on the tee of the par-3 seventeenth hole, he was back in a tie for the lead, with Glover and a surging Duval. He flared his 5-iron short and left of the green. A good pitch left Mickelson with a do-or-die six-footer. In Rancho Santa Fe, Amy and the kids were gathered around a TV, fighting back tears. A nation was riveted to Mickelson's quest. With so much riding on one par save, Mickelson's putter must have felt like an anvil. He didn't hit the putt nearly hard enough, his ball peeling away at the hole. Bogey. Needing a Hail Mary on eighteen, he pounded a driver into the narrow fairway, but his flip wedge flew well past the hole and he missed the last-gasp birdie putt. Glover played the last three holes birdie-par-par to nab the trophy. It was Mickelson's fifth runner-up finish at the U.S. Open, a dubious record that supplanted Sam Snead, another lavishly talented free-swinger whose flaws were serially exposed in the national championship. But unlike Winged Foot, or Shinnecock, or Pinehurst, or the previous spin around Bethpage, Mickelson was not devastated by this defeat. "Certainly, I'm disappointed," he said, "but now that it's over, I've got more important things going on, and, oh well."

Straight from New York, Phil flew home to pick up Amy and the kids and they jetted off for a tropical vacation, knowing it would be their last such trip for a while. Amy's ensuing surgery was a success, with strong indications the cancer had been caught in time. Still, she faced a long, tough road ahead. "There are different kinds of breast cancer and she got a very bad, very aggressive kind," says Julie Crenshaw. "It required a very aggressive form of treatment, and they knew if it ever came back, that was *no bueno*. They told Amy she was looking at five years of treatment."

Less than a week after Amy's surgery, the Mickelsons were hit by another thunderbolt: Phil's mom, Mary, was diagnosed with breast cancer, too. Amy may have helped to save the life of her mother-in-law. Said Phil, "I think it did have a little bit of an effect in that the awareness of it made her be more concerned if she were to feel a lump, and I think that led to her having something checked and getting a biopsy and having it come back positive."

Mickelson withdrew from the British Open to care for his loved ones, ending his streak of consecutive majors played at sixty-one, the longest in golf. He turned up at a few ensuing tournaments that summer, but played like a man with the weight of the world on his shoulders. However, he seemed more buoyant arriving at the season-ending Tour Championship. Mary had enjoyed a remarkable recovery, and Amy was rallying, too. The time away from the Tour had reenergized Mickelson, then in his seventeenth season. "I'm excited to play," he said. "I didn't realize how much I loved playing the game of golf. It's made me relook at some of my longer-term expectations as far as if I would cut back the schedule at what age, all that stuff. It just makes me realize how much I really enjoy what I do, how much I love playing the game of golf, how much I love competing on the PGA Tour, and how I don't ever want to take that for granted." He also had a little extra pep in his step thanks to Dave Stockton, a two-time major champion who in his golden years had become a putting whisperer to some of the game's top players. Mickelson had been unsatisfied with his putting for the better part of the preceding two years. He had been increasingly relying on Dave Pelz to be his putting coach, but the former NASA technician saw the game as science, not art. Finally, Mickelson charged Bones with coming up with a plan to get them out of their putting slump. The next day, Mackay came back with the recommendation to see Stockton, who in a matter of an hour or two got Mickelson back in touch with the longer, more free-flowing putting stroke of his youth.

Mickelson rolled his rock beautifully over the first three rounds of the Tour Championship, and heading into the final round he was in third place, four strokes behind leader Kenny Perry and two back of Woods. Tiger had reached out to the Mickelsons after Amy's diagnosis, sending a heartfelt text in which he included the sentiment that he hoped doctors would someday find a cure for cancer, which had struck Woods's father in 1998 and begun his declining health. Phil thanked Tiger for the note but, typically, couldn't resist including a zinger: "I hope they someday find a cure for your hook."

Now another showdown loomed. It's debatable how much Harmon had improved Mickelson's swing; Harmon himself harbored doubts. "I was talking to Butch one day," says Gary McCord, "and he said, 'All I tell him is not to straighten his back leg, which makes him overturn. Keep a little knee bend in there. He'll do that for four swings, then he's back to straightening that leg to turn as much as he can so he can hit bombs. He'll go home and struggle and call me up and ask what's wrong. And I tell him the same damn thing over and over: *Keep a little knee bend in there*. I don't know why he pays me. I really don't. There's only one thing that works, but he doesn't want to listen to it.' So that's Phil in a nutshell." Still, there is no question that having Harmon in his corner had altered Mickelson's dynamic with Woods, and it played out again in the final round of the Tour Championship. On the third hole, Mickelson buried a fifteen-footer for birdie, then topped that with a thirty-foot bomb on the next hole. Meanwhile, Tiger couldn't buy a putt. On eight, Mickelson knocked his approach stone-dead and then at nine made a slick twelve-footer for yet another birdie. He was now three strokes ahead of Woods and leading the tournament. The advantage was still two strokes when Mickelson attacked what he called a "salty" back-right pin position on the sixteenth hole. He flew his approach one yard too long, his ball burrowing into a nasty lie in the thick rough. His only play was an almighty rip with his 64-degree wedge. "That ball could have shot off in any direction," he says, but instead it disappeared into the hole. Double fist pump. Game over. Mickelson shot 65 to smoke Woods by five shots and win the thirty-seventh tournament of his career. Tiger earned a minor consolation prize, the $10 million bonus that came with winning the FedEx Cup points race, but that only meant he was compelled to take a bunch of photos next to Mickelson, who between cheesy smiles was whispering all manner of trash talk. This Tour Championship gave Mickelson another chance to trot out a cheeky line that had become one of his favorites: "If Tiger is the greatest player of all time and I start beating him regularly, what does that make me?"

They receded into the long off-season, heading in very different directions. Mickelson would be at home caring for his family. Woods had a trip to the Australian Masters, where he was to rendezvous with his mistress, Rachel Uchitel. (Unbeknownst to them, the *National Enquirer* would be staking out the hotel lobby.) Then Tiger was looking forward to a nice, quiet Thanksgiving with his wife and kids.

The 2010 Masters was always going to be a morality play in the pines. Woods arrived amid the tawdriest sex scandal of the internet age, and the day before the first round was subjected to the moralizing of Augusta National chairman Billy Payne, who, glossing over his club's ugly history of exclusion, said, "It is not simply the degree of his conduct that is so egregious here: it is the fact that he disappointed all of us, and more importantly, our kids and our grandkids."

Mickelson came in under the radar. Instead of feasting on the West Coast swing, per usual, he had a series of middling results. Amy was still not well enough to travel week-to-week and golf's most high-profile family man looked out of sorts without his best friend and support system. At the Houston Open, the week before the Masters, "Phil played as bad as I've ever seen him play," says Bones. But Mickelson is an emotional player who accesses his best golf on courses that stir the soul, like Pebble Beach and Riviera and, especially, Augusta National. More important, on Tuesday of Masters week, Amy decided she was well enough to travel to Georgia. "I wanted this week to be all about Phil," Amy told me in Augusta, her first public comments since her cancer diagnosis. "I didn't want to put him in a compromising position—does he hit balls or take care of me because I'm not feeling well?" Everything changed for Phil once Amy and the kids touched down in Augusta. "He has a different energy, a different excitement," Harmon said during the first round. "He's playing for something bigger than himself." Mickelson made birdies by day and held court at night over lively family dinners that included his parents and in-laws. (His mother was doing so well in her recovery she walked nine holes a day at hilly Augusta National.) With extra babysitters on hand, Mickelson even sneaked off on Friday morning to a coffee shop to play chess with daughter Sophia before his afternoon tee time. So giddy was Mickelson when he showed up to work that Bones began referring to Augusta National as "Phil's playground."

During the first round, Mickelson shot a 67 to tie for second with Tom Watson, one behind Fred Couples. Despite the star power on the leaderboard, the white-hot spotlight was fixed solely on Woods for his first competitive round in four months. He played in dark sunglasses, hiding behind them like the tinted windows of a prison bus, but there was no escaping the ritual humiliation of the scandal: he had arrived in Augusta just as *Vanity Fair* released a salacious story about his serial infidelities, complete with a photo gallery of buxom babes who claimed to have been his paramours. On the eve of the tournament, the *National Enquirer* leaked details of an alleged tryst involving one of Woods's Florida neighbors. For the first round, Woods's short walk from the clubhouse to the practice green and then to the first tee added to the mixed feelings; instead of a humble return, Tiger's arrival looked like a Secret Service procession, as he was flanked by a dozen grim-faced goons who acted as if their job were to protect a head of state from whizzing bullets, not a mere golfer who was in danger of being hit by nothing more than a few stray wisecracks. But Woods's private army had neglected to clear the airspace above Augusta National. With a nod to Woods's born-again Buddhism, a prop plane appeared towing a banner that read TIGER: DID YOU MEAN BOOTYISM? It was a stunning breach of Augusta's meticulously curated artificial reality. Amid this circus, Woods somehow gutted out a 68, which has to be considered one of the most remarkable rounds of his life.

In the second round, Mickelson shot a quiet 71, leaving him (and Woods) tied for third, two strokes back of the English lads Lee Westwood and Ian Poulter. Slumped forlornly against the ropes on the fourteenth hole, Harmon offered a succinct report on his pupil's game: "Playing beautifully. Putting horrendously."

On Saturday, Westwood competed with the fierce determination of a man desperate to shed the label Best Player Never to Have Won a Major. He birdied four of the first ten holes to open a whopping five-shot lead. It was right about then that Mickelson decided to play H-O-R-S-E with his golf clubs. He went with a risky drive that hugged the left side of the thirteenth fairway, hard against Rae's Creek, and was rewarded with only 195 yards to the flag. A 7-iron to ten feet followed. Eagle. After a good drive on fourteen,

Mickelson had 141 yards left. With his pitching wedge, he dropped his ball ten feet left of the pin with a little side sauce and it obligingly spun into the hole. Eagle, eagle. In Mickelson's gallery, as always, was his dad, who declared, "That's as loud as I've ever heard it here." Most players would have been elated with their good fortune. Stepping to the tee of the par-5 fifteenth, Phil the Thrill was getting greedy. "I was trying to make a third [eagle]," he said afterward, with one of his naughty schoolboy grins. A bad drive seemingly eliminated the possibility, but after laying up to eighty-seven yards, Mickelson danced his wedge shot over the hole, stopping the ball a few inches away. Augusta National shook, and Mickelson was only mildly disappointed to settle for a tap-in birdie.

After the round, Westwood's agent, Chubby Chandler, and his caddie, Billy Foster, commiserated behind the eighteenth green, trying to come to grips with what had befallen them. "Going down eleven, we were five up," Foster said. "Then all of a sudden we were one down."

"Twenty-seven minutes," said Chandler, smiling ruefully. "That's all it took."

"Bloody hell," said Foster.

Mickelson's bogey on the seventeenth hole allowed Westwood to reclaim the fifty-four-hole lead, at twelve under. Woods was tied for third, four strokes back, and he was lucky to be that close. Throughout the round, Woods had fought his swing and struggled with his speed on the greens, leading to a few slipups in his pledge to clean up his on-course language and comportment. But in a showing of sheer stubbornness, Woods made three late birdies to claw back into the tournament.

Mickelson didn't have time to be nervous on the eve of what was shaping up to be an epic final round because he stayed up late on Saturday awaiting the X-ray results after elder daughter Amanda injured her wrist while roller-skating. (She suffered a hairline fracture.) "I am so proud of Phil and how he has handled it all," said his dad. "To be the father that he is, I couldn't be more proud."

Mickelson came out parrying on Sunday, parring the first seven holes and then birdieing the par-5 eighth with an all-world up-and-down. Woods was battling his swing, and his coach detected a rare air of defeat. Says Haney, "At majors, we always looked to see what Phil shot. He was the one player Tiger didn't want to spot three or four shots to. I could tell by Tiger's demeanor he knew [a comeback] wasn't going to happen. He knew he was spotting the wrong guy a lead on the wrong course." Mickelson began to take control of the tournament on the twelfth hole, with a fearless tee shot right over the flag. When he rolled in his twenty-footer, the birdie served two purposes: it gave him a one-stroke lead over K. J. Choi and it thoroughly rattled the burly Korean known as Tank, as the roar was so loud that Choi backed off his shot in the thirteenth fairway. He followed with his first bad swing of the day, pulling his shot into a bunker behind the green.

When Mickelson arrived at thirteen, he hit his drive a little too straight and it ran through the dogleg, onto the pine straw. There were two trees directly between Mickelson's ball and the green. He had no shot. Or so it seemed. A couple of years earlier, at the Players Championship, Mickelson had talked about the difference between being a champion and just another Tour player who is content to cash bloated paychecks: "Sometimes you've got to take risks to win the golf tournament, and a lot of times people will wedge that out and play safe, and they don't put themselves in position to win. If you want to win tournaments against the best players in the world you've got to take some chances. The weeks I'm able to pull them off I have a chance at winning and the weeks that I don't, I get ridiculed. But you have to take chances to win."

Now an entire career—perhaps even a worldview—had been perfectly distilled into one moment, with the Masters on the line. As Choi futzed around on the thirteenth green, Phil and Bones talked over the strategy at hand. "TV does no justice to how narrow the gap in the trees was," says Mackay. "It looks fairly wide on television, but I can tell you that it was about as wide as the length of a box of a dozen balls. And there was a lot of pine straw. My biggest concern wasn't that Phil could fit it through the gap, it was that Phil would lose his footing, and then hit one of the trees as a result. So I gave him the yardage [206 yards to the flag]. He tells me, 'I'm going for it in two.' So, okay, I know that. Now, part of any caddie's job is, when you talk to your player, to figure out if they're a hundred percent in. Sometimes they're eighty percent in. And it's not hard to judge. But sometimes you may go back to 'em a little bit just to see where they are. The previous day, on Saturday, he had made two straight eagles, almost three, on thirteen, fourteen, and fifteen. I just reminded him, 'You're the best wedge player in the game. If you lay this up, you're going to have a very routine up-and-down for four.' And he said, 'I'm going.' Okay, now I know he's a hundred percent in. And that's great."

Watching on TV at a rented house near Augusta National, Amy yelled at the TV, "Use your veto, Bones!"

"That would have been a dumb play," Phil says of a layup. "That would have been a bad play, mathematically, to hit anything other than what I did. Because the gap that I had was so small that had I hit a higher-lofted club, there would've been a greater chance for a pine needle to get in between the ball and the face and cause it to shoot it a little bit left or right and hit the tree. So the shot was much easier with a square, flat-faced club. Could I have just chipped it down there with a 6-iron? Possibly. But the angle that I was hitting on and the way the fairway runs, it would've taken the ball right to the water. The high-percentage play, believe it or not, was actually the shot that I played. Not to mention, when you talk about shot dispersion for a left-handed player. If you're aimed at the pin and a left-handed player pulls it, it's gonna go longer right. And if he pushes it, it's gonna go shorter left. And that's how thirteen green sits. So I had a massive margin of error. If I push it a little bit or open up the face, it goes short left, on the green, and I have a sixty-footer. If I hit it perfect, I'm fifteen feet left of the hole."

This was all well and good until Choi missed an eight-footer to take a messy bogey just as a charging Anthony Kim was making another birdie. "Phil's a big scoreboard watcher," says Bones. "It's my job at this point to say to him, 'Hey, does the fact that you're leading change the way you want to play this hole?' And he looks at me and he says, 'Listen, if I'm going to win this tournament today, I'm going to have to hit a great shot under a lot of pressure. I'm going to do it right now.' And that is the ultimate *Get the eff out of the way* to your caddie. You know what I mean? He says, 'I've got it. You like 6-iron. I like 6-iron. I'm ready to go. I'm ready to do this thing.' I have now said what I need to say. And I get out of there as quickly as I possibly can. And he hits the most famous shot of his career."

"I shouldn't admit this," says Mickelson, "but I pulled it fractionally." His ball squeezed through the trees and fell out of the sky three feet from the hole. It was the ultimate rebuttal to Winged Foot. "A great shot is when you pull it off," he said after the round. "A smart shot is when you don't have the guts to try it." Put it on his tombstone.

Still flooded with adrenaline, Mickelson blasted his eagle putt by the hole on the high side, but steadied himself to make the comebacker. It was not an artistic triumph, but the birdie gave him a two-stroke lead. At fifteen, another laser with his 6-iron set up a two-putt birdie, pushing the lead to three. Amy jumped off the couch and headed for Augusta National, not wanting to miss out on the fun. As her hubby walked up to the eighteenth green, amid thunderous applause, Amy was standing discreetly a few paces behind the putting surface. Both Phil and Bones spotted her as they approached the final green. The day that Amy received her diagnosis, Mackay and his wife, Jennifer, drove all night to be there to comfort her, and they traveled to Houston to be by her bedside before and after surgery. Now Bones refused to make eye contact with Amy behind the green. "I really didn't want to look up, because I knew I was going to get choked up if I saw her," he says. Imagine how Phil felt. He rolled in one final birdie putt, an exclamation point on a bogeyless 67 and a four-round total of 16-under 272 that had been bettered only three times in tournament history. Then slowly he made his way to his bride. The Masters has a long history of freighted hugs, but the Mickelsons' embrace was cinematic in its sweetness. In public, Phil had been remarkably stoic throughout Amy's cancer battle, but as they hugged, a lone tear streaked his cheek. The golf world cried along with them. "I pretty much turned into a puddle," says Mackay. Nearby, Harmon was bawling like a schoolgirl. "I've never been this emotional when any of my guys have won," he says. "This was special. They're special people."

After the green jacket ceremonies, Amy was standing alone outside Butler Cabin, her eyes twinkling in the twilight. I asked her what the victory meant for her embattled family. She sighed, took a deep breath, and wiped away a tear. Words would not come. After another deep breath, she summoned a radiant smile. "I'm going to go join my husband," Amy said, and then she floated up the stairs, into the victory party.

CHAPTER THIRTEEN

Billy Walters's life reads like it could have been dreamed up by Mark Twain. He was born in 1946 with a plastic spoon in his mouth, in the backwaters of Kentucky. Walters's father, an auto mechanic, died when Billy was eighteen months old, and shortly thereafter his mom ran out on little Billy and his two siblings. His grandmother took Billy in. She preached that hard work was the ticket to a better life, and he brought an almost evangelical fervor to his jobs, beginning at age seven, when he secured a $40 bank loan—arranged by grandma—to buy a power lawn mower. Two years later, he borrowed another $90 to start a paper route. When he was fifteen, his grandmother died and Walters moved to Louisville to live with his mom and her new husband, who made him pay rent. He worked at a bakery in the morning and a gas station at night. Walters eventually became a used-car salesman in Louisville, papering the town with self-promotional leaflets and relentlessly cold-calling customers. In 1966, at the age of twenty, he cleared $56,000, equal to half a million dollars in today's money. Six years later, he founded Taylor Boulevard Auto Sales, selling wholesale cars throughout the Southeast. That was the seed of a business empire that would grow to include numerous car dealerships, commercial properties, and rental-car franchises.

Walters made his first bet when he was nine, wagering $125 of his paper route money, that the Yankees would beat the Dodgers in the 1955 World Series. That didn't work out so well, but he kept gambling and eventually began working as a bookie. "I probably came in as a gambler and I am going to go out as a gambler," he says. Indeed, in his twenties he lost his house playing cards. By 1981, Walters had left the car business and become a full-time sports bettor, running his own book. After run-ins with the law in Kentucky, he moved to Las Vegas in '82. Pit bosses soon learned to recoil at the sight of Walters. During one thirty-eight-hour binge at the Golden Nugget in Atlantic City, Walters won $3.8 million playing roulette. (Having observed a wheel bias, he bet 7-10-20-27-36 over and over.) Walters also won the 1986 Super Bowl of Poker, good for a $175,000 payout.

Walters's big breakthrough in the early 1980s was to employ computer analysis in sports betting. He partnered with an exciting venture that had a purposefully bland name: Computer Group. They began betting millions of dollars every week, and Walters would woof that over the next four decades he had only one losing year, with annual winnings often running into the mid-eight figures. Naturally, this drew scrutiny from law enforcement. The FBI raided the headquarters of the Computer Group in 1985, and Walters and his associates were charged with illegal interstate gambling. They beat the rap. In ensuing years, the state of Nevada indicted Walters for similar crimes on three separate occasions, but he was never convicted, turning him into a cult figure around Las Vegas.

One other thing about Walters: he loves golf and is always on the lookout for a pigeon.

How do you replicate the adrenaline rush of hitting a 6-iron off pine straw through a forest over a creek to win the Masters? You can't, really, but Phil Mickelson has always tried to get his fix through gambling. "He loves the action," says his old friend Rob Mangini. "There have been many times when Steve Loy said he could get him $500K for a corporate outing, but Phil turned it down, saying he wanted to be with his family. But if I called him up that same day and said, 'Hey, there's a guy at Whisper Rock who wants to play you for ten thousand dollars,' he would jump in his jet and fly over here, even though he was spending twenty-six thousand dollars or whatever on fuel. It's not about the money for him, it's always about the action."

Mickelson's persona on the PGA Tour is well-honed stagecraft, but what is he like in these private money games? Mark Baldwin, a well-traveled pro who has enjoyed a couple cups of coffee on Tour, got a firsthand look in the fall of 2014, after returning home from European Tour Q School. Baldwin was living in Las Vegas, where there is always action available to a pro golfer who wants to play against deep-pocketed duffers with questionable handicaps. Baldwin had a regular game versus a jewelry salesman and compulsive gambler with a vanity index of 8. Let's call him Tony. "He reminds me of Joe Pesci's character in *Goodfellas*, leaving aside the murderous tendencies," says Baldwin. "Short of stature with a hyper-caffeinated personality, a quick laugh, and he had likely conquered some disreputable hangouts." Tony knew a guy who knew a guy who played with Phil, and after some loose talk a game came together; Mickelson wanted to sharpen up before an upcoming Tour event and he had put the word out that he wanted to play against another pro. Knowing the stakes would be too rich for a mini tour grinder just barely getting by, Tony agreed to back Baldwin. Along with another gent we'll call Matty—a short hitter but clutch putter with an index of 3—they flew out to San Diego on the appointed day. They were driving to the golf course when Mickelson's partner for the round, a high-powered attorney, called to say the greens had just been punched and they were relocating the game to a different high-end private club in the area. "That felt like a cheap shot, like they were just messing with us," says Baldwin. Because of the change of venue and morning commute traffic, they arrived late. Mickelson was on the range, drinking a tall cup of Starbucks, and had clearly been working through a big pyramid of balls. Baldwin had made exactly two swings when Mickelson said they needed to tee off *right now* to get ahead of a big group on the tee sheet. More gamesmanship. Tony is a big personality and a loud talker and Mickelson admonished him on the first tee for being indiscreet in reciting the stakes of the match. "I don't think he'd ever been talked to like that in his life," says Baldwin. "But Phil clearly didn't want the folks at the club to know the size of the game." Despite the lack of warm-up, Baldwin, then thirty-one, smoked a good drive on number one. As they were walking off the tee, Mickelson said to Baldwin, "I hear you just came back from European Senior Tour qualifying." The young pro was dumbfounded; the Senior Tour is for players fifty and over. "It was a really weird opening piece of trash talk," says Baldwin. He replied that unless they had changed the rules to allow guys in their early thirties to play the Senior Tour, he was not yet eligible. "Phil paused for a second, nodded, and just kept walking," says Baldwin. "He totally meant to say that."

The betting games were ornate: Baldwin-Tony and Baldwin-Matty versus Phil and his guy and an individual match, pro against pro. Recognizing that he had home field advantage and a slightly longer résumé, Mickelson offered Baldwin either one shot per side or no shots but he could play from one tee box up. Baldwin took the shots mostly so he could club himself against Mickelson from the same tees on a course he'd never seen before. There was no blood on the first three holes and Mickelson continued to big-time Baldwin as they arrived on the tee of number four, an uphill, drivable par-4: "Phil says, 'Hey, man, this is my course, I'm gonna hit driver, because that's the way I play. But that's not the way you should play it. You should lay up with a 4- or 5-iron.'" Mickelson hit a pretty good drive toward the green and strutted away, even though Baldwin couldn't quite tell where the ball landed because of the hill. Without hesitating, Baldwin grabbed his driver and ripped a towering draw that never left the flagstick. They didn't find Mickelson's drive; Baldwin won the hole and his playing partner's respect. "His whole demeanor changed," says Baldwin. "Suddenly he was so cool and open and gracious, as if we were best buddies. We talked about all kinds of things, just full stream of consciousness."

Mickelson, whose game continued to be a little ragged, flipped another switch on the twelfth tee. "Man, am I really three down?" he asked.

Yep.

He fixed Baldwin with a hard look and said, "I promise you will not take a single dollar off me."

Mickelson proceeded to birdie five of the next six holes, his only par coming after he stiffed an approach shot but the short birdie putt horseshoed out. Along the way he didn't say another word to Baldwin. Arriving at eighteen, a shortish par-5, Mickelson was all-square in his match versus Baldwin, and an extravagant number of presses and side bets were on the line. Overwhelmed by the moment, each of Baldwin's partners blew their drives off the planet and were in pocket. Both pros hit good drives down the middle, and Baldwin played first, from 207 yards out, to a front pin. He produced a credible shot but his ball ran out on a firm green, leaving him a downhill forty-footer for eagle. "Oh, man, that's not good," Mickelson said. "That's the fastest putt on the whole golf course. You can't 2-putt from there." Says Baldwin, "He starts narrating his shot like he's Johnny Miller and it's the final hole of the Open. He was four or five yards in front of me and he says, 'I was deciding between 6- and 7-iron, but 6 brings into play the part of the green where you just went. Now I'm gonna hit the 7. But I can't get the 7 there. That's too far for a 7. I guess I'm gonna have to hit it totally perfect.'" Mickelson settled over his ball and took a ferocious swing. "I'll never forget the sound of the strike," says Baldwin. "It was like a two-by-four hitting a brick wall. Just absolute purity." Mickelson's ball tore through the sky, and even before it reached its apex, he intoned, "Ohhh, I did it." His ball took one hop, grazed the flagstick, and stopped six inches from the hole. "We looked at each other," Baldwin says of his partners, "and there was this morbid darkness in the air. We could feel the vise closing on us now." Baldwin narrowly missed his putt. Game over. He has a pro's discretion when it comes to revealing stakes, but pressed on how much Phil won, Baldwin says, "Tony bought him [the equivalent of] a nice car that day."

When it comes to betting on sports other than golf, Mickelson swims in even deeper waters. Tom Candiotti, the former big-league pitcher, was once among a big group of friends Mickelson invited to Las Vegas for the opening day of the NFL season. They woke up early in Scottsdale and flew to Vegas in Mickelson's plane. A cavernous suite at the Bellagio awaited, outfitted with a breakfast buffet and enough TVs to watch every game simultaneously. Mickelson had prepared a tip sheet with his thoughts on each game. The whole crew walked down to the sports book to place their bets. Says Candiotti, "We were kind of standing around, not sure if we should let Phil go first. Finally he says, 'You guys go ahead because when I place my bets it might move the line.'"

(Let that sink in for a minute.)

The entourage went back upstairs and it was like a frat party on steroids: the fellas were tossing around a football and tackling each other on the plush sofas. "Then the games started and things got serious," says Candiotti. "Phil swept every morning game. He was up over a million dollars." Mickelson lost only a game or two in the afternoon, increasing his haul. "We were flying home that night, but it's Phil's plane, so we're not gonna leave until he wants to, obviously," says Candiotti. "He goes down to play baccarat, and he's struggling. We practically needed a lasso to get him out of there. He stewed all the way to the airport because he gave a lot back at baccarat. *A lot.*"

Mickelson's heavy gambling increasingly brought him into contact with men of ill repute. In the mid-aughts, he began placing bets with a mobbed-up bookie out of Detroit named "Dandy Don" DeSeranno. (Mickelson's lawyer would later say Phil didn't know about the bookie's shady connections, which raises a different set of questions about the way he was tossing money around.) Recognizing that his famous client had no leverage and no muscle, Dandy Don simply refused to pay off Mickelson's winnings of over half a million dollars. This fleecing stayed a secret for a decade and a half before exploding into a public relations fiasco. (More on that later.) One of Mickelson's golf buddies at the Madison Club, in Palm Springs, was Bryan Zuriff, who would plead guilty in 2013 to his role in an illegal online gambling enterprise with alleged connections to the Russian Mafia; Zuriff, executive producer of *Ray Donovan*, paid a $500,000 fine and served six months of home confinement. In March 2010, a gambler named Greg Silveira accepted a wire transfer for $2.75 million. This touched off an investigation by the Internal Revenue Service's criminal investigation unit into what would come to be described as "an illegal gambling operation which accepted and placed bets on sporting events." Silveira was ultimately indicted on money-laundering charges. During his trial, the federal government produced evidence that "a well-known sportsman" had wired the $2.75 million to Silveira to cover gambling losses. An initial plea agreement with the U.S. Department of Justice signed in 2015 by Silveira and his attorney, James D. Henderson Sr., contained a reference to the "money laundering of funds from P.M." ESPN's *Outside the Lines* cited two sources alleging it was Mickelson who had transferred the money. (Phil and his lawyers have always refused comment on the matter.) California, where Silveira entered his plea, only prosecutes the recipient of the illegal "wages," not the person who places the wagers. The unsavory characters in Mickelson's life may or may not be the reason he tricked out his Ford Expedition with armored doors and bulletproof glass. His former PR guy T. R. Reinman offers an alternative explanation, saying "He likes to think of himself as James Bond."

Could Mickelson afford such staggering gambling losses? Maybe. From

2010 to '12, *Golf Digest* estimated his annual income at $41 million; in '14, it peaked at $52 million. "And Steve Loy was always complaining our numbers were too low," says Ron Sirak, the writer who put together the magazine's yearly list of golf's top earners. A separate question was whether or not Mickelson's heavy betting constituted a breach of PGA Tour rules. Its player handbook forbids its members to "associate with or have dealings with persons whose activities, including gambling, might reflect adversely upon the integrity of the game of golf." Tim Finchem was PGA Tour commissioner from 1994 to 2016, and when it came to player misconduct, he instituted Soviet-style secrecy: player fines and suspensions were never to be discussed publicly, to better uphold the image of Tour players as perfect gentlemen. I recently asked Finchem how closely the Tour monitored Mickelson's gambling. He replied, "We were aware of the basics of what was happening and that's pretty much all I would say."

But given the Tour's rules that prohibit associating with gamblers, shouldn't Finchem and his army of vice presidents have been watching more closely?

"It's a close call," he said. "People could look at it and argue both ways. Under our regulations it's certainly one thing if you go out and wager during a competition. But then outside of that we don't pay too much attention to what a player's doing on his own time. As long as he's not obviously doing something else that would bring disfavor on the sport."

But clearly the Silveira trial brought unfavorable coverage to the sport—was Mickelson ever fined or suspended as a result?

"Well, if we did sanction him, we wouldn't discuss it," says Finchem.

Okay, so you won't discuss specifics, but, Mr. Commissioner, can you at least declare publicly if Mickelson was ever fined or suspended as a result of his gambling?

"You can't have it both ways," says Finchem, a lawyer who worked as a Capitol Hill lobbyist before coming to the Tour. "You get to ask a question, but you've got to accept my answer. Rules of the road."

That Mickelson and Walters would become golf buddies had the inevitability of a runaway locomotive speeding toward a washed-out bridge. They had first met when they played in the same pairing at the 2006 Crosby Clambake. (Walters won the pro-am portion in '08 alongside Freddie "Junkman" Jacobson.) They became friendly after running into each other again at the Tour stop in Charlotte in 2008, when Walters played in the Wednesday pro-am. It quickly turned into a mutually beneficial relationship: Phil could pick the brain of a gaming legend, and Billy gained access to the accounts that Mickelson maintained, which was helpful since Walters would regularly get cut off from his own bookmakers because he enjoyed too much success. There is a misconception that Walters was Mickelson's bookie; in fact, they were partners, regularly pooling their money and splitting the winnings, though Mickelson lost plenty on bets in which Walters did not partake. (Billy once described Phil to a friend as a "rank sucker.") With Mickelson spending an increasing amount of time at Butch Harmon's golf school on the outskirts of Las Vegas, the relationship evolved to the point that Phil called Billy a mentor and Walters came to think of Mickelson as a little brother. "There was a real friendship there," says a close friend of Walters, who has also spent a lot of time around Mickelson; he would speak only on the condition of anonymity. "They're both larger-than-life characters who have seen and done a lot of things. They enjoyed each other's company and of course they loved betting against each other, too." Walters has said he's faced a putt worth as much as half a million dollars—he drained it—but in his on-course betting with Mickelson, they kept the stakes relatively low because they didn't want to add any strain to their partnership. According to a sworn statement by Mickelson's business manager, Phil delivered to Walters in September 2012 a cool $1.95 million to cover losses "related to sports gambling." These were for the games Mickelson bet but Walters passed on. Phil's business manager also acknowledged that his client "owed similar debts to Mr. Walters in the past, and had repaid them." If only there was a way for Mickelson to make some easy money to help cover such losses. Perhaps in the stock market?

Mickelson was unable to build on his 2010 Masters triumph because his body betrayed him. Two months after his emotional embrace with Amy at Augusta, he woke up in Pebble Beach and his limbs wouldn't work properly. It was the week of the U.S. Open, on a course where he had already won three times, but Mickelson had trouble just getting out of bed due to an attack of psoriatic arthritis. It took months of testing to dial in the right medication. (Naturally, Mickelson wound up as a paid endorser for Enbrel.) The onset of the arthritis occurred within days of his fortieth birthday, and it sent Mickelson down a new path of health and wellness that would ultimately set him up for a decade of age-defying success. But in the short term, he struggled to find his equilibrium, failing to win for the rest of the 2010 season and only once in 2011, while being a nonfactor in the majors.

Still, the holiday season of 2011 brought some joyous news: Mickelson had been elected to the World Golf Hall of Fame. He would be enshrined the ensuing May, during the week of the Players Championship. The ego boost of getting tabbed for the Hall gave Mickelson a little extra swagger at the start of the 2012 season. At the Crosby Clambake, he played well enough through three rounds to earn a spot in the penultimate pairing alongside one Tiger Woods.

On the eve of the final round, Mickelson attended, as he always does, a dinner party thrown by Jim Nantz in the wine cellar at the Sardine Factory, a swank restaurant near Cannery Row. Nantz often seats Mickelson next to Clint Eastwood but, knowing Phil's affinity for the NFL, on this occasion he was put next to Tony Romo. They hit it off famously. At one point, talk turned to the impending final-round showdown. "Phil says, with great bravado, 'There is absolutely no way I'm not winning tomorrow,'" says Nantz. "Tony is Tiger's pro-am partner, so he kind of pushes back and Phil says, 'Have you not been paying attention to the last four or five times we've been paired together? I'm in this guy's head.'"

Before the final round, Woods went to the far end of Pebble Beach's driving range, seeking solitude. Mickelson took his bag of balls and walked clear across the hitting area to set up right next to Woods. Tiger couldn't ignore him even if he tried, as they were nose to nose, with Lefty facing his right-handed adversary. In the two plus years since Woods ran over the fire hydrant, he had been badly diminished by scandal and injury. He remained winless since the summer of 2009. Now at Pebble Beach, the site of his most dominant victory, Woods had a golden opportunity to reassert himself, and he had clearly been buoyed by his easy chemistry with Romo. The Cowboys quarterback was so worried about upsetting his partner that at the end of the Sardine Factory dinner, Romo beseeched the other guests not to breathe a word to Woods about his new friendship with Mickelson. "If he finds out I've been sleeping with the enemy, I'm dead," Romo told Nantz. But Mickelson is a master of mind games and, walking off the first tee, at the outset of the final round, he shouted at Romo, who was one tee box ahead, "Hey, Tony, what a great night that was last night. I loved being with you, pal. Such a fun dinner."

Woods shot a glance at Romo, who mumbled something about having had no idea Mickelson was going to be at the meal. Phil half jogged to catch up to Tiger and his partner and continued to lay it on thick as they walked up the fairway: "What a pleasure to get to know you and [your wife] Candice. Thanks for all the great stories. . . ."

Says Nantz, "Tiger was not amused. And poor Tony wanted to run off the course and hide. He was completely shamed."

Looking like the cat that swallowed the canary, Mickelson birdied the second hole, then the fourth and fifth. After Woods tapped in for a birdie on number six, Mickelson poured in a twenty-footer for eagle on top of him. Just like that he had blown past Woods (and Charlie Wi) to seize the outright lead, and Tiger bogied three straight holes beginning at number seven, appearing ever more mopey with each miscue. He finally showed some signs of life at the twelfth hole, holing a bunker shot for birdie, but Mickelson then stepped up and buried a thirty-footer to save an unlikely par. An even longer putt on fifteen slammed the door. Mickelson shot 64 to roar to victory, trouncing Woods by eleven shots in the worst beatdown of his career. By the end of the round, the once-imperious Woods looked so out of his depth he elicited an unfamiliar emotion: pity. It was the fifth straight time Mickelson had shot a lower score than Woods when they were paired together in the final round, and Phil had now won three of those tournaments compared to zero for Tiger. Mickelson's fortieth career PGA Tour victory made him just the ninth player in Tour history to reach that whopping number.

After the champion's press conference broke up, Mickelson casually offered Tod Leonard, a longtime reporter at his hometown *San Diego Union-
Tribune*, a ride south on his jet. "In the awkward five seconds it took me to
answer," says Leonard, "a thousand things went through my head: *I've got a
story to write on deadline. . . . I have to return a rental car in San Jose. . . . This
is awesome. . . . Is this journalistically okay? . . . Will anybody on the plane talk
to me besides Amy?*" Leonard declined the invitation, which he says left him
"shaking." But to him the moment was revealing of how much the resounding
victory over his old nemesis meant to Mickelson. "He was just so out-of-his-
mind happy," says Leonard. "Other than the majors he's won, I've never seen
Phil happier."

In the ensuing two months, Mickelson nearly won at LA and Houston,
and he rode that momentum into Augusta. Rounds of 74-68-66 left him in
second place, a mere stroke behind European tour fixture Peter Hanson. A
fourth green jacket was well within Mickelson's grasp, a tantalizing prospect as
that would tie him with Woods and the great Arnold Palmer for the second-
most ever, behind only Big Jack's six. But on the tough par-3 fourth hole,
Mickelson suffered maybe the worst break of his career. With the pin in a
perilous position front-left, his preferred miss off the tee was left of the green,
which would leave an uphill chip. Alas, he pushed his tee shot a bit too much.
Mickelson was unbothered as his ball drifted toward the grandstand left of the
green; a free drop would leave him a good angle to save his par. But instead of
settling in a fan's lap, Mickelson's ball clanged off a metal railing and shot dead
left into a bamboo thicket lining the edge of the Augusta National property.
He had no room for a backswing but couldn't take an unplayable penalty because the only place to drop no nearer the hole was deeper into the shrubbery.
Mickelson could have swallowed the stroke and distance penalty and returned
to the tee box, but for his third stroke he would be replaying one of the toughest shots on the course and he'd have to work hard to make a double bogey
from there. So, he took the calculated risk of trying to gouge his ball out of
the hedge . . . right-handed. His first attempt moved the ball about six inches.
The next right-handed swing advanced it a dozen steps forward, onto trampled
turf where the gallery had been standing, which was muddy after days of rain.

Mickelson dumped the ensuing shot into the bunker. When the hole had mercifully ended, he took a triple bogey, tumbling down the leaderboard. Mickelson birdied the three ensuing par-5s to stay in the fight, but ultimately finished two shots out of the Bubba Watson–Louis Oosthuizen playoff. Hanson offered a succinct summary of the bad bounce Mickelson suffered on the fourth hole: "He got buggered."

Yet a few weeks later, Mickelson lit up the Hall of Fame induction ceremonies for a glittering class that included Dan Jenkins, the *Sports Illustrated* scribe who invented modern golf writing; Sandy Lyle, the onetime world number one who won a Masters and Open Championship; and Hollis Stacy, winner of three U.S. Women's Opens. Mickelson commanded the stage as he told a series of amusing stories that showcased what he called "my own little sick sense of humor." His voice cracked slightly a couple of times as he offered heartfelt words to his loved ones and reflected on his journey. "I would just like to say that since I was a kid and first picked up a golf club I have been living my dream," Mickelson said. He added, "I want to thank the fans because they have made this such a fun ride. There have been a lot of highs and lows that we've shared together. There have been a lot of times I've struggled and it's been their energy that pulled me through. I've tried to reciprocate by launching drive after drive in their general direction."

It was a good line. Mickelson had no way of knowing that the highs were about to get much higher, and the lows a heckuva lot lower.

CHAPTER FOURTEEN

I n 1930, Bobby Jones arrived at Merion Golf Club outside of Philadelphia attempting to complete the final leg of the Grand Slam. On the eve of that U.S. Amateur, he received a telegram from a friend, written in Greek: *E tan e epi tas.* This was something mothers in ancient Sparta told their sons as they carried their shields to battle: "With it, or on it."

That, on a lesser scale, is the brutal reality of tournament golf at the highest level—a player takes into combat fourteen clubs, and they will lift him to triumph or bury him. It took Jones two fingers of corn liquor to soothe his nerves after a tournament round, and the crushing pressure chased him from the game at twenty-eight, less than two months after he completed the Slam. Arriving for the 2013 U.S. Open at Merion—the first it had hosted in thirty-two years—Phil Mickelson could empathize with the metaphysical challenges Jones faced. The Open had become an annual psychodrama for Mickelson, a reminder that the national championship is a personality test as much as a golf tournament. It reveals more about a man's mental makeup than it does his golf game. The relentless difficulty of the course setup pushes players to the breaking point—mentally, physically, spiritually—which is why golf's most revered champions have been defined by their Open conquests, beginning with Jones, who won four. Ben Hogan and Jack Nicklaus matched that number, while Tiger Woods has snagged three.

Now Merion presented Mickelson, forty-three, with a unique opportunity. Even retrofitted for the modern game, it would play less than seven thousand yards, allowing him to drop the most unreliable club in his bag— the driver—in favor of a fifth wedge. More than that, Mickelson is a golf romantic, and to perform his best he has to fall in love with a course. The great golden-age course designer A. W. Tillinghast once described Merion as a "coy but flirtatious maiden with mocking eyes flashing at you from over her fan," and Mickelson fell hard. During a scouting trip the week before the Open, he took time to admire the old black-and-white photos in the clubhouse and leaf through the vast historical archives.

Mickelson's love affair with Merion continued during the first round as he shot a three-under-par 67 that propelled him into the lead and burnished his iconoclastic image. The day before, golf's most high-profile family man was at home in California for the eighth-grade graduation of his daughter Amanda, and he then flew overnight to Philly, touching down at 3:30 a.m., less than four hours before his tee time. Amanda's birthday has figured in U.S. Open weeks going all the way back to Pinehurst; she turned two when the family was in Tulsa for the Open at Southern Hills, so her parents threw a huge party that featured ponies and a life-sized Barney. Famously a psychology major at Arizona State, Mickelson didn't feel disadvantaged by his whirlwind arrival into Merion because, he says, "I think that mental preparation is every bit as important as physical, and I was able to take the time on the plane to read my notes, study, relive the golf course, go through how I was going to play each hole, where the pins were, where I want to miss it, where I want to be, study the green charts. It gave me a great few hours to get mentally prepared."

On Friday, Mickelson was unnerved by the extreme pin placements the USGA used to help the old girl maintain her reputation. (One prominent caddie memorably said that, tee-to-green, it was the best U.S. Open setup he had ever seen, but "the USGA monkey-fucked us on the hole locations.") Mickelson didn't make a birdie until the final hole, grinding out a 72 that kept him atop the leaderboard. Justin Rose putted beautifully en route to a 69 that left him one stroke off Mickelson's lead. He, too, was smitten with Merion. Noting the ebb and flow of the routing, he quoted a maxim popular among the club's caddies: "The first six holes are drama, the second six are comedy, and the last six holes are tragedy."

Mickelson kept his lead on Saturday with a hard-fought 70, putting him at one under, the only player below par. (Rose was two back.) The tournament was Phil's to lose, and it would be a solitary pursuit as his wife, Amy, stayed home to tend to Amanda's siblings, Evan and Sophia, both of whom had strep throat. Speaking by phone, she predicted her college sweetheart would have a restless night. "He doesn't sleep much the week of majors—he can't turn off his brain," said Amy. "He'll lie there doing mental rehearsals of the next day's round." Indeed, Phil sent me a text at 3:34 a.m. on Saturday apologizing for having made a biting (but undeniably funny) crack about my physique hours earlier.

Mickelson, who has a side business designing golf courses, can be shrill when discussing championship setups. His critical eye began his undoing in the final round. After lipping out birdie putts on the first two holes, his mood further soured when he arrived at the tee of the downhill par-3 third, which was playing 274 yards and into a twenty-mile-per-hour wind. "I needed a driver," he later said mournfully of his absent club. Instead, he tried to smash a 3-wood and his ball skittered into an awkward lie on the edge of a greenside bunker. A chip and three putts followed, leading to a double bogey. Mickelson was still steaming coming off the fourth tee when he spied Mike Davis, the USGA executive director who had long overseen Open setups. Mickelson veered in Davis's direction and barked some choice words about the third hole playing unfairly long. Nicklaus always said he loved to hear competitors complain about a course setup because it meant they were already beaten mentally. Davis, in an interview, claimed that a different wind had been forecast for Sunday. "Maybe Phil was right," he said. "In that wind, maybe it was too long." But the larger point is that anyone who wants to win an Open has to spend his energy saving par, not griping about the course. Mickelson made another ugly double bogey at the fifth hole when he drove into a hazard and three-putted again. The composure and patience that carried him the preceding three days were long gone.

But Mickelson has always been able to take a punch. On the par-4 tenth, he holed a seventy-five-yard approach for an eagle that vaulted him into the lead. Phil the Thrill was back, and the crowd was suddenly at full throat. "We had been struggling all day and there wasn't any energy out there," says Hunter Mahan, paired again with Mickelson for the final round of the Open. "When he holed that shot, the whole feeling flipped. It felt like it was finally his time."

Rose responded to Mickelson's eagle by birdieing the next two holes to reclaim the lead. Onions.

Mickelson arrived at the petite par-3 thirteenth and had to pick between one of his five wedges. With the pin back-right, perched atop a vertiginous slope, long was dead; most competitors were playing cautiously to the center of the green, leaving an uphill birdie putt. Mickelson took dead aim at the flag, but the pitching wedge was too much club, a whopping mental blunder. His ball bounded into the back bunker, pretty much guaranteeing a bogey. Still, Mahan doesn't fault the play. "He was probably going to need one more birdie to win," he says. "He's got a wedge in his hand, the ball is on a tee—can't think of a better time to be aggressive. But I was definitely surprised he flew it that far."

At fifteen, Mickelson was again between wedges. This time he decided to hit a hard gap wedge, but he never quite committed to the shot and his ball expired short of the green, leading to another killer bogey. "I quit on it," Mickelson said. After missing a ten-foot birdie putt on sixteen, Mickelson needed to birdie the stern eighteenth to have any hope. Alas, he fanned his drive deep into the left rough. The only consolation? It wasn't quite as off-line as the final, doomed drive at Winged Foot.

Rose, meanwhile, locked up the trophy with two perfect shots on the seventy-second hole. His drive had finished four paces from the plaque that commemorates Ben Hogan's one-iron on the seventy-second hole of the 1950 U.S. Open, maybe golf's most famous single swing. "It's hard to play Merion and not envision yourself hitting the shot that Hogan did," Rose said. "And even in the moment today, that was not lost on me."

Mickelson was left with a familiar emptiness after letting another Open slip away. "This one's probably the toughest for me," he said with glassy eyes, "because at forty-three and coming so close five times, it would have changed the way I look at this tournament altogether and the way I would have looked at my record. Except I just keep feeling heartbreak." Only one person is truly qualified to psychoanalyze Mickelson's serial crack-ups at the U.S. Open and he speaks from the grave. Sam Snead remains tied with Woods as the Tour's all-time leader in victories—including three at the Masters, which rewarded his freewheeling play—but he lacked the discipline and course-management skills to ever conquer the Open. His signature blowup came in 1939, across town from Merion at the Philadelphia Country Club, when he triple-bogeyed a waterless seventy-second hole to finish two shots out of a playoff. "I'll tell you about these Opens," Snead once said. "They get tougher and tougher on the mental side. You keep remembering the mistakes you made in the past that cost you an Open title. I guess you keep trying too hard."

Leaving the grounds at the end of a wrenching Father's Day, Mickelson's dad talked about how proud he was of his son. "He has a lot of resiliency," he said. "No matter how many times he gets his heart broken, he keeps throwing himself into the fray."

Mickelson conducted himself with his usual dignity in the aftermath of blowing another U.S. Open, but in the privacy of his home he felt the full weight of defeat. "He stayed in bed for two days with this blank look on his face," says Amy. "He was a shell of himself." On the third day, Mickelson finally rose, to leave for a long-scheduled family vacation to the Yellowstone Club in Montana, which is a sleepaway camp for the ruling class. (Other members include Bill Gates, Google founder Eric Schmidt, Dan Quayle, and investor Peter Chernin, as well as Tom Brady, Justin Timberlake, and Ben Affleck.) Part of Mickelson's charm is that, despite all the trappings of middle age, he has never really grown up. Alongside his three kids, he lost himself in whitewater rafting, rock climbing, archery, skeet shooting, and various other kinds of fun. At the Yellowstone Club, Mickelson often organizes dodgeball games in which he is the only adult. "I find it very therapeutic," he says with a laugh.

When he returned home to Rancho Santa Fe, a refreshed Mickelson was ready to go to work. How would he pick himself off the mat yet again? "Because he's Phil," said Bones. "He's resilient. And there are birdies to be made." Mickelson's commute had been greatly reduced: in his backyard he had built a practice facility that stretches for three hundred yards, with numerous bunkers and five greens, each with a different grass and design style. A full-time greenkeeper tweaks the putting surfaces to Mickelson's every whim. Before the 2013 Masters, one green was stimping at 14.5 to replicate Augusta National's speed, while ahead of the Open Championship, two greens were slowed to 10. Since turning forty, Mickelson had been beset with putting problems, leading to dalliances with a belly putter (2011) and an unorthodox claw grip (2012). But in 2013, Mickelson had been saying he was putting better than at any point in his career, and, indeed, Merion was his fifth top-three finish of the season. The improved putting was due to old-fashioned hard work, with a dash of Cali swag. "He loves to go out there in shorts and flip-flops," says Amy. "He just loves to practice." Dave Stockton remained his putting guru and continued to try to negate the influence of Dave Pelz, who was charged with overseeing the wedge game. "I was amazed he worked with Pelz and me at the same time because we don't exactly have the same philosophies," says Stockton. "Pelz would have him think more, I would try to have him get more creative. I could always tell when Phil had gone to Pelz. He would say something like 'I got a question for you: What do you think is a tougher putt, uphill or downhill?' Aww shit, he's been to Pelz again. Pelz told him downhill, but I said uphill is definitely much tougher. Phil says, 'No way, that's not right.' I said, you're an aggressive putter, right? On a downhill putt, if you rip it by the hole, you can see how it breaks and then you have an uphill comeback. That makes it much easier. On an uphill putt, if you rip it by, now you have four feet downhill coming back, which is definitely worse. Phil just looked at me and said, 'I love it. I needed to hear that.'"

Mickelson continued to try to better himself into his forties. He had begun working with sports psychologist Julie Elion in 2011, and one of their focuses was changing his attitude at the Open Championship. She encouraged Mickelson to think of the quirky linksland as a playground that could unlock his imagination. That summer he finished tied for second at Royal St. George's, his first time contending at the Open since 2004.

A couple of weeks after Merion, Mickelson turned up for the Scottish Open—at a firm, fast, rollicking Castle Stuart—and played a dizzying variety of shots en route to his first victory on European soil since a B-list event in France in 1993. That British Open tune-up was part of Mickelson's ongoing education in links golf. For most of his career he had tried to impose his game on the course, pounding towering drives and high, spinning iron shots, wind be damned. Nick Faldo was paired with Mickelson at the 2002 Open, at Muirfield, and he says, "His course management was horrendous. He kept hitting wrong shot after wrong shot. It was baffling, actually." Only in the last couple of years had Mickelson learned to embrace the ground game and strategic play necessary on these ancient courses where land meets sea. "He's the most creative player in the game," said swing coach Butch Harmon. "He just needed to change his thinking."

Muirfield, the site of the 142nd Open, presented the ultimate test. Most Open venues are blondes, with long fescue waving in the breeze, but Muirfield was a brunette, the dying greens and fairways turning browner by the day, thanks to an ongoing heat wave. The brick-hard greens and crazy-fast fairways dotted by ball-gobbling pot bunkers made for a brutally tough setup. Mickelson played well but not quite well enough over the first three rounds; at two-over par he was tied for ninth, five off Lee Westwood's lead, and staring up at Woods (one under) and Adam Scott (even), among others. But Mickelson was typically jaunty on Sunday morning. On his way out the door, he told Amy, "I'm gonna go get me a Claret Jug." He called his buddy Rob Mangini, who recounts Mickelson's monologue: "I'm playing so good. Jesus Christ, if I don't show up today I'm gonna be so pissed. I have to show up. All of it means nothing if I don't show up."

A mistake-free front nine put Mickelson in position, and then he simply blew everyone else off the course. Three strokes off Scott's lead playing the par-3 thirteenth hole, Mickelson flagged a 5-iron. "It was a putt that was going to make the rest of the round go one way or another," he said afterward of a testy eight-footer. "Because I thought if I made it, it would give me some momentum and get me to even par for the championship, a score I thought had a good chance of being enough [to win]. And that putt went in and it just gave me a nice momentum boost, because it's very hard to make birdies out here." On fourteen, he played a crafty links shot, landing his ball short of the green and letting it bounce and trickle all the way to a back flag. When he made the curling twenty-footer, he was just one off the lead. Then Scott lipped-out his par putt at thirteen. Tie ball game.

Scott continued to fade, sending Mickelson into the lead. He was one ahead of Henrik Stenson, standing in the fairway of the par-5 seventeenth hole, having found the fraught fairway with a bullet 3-wood that tore through the wind. He used the same club, and trajectory, on the next shot, and his ball rolled out seventy or eighty yards into the heart of the green. "When I was walking up seventeen, that was the moment that I had to kind of compose myself, because I'd just hit two of the best 3-woods I've ever hit," he said. "As I was walking up to the green, that was when I realized that this championship is very much in my control. And I was getting a little emotional. I had to kind of take a second to slow down my walk and try to regain composure." He deftly two-putted for birdie, pushing his lead to two strokes. Then at eighteen, Mickelson hit another perfect drive and precise approach, and one last birdie put an exclamation point on a back-nine 32 that was every bit as thrilling as his closing 31 at the 2004 Masters. Walking off the green, he dissolved into a long hug with his wife and kids. Mackay, fighting back tears afterward, called the 66 the best round his boss had ever played, and Zach Johnson, who was in the group behind Mickelson, added, "That will go down as one of the greatest rounds ever at a major championship."

"I don't want anybody to hand it to me, I want to go out and get it," Mickelson said. "And today I did."

Phil's fifth career major championship victory tied him with two players he has patterned himself after: swashbuckling escape artist Seve Ballesteros and Byron Nelson, the ultimate golfing gentleman. He was now three-quarters of the way to becoming just the sixth player to win the career Grand Slam. But for all the historical import, this victory was deeply personal for Mickelson. "I'm so proud to be your champion," he said at the trophy ceremony. "I never knew if I'd be equipped, if I'd have the shots, if I'd have the opportunity to win this tournament. To play some of the best golf of my career, and break through and capture this Claret Jug is probably the most fulfilling moment of my career." Two hours later, having cured his U.S. Open hangover in the most audacious way imaginable, Mickelson found himself at a party holding a flute of champagne in one hand and the Claret Jug in the other. Amy motioned toward the trophy her hubby was lugging around. "Why don't you drink it out of that?" she said with a mischievous grin. Phil glanced around the room at the assembled tweedy gents from the R&A. With a little smile, he said, "Not here." But definitely somewhere else. And soon.

CHAPTER FIFTEEN

P hil Mickelson failed to notch a victory in 2014, only the third winless season of his career. He did contend until the bitter end at the PGA Championship, but Rory McIlroy nipped him in the twilight at Valhalla. That autumn's Ryder Cup, then, offered a chance to redeem a frustrating year . . . and a vexing Cup career.

Just as in 2008, Tiger Woods would miss the '14 Ryder Cup as he recovered from surgery, further cementing Mickelson's standing as the leader of Team USA. In the early and mid-aughts, Mickelson was paired with old dogs like David Toms and Chris DiMarco at the Ryder Cup. In '08, when the Americans won for the first time in the twenty-first century, he began to transition into the elder statesman role, charged with shepherding younger players. "Even though a couple of guys brought home more points, Phil was the heart and soul of that team," says Paul Azinger, captain of the 2008 Ryder Cup team. "He took all those kids under his wing and showed them the way." Mickelson had a particular chemistry with Anthony Kim, the vastly talented but enigmatic young star. Zinger sent them out in the tone-setting first match of each Friday session, and they delivered 1.5 points as the U.S. raced to a 5.5–2.5 lead that proved insurmountable. "I let Phil figure out who his partner was going to be," says Azinger. "Those two together were a real dynamic duo. Phil wasn't going to be able to out-confident AK. The bling of his belt multiplied by Phil's flashiness, it became a dynamic energy that lifted the whole team."

The following year's Presidents Cup was notable for Mickelson's mentorship of Sean O'Hair, whose fragility became apparent over the first two days when his shaky play led to a pair of losses. The U.S. was up only one point versus a stout International team that featured eight major championship winners. Mickelson had won both of his matches, paired with AK and then Justin Leonard, but for a crucial Saturday, which featured both morning and afternoon matches, he volunteered to take on O'Hair as a reclamation project. "The special thing about Phil is he brings so much energy to any team he's on," says O'Hair. "I was struggling with my self-confidence and he brought an enthusiasm I didn't have. He made it fun and allowed me to play a little looser and get out of the funk I was in. There was so much positive self-talk. Everything I did was great and amazing. He'd say, 'Go ahead and aim at that flag and it's no big deal if you miss the green because I guarantee I'll chip it up close.' Or 'Swing as hard as you want and don't worry where it lands because I'll take care of the next shot.' I had been feeling like I had a ton of pressure on myself, but he put all the pressure on him and just let me play." In two matches together they won 1.5 crucial points, and then a rejuvenated O'Hair thumped Hall of Famer Ernie Els 6 & 4 in singles as the U.S. pulled away. Paul Tesori, who was then caddying for Vijay Singh, got a close look at Mickelson's coaching during the Saturday afternoon four-balls. "It's one of most incredible things I've ever witnessed a player do for another player," Tesori says. "I believe in my heart that when Sean is telling his grandkids about his career, he is going to start with that Presidents Cup, and how meaningful Phil's generosity was."

At the 2010 Ryder Cup, Mickelson was asked to shepherd Dustin Johnson (then twenty-six) and Rickie Fowler (twenty-one). They bonded to the point that both would become part of Phil's Tuesday money games on Tour; alas, Mickelson and his partners went 0-3 in those matches during the U.S. loss. But the following year he was 3-0 in partner play at the 2011 Presidents Cup at Royal Melbourne, maybe the best course in the world. During that Cup, Mickelson continued his cold war with Steve Williams, who had left Tiger Woods's bag and was then caddying for Adam Scott. "As they're going around, when Phil hits one off-line, Stevie is yelling, 'Foooore riiggghhht!' and 'Fooooore left!'" says Steve Stricker, a member of the American team. "Like really yelling. More than was needed. It happens three, four times and it's really getting under Phil's skin. They get up on sixteen, a dogleg left where there's stands down the right side, and Adam flares one toward the stands. Phil yells as loud as he can, 'Foooooooorrreee riiiighhhhhhht!' But Adam's ball lands in the fairway. That was awkward."

At the 2012 Ryder Cup, Mickelson was given the reins to Keegan Bradley, twenty-six, who is high-strung and fidgety even in the best of circumstances. Now Bradley was going to have to hit the opening tee shot in the second match of the Cup, in alternate shot against one of Europe's strongest teams, Sergio Garcia–Luke Donald. "I was freaking out," Bradley says of the walk to the first tee. "I mean, two years earlier I was playing the Hooters Tour. Phil could sense that, so he calls me over and says, 'Listen, Keegan, I don't want a 7-iron in. I don't want an 8-iron. I want an f-ing sand wedge.' He made me laugh when I didn't think it was possible to laugh. I stepped up and hit the best drive of my life, and he did have a sand wedge in"—actually, it was a seventy-eight-yard lob wedge on a hole playing 433 yards—"and he hit it to a foot and we were off and running." They went 3-0 together over the first two days, including an overwhelming 7 & 6 victory against Donald and Lee Westwood in alternate shot. Mickelson was gassed by Saturday afternoon and asked to sit out; U.S. captain Davis Love would take some shrapnel for not insisting his hottest team keep playing, especially after Europe won the last two matches on the eighteenth hole to end the day with a huge morale boost. Still, the U.S. had a formidable 10–6 lead heading into singles. Then came the "Miracle at Medinah." The whole Ryder Cup flipped when Justin Rose buried a big-breaking fifty-footer on the seventeenth hole against Mickelson, keying Rose's 1-up victory. But in an enduring showing of sportsmanship, Mickelson stood next to the green and applauded the putt.

Despite the stinging loss, the 2012 Ryder Cup was edifying for Mickelson. It marked the first time a true contemporary had been captain. Davis Love III is a gentle soul and natural consensus-builder. He recognized Mickelson was the biggest personality on the team and treated him deferentially. "Phil had a big voice in everything we did," says Love. That began well ahead of the Ryder Cup, when Love organized a dinner at a steakhouse for probable team members to engage in male-bonding rituals. Given the casual setting, he didn't plan to make any opening remarks, but Mickelson admonished him. "Phil said, 'Get up and say something—you're our captain and we want you to act like it,' " says Love. That dinner was also notable for the banter between Mickelson and Woods, who, in the wake of his sex scandal, had been humbled enough to need more human connection with his teammates. "There was a lot of stuff said between them that I can't repeat," says Brandt Snedeker. "It was the first time I saw a real friendship there. But there were a few moments where it was like, Are they gonna laugh, or get pissed off? Like, man, I don't know if you can say that. That's borderline—it could end in blows. By the end of the night, Phil had Tiger laughing so hard Tiger almost went under the table. Me and Davis were laughing so hard we were crying."

Given Mickelson's elevated status within Team USA, imagine his shock when, out of left field, he was informed that sixty-five-year-old Tom Watson would be captain for the 2014 Ryder Cup. Strident, old-school, and set in his ways, Watson was a hard-ass who loved to work the land on his farm in Kansas City. Mickelson had caught wind of enough of Watson's diatribes to know they saw the world in very different ways. He once described Watson to me as "rarely right, but never in doubt."

Watson's surprise appointment exposed the serial flaws in Team USA's fractured approach to the captaincy. Overseen by the PGA of America, the American effort had to start over willy-nilly every two years when a new PGA president was installed. Watson, who was totally out of touch with modern Tour players, had been handpicked by an Indiana golf course owner turned PGA president named Ted Bishop, who thought it would be cool to pal around with one of his idols. There was minimal communication between Watson and Love, typical of the lack of collaboration between administrations. This was a stark contrast to the European way. Its Ryder Cup committee is run by current players and former captains and stresses continuity in the leadership. Captains are groomed with apprenticeships as Ryder Cup vice captains and, previously, with managerial positions at the Seve Trophy, a biennial competition held from 2000 to '13 that pitted Great Britain & Ireland against Continental Europe.

The meltdown at Medinah meant the U.S. had lost five of the preceding six Ryder Cups, so Watson had no qualms about doing things his way. He didn't exactly endear himself to his players when, in the run-up to the Cup, he said in an interview he wouldn't be afraid to "tell one of these prima donnas they were going to sit, or play."

Mickelson, as always, had his own idiosyncratic ideas. "He's really into numerology, he talked about it a bunch with me," says sportswriter Rick Reilly. "What it means for his future, which tournaments he's going to win. Phil thinks he can use it to predict the future." Adds Jordan Spieth, "He's a big energy guy. How the sun and the moon are positioned and how that can bring you certain energy." Mickelson has been known to expound on things that are even more out-there. "There's a famous story about Phil telling a few of the guys that aliens were captured in the U.S. in the early 1940s and that was how we got the technology to develop the atomic bomb," says Shaun Michael. "I don't know if he was serious. You can never tell with him." Anyway, ahead of the Ryder Cup, Mickelson buttonholed Bishop to explain his groovy chemistry with Freddy Couples, a fellow Californian who captained the U.S. at three straight Presidents Cups beginning in 2009. "Certain players are just going to have good or bad weeks based on the position of the sun," Mickelson told Bishop. "There are charts that depict this, and Fred studies them." Bishop asked Mickelson if he had shared this information with Watson. "No, Tom would never listen to that," Phil said, quite correctly. "He has his own way of doing things." But in the months before the 2014 Ryder Cup, Mickelson had employed his own team of what he called "Ivy League statisticians" to make models that forecasted the most effective pods and pairings for the U.S. team. He had screenshots of all the notes on his phone and pressed them upon anyone who would listen. "He was so invested in it," says Mark Baldwin, whose money match with Mickelson took place a couple of weeks after the Ryder Cup, "and he thought it was the most brilliant thing ever. But the longer he talked about it, the less it sounded like astrophysics and the more it sounded like astrology. There were definitely components of that in this formula." Mickelson did eventually present the reams of data to Watson, and was embittered when the captain blew it off.

Watson had already raised eyebrows when he admitted to reporters that Webb Simpson basically talked his way into a captain's pick with an early-morning text volley on the day the picks were to be announced. Once the U.S.

team arrived at Gleneagles, in Scotland, Mickelson began to question Watson's acuity. Early in the week, the captain asked Mickelson for his phone number, which was baffling since there were so many ways Watson could have previously acquired it. He had a stray golf ball in his pocket, so he used a Sharpie to write Mickelson's number on the ball, embellishing it with the initials *PM*. Shortly after that, Watson encountered some fans who beseeched him for a souvenir and he absentmindedly tossed one of them the ball. Almost immediately, Mickelson began getting random phone calls and texts at odd hours. He had to have an associate change his phone number in the middle of Ryder Cup week.

The day before the competition was to begin, Watson and Mickelson had words about a money game Phil had organized during a practice round; the captain preferred a more rigorous approach to preparation. "There was a tension between them all week," says Bishop. "They're two very stubborn, very headstrong individuals who are used to getting their way. It was probably inevitable they were going to butt heads."

On the first morning of the Ryder Cup, Watson sent out Mickelson-Bradley to face the powerhouse European team of Rory McIlroy and Sergio Garcia in better ball. Before heading out to play, the American duo found themselves alone in the dead-quiet locker room. "I think about this all the time because it's one of the favorite moments of my career," says Bradley. "Rory and Sergio were one and three in the world. I was freaking out to the point that I was having trouble breathing. And Phil says to me, 'Hey, I'm really nervous right now, give me a pep talk.' He just turned the energy around and made me focus on something besides my own nerves. I said, 'I can't believe this is happening to me. If you'd told me as a kid I would be playing with and against my idols, in Scotland, representing my country, I'd never have believed it. This is the honor of a lifetime.' And we both got so pumped up." Then they went out and won an emotional match, 1-up, raising their Ryder Cup record together to 4-0. Watson had no choice but to send them back out that afternoon, even though it altered his scripted pairings. Both Mickelson and Bradley drove the ball poorly during alternate shot foursomes. On the ninth tee, Watson approached them and barked, "When are one of you two guys actually going to hit a fairway?" That was his version of a pep talk.

Mickelson-Bradley got beat 3 & 2 by Graeme McDowell–Victor Dubuisson, part of a lost afternoon for the Americans, who won only half a point to put themselves in a 5-3 hole. Watson sat Mickelson-Bradley the next morning, a curious choice given that better ball played to their strengths as occasionally wayward birdie machines. Presumably, that meant Watson would have to trust them in the more awkward alternate shot format. Per usual, Watson hadn't consulted any players in his decision-making. If Love and Azinger had run their teams as democracies, Watson's style was far more dictatorial. The U.S. won 2.5 points in the morning to close the gap. Mickelson and Bradley were warming up on the range when they received word that they were benched for the afternoon session, too. Watson was out on the course, so Mickelson began texting him furiously, begging his captain for a chance to play. Watson remained unmoved. (He sent out Rickie Fowler–Jimmy Walker for a fourth straight session, even though they had halved their previous three matches in intense battles; they were visibly drained and got trounced 5 & 4 by McDowell-Dubuisson, and Watson later lamented that he had leaned too hard on "tired" players.) Watson returned to the clubhouse to try to talk down Mickelson. It didn't go well. "Phil said it got so heated, that they had such an extremely confrontational exchange, that if Tom hadn't done what he's done in golf and if he were a few years younger, it could have gotten physical," says Baldwin.

The U.S. again won only half a point in alternate shot, falling behind by the score of 10–6. They gathered in the team room that night hoping to find some inspiration and camaraderie. Addressing the team, Watson said, "You guys suck at foursomes." If that was his version of levity, it didn't exactly lighten the mood. The team had made a replica of the Ryder Cup trophy to give to Watson as a gift. Befitting his standing on the team, Mickelson had been tabbed to present the bauble, but now he begged off, saying, "You don't want me up there talking tonight." Jim Furyk did the honors, but Watson dismissed the gesture, saying he only wanted "the real thing." That bruised some feelings. When he left the room, Mickelson stood up and offered a pep talk to his teammates, trying to breed a little solidarity. It didn't work: Team USA went down meekly in singles, losing yet another Ryder Cup. (Mickelson prevailed in his match versus Stephen Gallacher, making him one of only three Americans with a winning individual record.)

What followed was one of the most exquisitely awkward press conferences in golf history. Watson and all of his players were seated on a dais at the front of a drafty tent, facing their inquisitors. The captain was asked what formula the U.S. needed to actually win a Ryder Cup. "Well, the obvious answer is that our team has to play better," he said. "I think they recognize that fact; that somehow, collectively, twelve players have to play better."

It was a simplistic response. The players can't just magically play better without a culture change achieved through cohesive and supportive leadership. Another reporter raised his hand and asked, "Anyone who was on the team at Valhalla, can you put your finger on what worked in 2008 and what hasn't worked since?" (At that Ryder Cup, Azinger had instituted a ballyhooed "pod" system in which players were broken into groups of four, so they could practice and bond together, knowing who their playing partners would be in the upcoming matches.) With a glint in his eye, Mickelson leaped at the question.

"There were two things that allowed us to play our best I think that Paul Azinger did, and one was he got everybody invested in the process," Mickelson said. "He got everybody invested in who they were going to play with, who the [captain's] picks were going to be, who was going to be in their pod, when they would play, and they had a great leader for each pod. In my case, we had [vice captain] Ray Floyd, and we hung out together and we were all invested in each other's play. So we were invested in the process. And the other thing that Paul did really well was he had a great game plan for us, you know, how we were going to go about doing this. How we were going to go about playing together; golf ball, format, what we were going to do, if so-and-so is playing well, if so-and-so is not playing well, we had a real game plan. Those two things helped us bring out our best golf. And I think that, you know, we all do the best that we can and we're all trying our hardest, and I'm just looking back at what gave us the most success. Because we use that same process in the Presidents Cup and we do really well."

Mickelson's words hung in the dank air. The players on the dais fidgeted uncomfortably. Reporters were arching eyebrows at one another. Blood was now in the water and the sharks immediately went in for the kill. "That felt like a pretty brutal destruction of the leadership that's gone on this week," a reporter responded.

"Oh, I'm sorry you're taking it that way," Phil said in classic Mickelsonian bullshittery, because that's exactly how he had wanted it to be taken. He continued, "I'm just talking about what Paul Azinger did to help us play our best. I don't understand why you would take it that way. You asked me what I thought we should do going forward to bring our best golf out and I go back to when we played our best golf and try to replicate that formula."

"That didn't happen this week?"

"Um"—here Mickelson paused dramatically—"no. No, nobody here was in any decision. So, no."

Now the energy in the room shifted again, from disbelief to low-grade giddiness. Something unprecedented was happening, and reporters' thumbs began twitching wildly, tweeting the news that a full-blown insurrection had broken out at Gleneagles. An otherwise run-of-the-mill U.S. defeat belatedly had its defining moment.

Watson was asked, "Do you think that Phil is being disloyal? Because it sounded like that."

Watson's ramrod posture never changed. "Not at all," he said. "He has a difference of opinion. That's okay. My management philosophy is different than his." For all the mistakes Watson made as captain—and they were legion—this was his finest moment, a showing of restraint, class, and discretion with the whole world watching. Per Omar Little, a man gotta have a code. This proud champion would live his, even while getting clowned by his own player.

The blowback from the fractious loss and contentious press conference was so intense that Watson's vice captains—Floyd, Andy North, and Steve Stricker—made a vow that night to never discuss the inner workings of that Ryder Cup publicly, for fear of further inflaming the hard feelings. But with Watson's blessing, North agreed to be interviewed for this book. (Watson himself declined, saying in an email, "Sorry, but the story that you want from me is not for public knowledge.")

"It was one of the worst thirty minutes of my life," North says of the Team

USA press conference. "It was shocking. I couldn't believe what was transpiring. No captain will ever put as much into that event as Tom did for two years. I know it meant more to him than anything in the world. It's sad that what he'll be remembered for is that press conference. It's not right. Phil was upset, so he thought it would be okay to throw a great man under the bus? No, that was totally unacceptable. He wanted more of a voice, but at what cost? I wonder if he thought about that before doing what he did."

Of course he did—Mickelson almost never opens his mouth without an agenda. Was he fueled by personal vendetta? Definitely. But, with an eye on the big picture, he also made the calculated decision that the only way to create the necessary momentum for reform was to take his grievances public, even if it meant savaging Watson in the process. I said as much in a story I wrote that dark night in Scotland. When it dropped online, Mickelson texted me his approval: "It's like you can read my mind."

CHAPTER SIXTEEN

Phil Mickelson shot a four-round total of 274 (–14) at the 2015 Masters, a score that previously had been bettered only four times in tournament history. Unfortunately for Mickelson, Jordan Spieth was four shots better. It was the second major championship in a row that he brought out the best in one of the game's brightest stars. (And an epic duel in the fog with Henrik Stenson was still coming.) "I'm a fun guy to beat," Mickelson says, by way of explanation. "I really am. Because when you don't beat me, I really stick it to you. So I think guys really get a lot of enjoyment out of beating me. I know I would. I think that I have a very positive energy. The way I view life is so positive. I don't really have much negativity. I love my life all the way through, from what I do for a living, to my family, my kids, the people I spend time with, the friends I have, everything. I just have a very positive outlook and I guess [opponents] feed off that positive energy. I don't try to stare 'em down or I don't try to be mean or use gamesmanship or anything like that. I just have fun and play. And I think in that environment, it allows me to play my best when I'm talkative and smiling and having fun. And I think it does the same for others, too."

Mickelson brings that same energy to his famed practice-round money games on Tour. The stakes are not that big—rarely does more than a thousand dollars change hands—but the competition is cutthroat. One of Mickelson's favorite battles came at the 2015 Players Championship, when he and Rickie Fowler took on Keegan Bradley and Brendan Steele. "Keegan was about ready to bow out of these games 'cause he's never won," Mickelson says. "It's been a year and a half and he's had to pay every time. It gets demoralizing. So he's like, 'If I don't win today, I'm out. And this is the day I'm gonna win.'"

Fast-forward to the twelfth hole. Bradley-Steele are 2-up. Mickelson has a fifteen-footer for birdie, while Bradley faces twelve feet for a bird of his own. Says Mickelson, "As I'm standing over this putt, I back away. And I say, 'Oh, my goodness, this putt is the entire match.' And Keegan bites. He goes, 'Oh, yeah? How so?' Which is what I was hoping he would say. And I said, 'If I miss, you're gonna make your putt. You'll have momentum, you're gonna make it. And you're going to be three up with six to go and you guys are gonna win. But if I make it, you're gonna quick-peel yours on the low side. You're gonna be so pissed off, you and Brendan are gonna give us a hole. Next thing you know, we're gonna be tied. Then Rickie and I will have the momentum. We'll make a birdie or two comin' in, probably beat you 2 & 1.' So I knock it in. And of either side that Keegan could've missed his putt on, he missed it low side. He quick-peeled it low side. Now they're so pissed off they both bogey the next hole. And we get that hole. Now we're tied. So Rickie and I birdie fifteen, sixteen, and seventeen, and win 2 & 1. And I chuckle about that story every time because it's just funny. And I don't care about the money—I get to give him smack about this every time I see him."

"Most of Phil's stories are fabricated," says Bradley with a sigh, "but unfortunately that one is totally true. I want to beat him so bad and it pisses me off when I don't."

Bradley wound up excusing himself for a while from further money games with Mickelson. "He picked up his toys and he went home," Phil says. "He took a one-year sabbatical. But he eventually came back. He pulled up his big-boy panties and came back out. And he's had some success, he's won some matches and he's no longer totally defeated."

Mickelson is a big believer in the maxim that fast pay makes fast friends. At the 2014 Ryder Cup, he and Bradley beat Fowler and Jimmy Walker two days in a row in practice rounds. Since they were in Scotland, Walker claimed not to have any U.S. currency, so Mickelson agreed he could settle his debt the next time they saw each other on the PGA Tour, which turned out to be when they were paired together at Torrey Pines at the outset of the 2015 season.

"Naturally, what are you gonna do?" asks Mickelson, already knowing the answer. "The first thing you're gonna do is square up, that's what you do. You walk over and say, 'I haven't seen you in a while, here's the money I've owed you for four months.' Didn't happen. So I felt the need to drop Jimmy a line: 'Hey, dude, tomorrow after the round, go to the bank, we'll square up in the morning.' And he didn't do it."

Walker finally paid up a couple of weeks later.

"So then we're at Doral," Mickelson says, "and he and [Brandt] Snedeker were talking smack: 'Oh, yeah, we're gonna play you at the Masters, blah, blah, blah.' And I said, 'Well, that's great, Brandt—I would love to play with you. But you're gonna have to get another partner because Jimmy is suspended a match.' And he thought that I was kidding. I wasn't kidding. He had a one-match suspension. The commissioner has to draw the line somewhere, right?"

For all the verbal fireworks, these matches can be quite instructive, especially for Mickelson's opponents. "He's taught me so much about the game and about myself," says Steele, a three-time winner on Tour. "For a long time he beat me every time we played." Steele vividly recalls one occasion when both players were in the fairway but Mickelson missed the green with his approach, his ball settling in a bad spot. Steele followed with a cautious play to the center of the green, leaving himself a forty-foot birdie putt. Mickelson chipped to gimme range and then Steele had to rattle in a four-footer just to halve the hole. The Hall of Famer scolded his young adversary: "The mistake you made there," Mickelson said, "was as soon as I missed the green you thought you were gonna win the hole. I will never hand you a hole. Ever. If I miss a green, you have to get more aggressive, not less, because that's your chance to win a hole with a birdie." Other lectures would follow. At the 2011 PGA Championship, Steele was tied for the lead heading into the final round, but on Sunday he double-bogied the first hole and then, in his words, "completely unraveled." Mickelson told him, "The mistake you made was not that you got off to a bad start, it was not understanding you have eighteen holes to shoot a score. Everyone stumbles at some point—you have to use all eighteen holes to make your score. Maybe you birdie the last three holes and that's what it takes." At the 2016 Texas Open, Steele enjoyed a three-shot lead at the halfway point. But he had a mediocre weekend and faded to eighth place. Mickelson came through with another life lesson: "Your mistake was not how you played

on Sunday, it was your approach on Saturday. You were obviously playing incredible golf to be leading. You should have birdied three of the first five holes
on Saturday and put your stamp on the tournament and let everybody know
they're playing for second place. But you played defensive and tried to protect
the lead and got run over."

Says Steele with a laugh, "He doesn't sugarcoat things, but he's pretty
much always right."

Despite Mickelson's continued success during the practice rounds, 2015 was
another frustrating year as he again went winless on Tour. That November, he
flew to Las Vegas to break up with Butch Harmon in person. After eight years
together, he felt he owed him that. "We talked for about two hours," Harmon
said at the time. "I completely agreed that sometimes you need to hear things a
different way, get a different perspective on things. He's been frustrated the last
two years. I thought it was a good idea that he would do this. He needs to hear
things differently that maybe get him rejuvenated and get him back to what
we all know he can be." Mickelson hired an Aussie named Andrew Getson
as his new coach. He knew Getson through their association with Grayhawk
Golf Club in Scottsdale, where Getson had been teaching for the preceding six
years. Getson worked with other pro golfers, including Kevin Streelman, who
had long been celebrated for having one of the simplest and most repeating
swings in the game. Mickelson made all the usual noises about tightening up
his action and hitting more fairways.

If he had hoped 2016 would be all about reinvention, the headlines
throughout that spring and summer made it clear that Mickelson was not going
to be able to outrun his past, as he was once again ensnared in a messy insider-
trading case. Back in May 2014, two FBI agents had approached Mickelson
after his first round at Jack Nicklaus's Memorial Tournament as part of a probe
related to allegations of suspicious trading of Clorox stock by billionaire investor Carl Icahn and Phil's guy in Las Vegas, Billy Walters. The case garnered a
huge amount of media coverage given the outsized profiles of all three protago-
nists. Mickelson maintained his innocence, and two weeks after the awkward

encounter at the Memorial, the *New York Times* reported, "The F.B.I. and the Securities and Exchange Commission have found no evidence that Mr. Mickelson traded Clorox shares. The overstated scope of the investigation came from information provided to the *Times* by other people briefed on the matter who have since acknowledged making a mistake." But buried in that piece was this ominous passage: "Although Mr. Mickelson is not connected to the Clorox trades, he is not in the clear. The F.B.I., federal prosecutors in Manhattan and the S.E.C. continue to investigate well-timed trades made by Mr. Mickelson and Mr. Walters in shares of Dean Foods in the summer of 2012, the people briefed on the matter said. The authorities are pursuing a theory that a source inside Dean Foods gave Mr. Walters a heads-up about the company's plan to spin off its WhiteWave Foods subsidiary in an initial public offering, though it is unclear what exactly prompted Mr. Walters and Mr. Mickelson to trade. Shares of Dean Foods surged 41 percent on August 8, 2012, the day after the company officially announced the spinoff in a news release."

For two years Mickelson lived under that cloud of suspicion, and then in May 2016 the Dean Foods case exploded into the public sphere. Walters was indicted on insider-trading charges, with the SEC alleging that he made $43 million on illegal stock tips provided by Thomas C. Davis, a Dean Foods board member who had taken loans from Walters while running up a massive gambling tab. (Davis is a former club president at Preston Trail Golf Club.) Mickelson was named as a relief defendant, meaning he was not accused of wrongdoing, but the SEC still recovered "alleged ill-gotten gains from schemes perpetrated by others." Mickelson neither admitted nor denied the allegations in the SEC's complaint; he agreed to disgorge trading profits totaling $931,738, plus interest of $105,292. The SEC laid out a damning case of alleged collusion between Billy and Phil: "In July 2012, Walters called Mickelson, who had placed bets with Walters and owed him money at the time. While Walters was in possession of material nonpublic information about Dean Foods, he urged Mickelson to trade in Dean Foods stock. Mickelson bought Dean Foods stock the next trading day"—in all, he would purchase 200,240 shares at a cost of $2.46 million—"in three brokerage accounts he controlled. About one week later, Dean Foods' stock price jumped 40 percent following public announcements about the WhiteWave spin-off and strong second-quarter earnings. Mickelson then sold his shares for more than $931,000 in profits. He repaid his debt to Walters in September 2012 in part with the trading proceeds."

Why would Mickelson be waiting on a Wall Street bonanza to pay back Walters? The massive scale of Phil's gambling losses has never before been made public, but as part of the Dean Foods investigation, a forensic examination of his finances was conducted by government auditors. According to a source with direct access to the documents, Mickelson had gambling losses totaling more than $40 million in the four-year period (2010–14) that was scrutinized.

Mickelson had never previously traded Dean Foods stock, and phone records showed that around the time of his buying and selling he was texting frequently with Walters—so how on earth did he avoid criminal charges? Pure dumb luck played a big part. In December 2014, as investigators were building their case against Walters and, potentially, Mickelson, the United States Court of Appeals for the Second Circuit threw out the conviction of a man named Todd Newman, who had traded stocks based on a tip from someone who received it from a corporate insider. Cashing in on secondhand information, as the government alleged Mickelson had done, meant he was in a comparable position to Newman. According to the Second Circuit decision, a secondhand beneficiary like Mickelson could only be found guilty of insider trading if he knew that the source of the information (Thomas Davis, in Phil's case) benefited by giving it to the middleman (Walters). Mickelson denied knowing about Walters and Davis's relationship. In the absence of evidence to the contrary, and under the case law of the Newman ruling, Phil could not be charged.

Walters went to trial in March 2017. Mickelson was not called to testify by either the defense or prosecution because his lawyer Gregory Craig—former White House counsel to Presidents Bill Clinton and Barack Obama—had made it clear that his client would exercise his Fifth Amendment right to protect himself from self-incrimination. Still, Mickelson had a starring role in the trial, being mentioned by name more than a hundred times. In his opening statement to the jury, Walters's lawyer built his defense largely on the notion that his client was too sophisticated an investor to give insider information to his celebrated friend: "When there is a big event for a company, whether it's a merger, acquisition or a spinoff, the Securities and Exchange Commission looks to see who are the buyers leading up to that, and they investigate; that's what they do. So if you're Bill Walters, I would submit, and you believe that someone has given you illegal inside information, the last thing you would do is give it to Phil Mickelson, one of the most famous athletes in the world. That is immediately going to attract regulatory scrutiny and lead back to Bill Walters." Walters had been a Dean Foods shareholder going back a decade. When Mickelson asked for a stock tip, as he is wont to do, Walters had indeed recommended Dean Foods, but he has always maintained his confidence came from readily available public information. After Mickelson's sell-off in the summer of 2012, Walters still held on to four million shares of the stock because he believed in its long-term potential. The prosecution saw it differently. "When [Walters] knew he had a sure winner, he let his friends in on the action," U.S. attorney Brooke Cucinella said in her closing argument. "Mickelson made just under $1 million—money that ultimately he transferred right back to the defendant because of a gambling debt. Of course, Phil Mickelson could pay it back, but this was another way for Billy Walters to feed himself, by giving Mickelson this sure thing. Information that he knew was going to happen, he knew that the money would come back around, and that's exactly what it did."

The jury found Walters guilty on all ten counts against him. Speaking to reporters after the verdict, he said, "I just did lose the biggest bet of my life." At the age of seventy, he was sentenced to five years at the Pensacola Federal Prison Camp, a minimum-security facility housed on a naval air station in the Florida Panhandle. Walters lost his appeal; Mickelson again loomed large in absentia. "It was clear from the pleadings, the public documents during the trial, Mickelson was interviewed on more than one occasion [by FBI agents]," says Richard Wright, Walters's longtime personal attorney. "And he denied any wrongdoing on his behalf as well as Bill's behalf. Essentially denying he got any tips. He had denied that to the government. If he had testified, he would have denied he had any insider information from Bill Walters. In my judgment, it would have helped us."

Walters's view, more succinctly, is that he got sold down the river by Mickelson. "Here is a guy that all he had to do was come forward and tell the truth," he told ESPN shortly before reporting to prison in October 2017. "That was all he had to do. The guy wouldn't do that because he was concerned about his image. He was concerned about his endorsements. My God, in the meantime a man's life is on the line."

If Mickelson did not receive any inside information—as both he and Walters contend—why did he pay back more than $1 million to the government? "Anyone of Phil's stature in that situation would gladly write a check to make the whole thing go away," says a friend of Walters. "The problem is, by doing that he made Bill look guilty as hell. And then to not testify on Bill's behalf, when he could have saved his skin, that was the ultimate betrayal. Phil had nothing to lose—he had already cut his deal. If there were any questions he didn't like, he could have taken the Fifth [Amendment] up on the stand. But to hang Bill out to dry the way he did, after calling him a friend and a mentor, that tells you a lot about the character of the man."

A member of Mickelson's inner circle sees it quite differently: "Look up the meaning of 'relief defendant'—it means you're an innocent bystander to someone else's crimes. Phil gave the money back because he was required to by law, but even the government admitted there was no wrongdoing. They would have loved to nail him to the cross, but they had nothing on him. Why on earth would he testify? He wasn't part of Billy Walters's case at all—that was between Billy and Tom Davis. Phil just got dragged into it because the government wanted to make headlines. If there was a betrayal it was by Billy Walters, because he gave Phil tainted information without telling him the source."

This legal saga had one final plot twist. In December 2016—long after the charges against Walters were filed and three months before he went to trial—the Supreme Court ruled on *Salman v. United States*, a case from California that had limited insider-trading law in virtually the same way that the Newman verdict had done in New York. In a unanimous decision, the Supreme Court rejected parts of the Newman ruling and, according to a lawyerly analysis in *Golf Digest*, "held that recipients of inside information could be prosecuted even if they didn't know what the original tipper received." Ergo, if Mickelson's case had arisen before December 2014 or after December 2016, it's much more likely he would have been indicted for insider trading and been staring down the gun barrel of prison time. But because the Newman case was the law of the land when his case came due, he skated. This was the greatest escape in a life defined by them.

Mickelson is a master compartmentalizer. In his first start after the news broke about his settlement with the Securities and Exchange Commission, he held a pretournament press conference at the Memorial, site of his chat with FBI agents two years earlier. "I'd like to say that I'm disappointed to have been a part of that whole thing, but after a thorough investigation, I'm pleased that it's behind me, that it's over," Mickelson said. "I'm appreciative of my family and friends and my companies and their faith in me and their support of me." Asked what lessons he had learned, Mickelson responded, "I have to be responsible for the people I associate with. Going forward, I'll make the best effort I can to make sure I represent myself, as well as my family, as well as my companies, in the way that I want to and they deserve." The emphasis on his corporate partners was unrelenting. A reporter pointed out that Billy Walters had been a regular in PGA Tour pro-ams and asked if the sport needed to examine its intimacy with such a notorious gambler. "I'm not singling out anyone," Mickelson said. "I just think that I just need to be more careful because, as a representative of companies which I take a lot of pride in, those relationships mean a lot to me, and I need to make sure that I represent them as well as myself in the best possible way."

Clearly there would be no public soul-searching from Mickelson. The side-eye from colleagues or stray barbs from the gallery didn't seem to affect him in the slightest, as he finished twentieth at the Memorial and then tied for second in his next start, at Memphis. This momentum traveled with him all the way to Royal Troon. Walking to the eighteenth green in the first round of the Open Championship, Mickelson said to Bones, "I need your best read. I don't know if you know this. . . ."

"Oh, I know," Jim Mackay said. The right-to-left eighteen-foot birdie putt they were facing was for a 62, what would be the lowest round in the history of the major championships. They played it two balls outside-right, and Mickelson hit a perfect putt. A couple feet out, there was zero doubt his ball was going in, but in the last few inches it inexplicably wiggled to the right, leading to a vicious horseshoe. It was eerily similar to the final-hole lip-out that denied Mickelson a 59 at the 2013 Phoenix Open (and Tiger Woods a 62 at the 2007 PGA Championship). "It was one of the best rounds I've ever played and yet I want to shed a tear right now," Mickelson said afterward. "That putt on eighteen was an opportunity to do something historical. I knew it, and with a foot to go I thought I had done it. I saw that ball rolling right in the center. I went to go get it, I had that surge of adrenaline that I had just shot 62, and then I had the heartbreak that I didn't and watched that ball lip out. Wow, that stings. I mean, if I had just hit a weak flail-off and never had a chance and left it short, so be it. But this ball was hunting right in the center and didn't go in. It was just heartbreaking."

Mickelson became the twenty-eighth player to shoot 63 in a major. How to explain that not one of these players was able to shave off one more stroke? "Well, it was obvious right there that there's a curse, because that ball should have been in," he said. "If there wasn't a curse, that ball would have been in and I would have had that 62." (Branden Grace would finally shoot a 62 at the 2017 Open Championship.)

Phil, do you believe in golf gods?

"I didn't, but I do now."

The most disappointing 63 in golf history gave Mickelson a three-stroke lead. The second round featured much colder, windier conditions. Mickelson shot 69, but his lead was trimmed to one stroke by Henrik "Iceman" Stenson, who posted a sizzling 65. Stenson, the Swedish Iron Byron who had inherited the good news/bad news title of Best Player Never to Have Won a Major, went around in 68 on Saturday to take a one-stroke lead over Mickelson, who said, "I was off today. I didn't have my best stuff. My rhythm was a little quick from the top as we started downwind. I was a little bit jumpy." Still, he was five shots clear of the player in third place, Bill Haas, setting up a Sunday duel between fire and ice.

Before the final round, Mickelson had a long practice session with his new swing coach Getson, who, unlike the very in-demand Harmon, is always on call. On the first hole, Mickelson flagged his approach shot for a birdie and Stenson 3-putted from sixty feet, a two-shot swing that propelled the left-hander into the lead. Stenson punched back with three straight birdies, but Mickelson countered with an eagle at four. They both birdied six, then Stenson stuck his tee shot to ten feet on the short par-3 eighth, the famed Postage Stamp, to make birdie and retake the lead. On the long, tough par-4 tenth hole, both hit flawless approach shots and rolled in their birdie putts. How long could perfect golf be played? There was a giddiness in the air. The entire golf course had tilted in the direction of the final group—J. B. Holmes would finish third, eleven shots out of second place. The Scots knew they were witnessing something historic and TV producers began unspooling archival footage of the 1977 Open, Nicklaus and Watson's fabled "Duel in the Sun."

Stenson bogeyed the eleventh hole and they were once again in a tie, which Mickelson preserved with a gritty fifteen-footer to save par on twelve. But Stenson birdied fourteen and then on the next hole landed a round-house, a fifty-footer from the fringe. Mickelson was two down and on the ropes, but at the par-5 sixteenth, playing into the wind, he nuked a 3-wood from 279 yards out to within thirty feet for eagle. His putt singed the edge of the cup. Stenson matched the birdie with a slick downhill five-foot putt that he later called the nerviest of the whole round. Mickelson couldn't get a putt to drop on the last two holes. He shot a bogeyless 65, but Stenson did him two strokes better. Mickelson's four-round total of 267 (17 under) had never been bettered in the history of golf's oldest tournament. It was his eleventh career runner-up finish in a major, the second most all-time behind only Jack Nicklaus (nineteen), who leads in wins, 18–5. "It's probably the best I've ever played and not won," said Mickelson. "I think that's probably why it's disappointing in that I don't have a point where I can look back and say, I should have done that or had I only done this. I played a bogey-free round of 65 on the final round of a major—usually that's good enough to do it, but I got beat by ten birdies. You know, it's not like I have decades left of opportunities to win majors, so each one means a lot to me. I'm happy with the way I played, but even more disappointed that it wasn't enough, because you look back and say, What do I need to do?"

The PGA of America had to act after Mickelson flayed Tom Watson at Gleneagles, so a Ryder Cup Task Force was created within three weeks of the infamous press conference revolt. It included three PGA of America officials; past Cup captains Davis Love III, Ray Floyd, and Tom Lehman; and current players Rickie Fowler, Jim Furyk, Steve Stricker, Tiger Woods, and, of course, Mickelson. The first gathering was held in December 2014 at the PGA of America headquarters in Palm Beach Gardens, Florida, and Mickelson flew cross-country to be there "on his own dime," said Furyk, for added emphasis. The Task Force—capital letters were needed to add gravitas—was charged with reexamining every aspect of how Team USA selected and prepared its players and chose its captains and vice captains. The collaboration between Woods and Mickelson took their relationship to a different level; in early 2015, when Tiger suffered a case of the chip-yips, Phil offered to meet him for a private lesson, a deeply empathetic gesture. But Woods was destined to have a smaller role in the Ryder Cup effort—with his body breaking down, he missed the 2008 and '14 Cups and would be sidelined again in '16. (Incredibly, Woods has played on only one winning Ryder Cup team, way back in 1999.) "Phil had the loudest voice," says Love. "Since 2014, on any question about what we should do, Phil is the first person I call."

The Task Force revamped the qualifying timeline for players and codified how captains and vice captains would be selected going forward. Those on the outside looking in were not impressed: Nicklaus called it "overkill," while Billy Horschel, who has never actually played in a Ryder Cup, offered, "I think the Task Force is a lot of political B.S." Jimmy Walker, whose relationship with Mickelson has become frosty, says, "There's cliques for captains, cliques for vice captains, cliques for captain's picks. There's a club and it's tough to get into the club." How does he see Mickelson's role? "He gets in the middle of everything, for sure," says Walker.

Including the selection of the 2016 Ryder Cup captain. Mickelson wanted an insider who had bought into his vision of how things should be done and—voilà—Love was named captain again. Internally, Love had been a vocal supporter of Mickelson's activism. "I hated that it played out publicly, but Phil was one thousand percent right calling for a system of consistency and continuity that we didn't have," says Love. "We all knew it and were thinking it, but he was the only one who had the guts to say it out loud. That took leadership."

Mickelson's spectacular play at Royal Troon guaranteed him a spot on the U.S. team, and heading into the Ryder Cup at Hazeltine, he knew there was a giant target on his back. "The pressure started when some dumbass opened his mouth two years ago in the media center," he said. Love sent out Mickelson in the second match of the Cup, paired with his Task Force buddy Fowler against Rory McIlroy and Andy Sullivan. The Americans won a tense match, one-up. After two years of controversy and recriminations and questions about their chemistry, the Yanks had fire in their eyes and swept the Friday morning alternate shot, the first time Team USA had won all four matches in a session since 1981. Mickelson sat in the afternoon as Europe took three of four matches to claw back into the Cup, and then he and Fowler lost in the Saturday alternate shot as Europe closed the gap to 6.5–5.5. That made Saturday's better-ball session monumentally important. Paired with Matt Kuchar, Mickelson made a bevy of birdies in a 2 & 1 win, which helped stake the U.S. to a 9.5–6.5 lead. "This is like playing with my big brother," Kuchar said. "It was such a thrill. I have seen him do it so much from the other side as a competitor. As a friend, to watch him down the stretch go after it, he hit great shot after great shot, and I was so proud to be alongside of him."

For singles, Mickelson wound up with a delicious matchup versus Sergio Garcia, Europe's emotional leader. (Ian Poulter didn't make the team.) Over the first six holes, Sergio threw four birdies at Phil . . . and the match was all-square. Of the first four singles matches to conclude, Europe won three of them, drawing within one point and putting intense focus on the Mickelson-Garcia tussle. They kept trading blows—Garcia didn't make a bogey and shot an unofficial 63, but Mickelson countered with ten birdies. It ended the only way it could, with Garcia gutting a fifteen-footer on eighteen for a halve. "It was amazing," Sergio said afterward. "Obviously to shoot nine-under and end up tying the match, it was heartbreaking. I gave it everything I had, but Phil just made it from everywhere."

The Task Force enjoyed one final validation. One of its tweaks to the process was to delay the last of four captain's picks until after the Tour Championship, which ended the Sunday before Ryder Cup week began, the theory being this allowed the captain to pick a player who had suddenly gotten hot. That pick turned out to be Ryan Moore, who lost in a playoff to McIlroy at the Tour Championship. Seven days later, Moore delivered the Ryder Cup's clinching point with his singles win over Lee Westwood. The U.S. victory validated Mickelson's rebellion, and he helped salvage his reputation with fine play: only three players on the winning team delivered more than his 2.5 points. Mickelson had survived what Bones called "definitely one of the most pressure-packed weeks" of his boss's career.

Still, a few barbs were inevitable. As Team Europe shuffled in for its press conference behind its captain, Darren Clarke, McIlroy bellowed, "Oi, Darren, it's the end of the Ryder Cup. Is this where I throw you under the bus?"

Replied Clarke, "You gonna do a Phil?"

CHAPTER SEVENTEEN

O n June 20, 2017, a thunderbolt hit the golf world. "After 25 very rewarding and memorable years, Bones and I have mutually decided to end our player-caddie relationship," Phil Mickelson said in a press release sent out by his management team. "Our decision is not based on a single incident. We just feel it's the right time for a change. Bones is one of the most knowledgeable and dedicated caddies in the world. He is always prepared and has the ability to make decisions in pressure-packed situations. Bones is without a doubt one of the most thoughtful people that I have ever known. The next player to work with him will obviously be very lucky."

"When Phil hired me in 1992, I had one dream: to caddie in a Ryder Cup," Jim Mackay said in his own press release. "Last year, at Hazeltine, Phil played in his 11th straight Ryder Cup. It was so cool to have a front row seat. I wish Phil nothing but the best. His game is still at an elite level, and when he wins in the future (definitely the Masters), I will be among the first to congratulate him."

"He has been one of the most important and special people in my life since the day we met and I will always be grateful for everything he has done for me," Mickelson's press release continued. "Amy and I, and our children, will always think of Bones, Jen, Oliver and Emma as family. We are looking forward to sharing life and friendship with them forever."

The overriding emotion in golf circles was disbelief. "It felt like your parents were splitting up," says John Wood, a longtime Tour caddie and now an NBC/Golf Channel commentator.

The press releases made the divorce sound amicable but it was all bullshit. Bones had actually fired Phil three weeks earlier at the Memorial, over some long-simmering grievances. The chummy public statements were a way for Mickelson to save face and Mackay to make a graceful exit that kept various career options alive. Adhering to the caddie code of omertà, Mackay declined to comment for this book, but those with direct knowledge of the situation say money was a longtime source of contention. The FedEx Cup debuted more than a decade into their working relationship; Mickelson made various promises to distribute to his caddie a percentage of the bonuses he won but for a full decade failed to pay up. By Mackay's calculations, he was owed $900,000. In the months before the breakup, as things were becoming increasingly strained between them, Mickelson paid Mackay $400,000 toward the FedEx Cup debt, but Bones was miffed to not get the full amount. He was also increasingly irked by Mickelson's disregard for his advice and habit of showing up later at the golf course than he told his caddie to arrive. Then there was the dispute about the eighteenth-hole flags from their victories. Mickelson had always insisted on nabbing these keepsakes for his grandfather's kitchen wall. This included the 2004 Masters, four months after Nunu's death; Phil had that one framed and presented it to his grandmother Jennie, Nunu's widow. Mackay understood and respected that gesture, but nineteen more Tour victories would follow, including four majors, and he never got to keep a single flag. "That's a giant fuck-you to a caddie," says someone very close to Mackay. "When Phil wins the Masters, he gets the green jacket, the trophy, the big check, all the glory. He had to take the flags, too? Every other caddie who has ever won the Masters got to keep the eighteenth-hole flag. For Phil not to follow tradition was hugely disrespectful." During the week of the Phoenix Open, the Mackays would often host dinner parties for players and caddies at their home, and a frequent question was "Where are all the flags?" It nettled Mackay in a way that is hard for any outsider to understand.

A week after their bust-up, during which Mackay finally aired all of his gripes, Mickelson paid his caddie another $400,000 of overdue FedEx money and overnighted to Bones the flags from their wins at the PGA Championship, British Open, and the 2006 and '10 Masters. But Phil autographed them in comically large letters, which Mackay felt disfigured the keepsakes. Bones has never displayed them in his home and, according to the source, has plans to someday sell them and donate the money to charity. As for the flags from their other Tour victories, Mickelson's motivation in continuing to keep them may transcend sentimentality. Like a few other top pros, including Tiger Woods, Mickelson habitually declines to autograph golf balls because it's difficult to execute a clean signature on a round, dimpled surface, which looks sloppy and is also easier to forge. But locked away in a safe-deposit box are dozens of golf balls Mickelson has painstakingly signed and set aside for his kids as part of their inheritance. Perhaps someday he will also try to monetize the victory flags.

Only a couple of weeks after the breakup, Mackay signed on with NBC/Golf Channel to become an on-course reporter. He had already displayed serious chops in a two-day tryout at the Sea Island tournament in 2015. Given that Bones had both of his knees replaced in October 2016, it made sense that he would take a sabbatical from lugging around a Tour bag that can easily weigh forty pounds. Mickelson has always kept an insular circle, so for Mackay's replacement he eschewed any established caddies and turned to his brother, Tim.

Seven years younger, Tim grew up in the shadow of his celebrated big bro. He was a good-but-not-great junior player with just enough game (and legacy standing) to be given a spot on the Arizona State team. After college, he got into coaching, ultimately earning the top job at the University of San Diego. Tim tooled around town in a jacked-up pickup truck with the school mascot, the Torero, stenciled on the doors. "He's a grinder," says Casey Martin, the former Tour player and now longtime head coach at Oregon. "I pride myself on spending a lot of time on the recruiting trail and going places that other coaches don't, but along the way I kept bumping into Tim. We would just nod at each other like, *Okay, I see you.*"

In 2011, Tim leveraged his famous last name to help land the head coaching job at Arizona State. Tim's most impactful recruit was a Spanish savant with thighs that looked like redwood trunks. When Jon Rahm turned pro in 2016, Tim followed Steve Loy's playbook and became the phenom's agent. Business was booming, but Tim couldn't turn down his brother when he offered him the chance to step on the other side of the ropes. Having a different voice in his ear gave Phil the little jolt he needed to break a five-year winless streak, at the WGC-Mexico Championship in February 2018. On the seventy-second hole, the Mickelsons faced a knee-knocker to force a playoff against Justin Thomas. Given the slippage in Phil's putting in the preceding years, those three feet looked like three miles. "I was standing on the back of the green and he came up behind me and whispered in my ear," Phil says. "He didn't mess up my concentration, he just whispered exactly what was in my head: 'Control your breathing and connect with the target, connect with the hole.' It's exactly what I was thinking. And so he's very in sync with me and that brings out my best."

There's one other thing Mickelson likes about having his kid brother on the bag: in contrast to Mackay's grinding, slightly oppressed seriousness, "Tim and I have a very similar sense of humor," says Phil. "We often say the same punch line simultaneously. So naturally, I find him extremely funny."

Rancho Santa Fe is a hilltop hamlet a half hour north of San Diego, a sun-splashed Mayberry for the 1 percent. On a sleepy spring morning, the procession of Teslas and drop-top Bentleys down the main drag was interrupted by a middle-aged dude in a golf cart with a leather Tour bag bulging out the back. He was turned out in baggy shorts, flip-flops, and a Whisper Rock cap, carrying an oversized tumbler of coffee. Stepping into Caffe Positano, this jovial patron was sized up the same way Sam Malone gazed upon Norm Peterson. "You want the usual, Phil?" asked the barista. She dumped five shots of espresso into the tumbler, and then Mickelson took a seat at a table on the sidewalk to explain his coffee infatuation, which was born from his ongoing efforts to improve his health and longevity.

It was May 2018, and Mickelson, a month shy of turning forty-eight, was hosting me for a state-of-Phil cover story for *Golf Magazine*. He had a wistful vibe because Amy was back east, moving their eldest daughter out of her dorm room at Brown at the end of her freshman year, just another mileage marker as he sped into middle age. Phil had skipped the 2017 U.S. Open to attend Amanda's high school graduation, at which she gave the valedictorian speech, part of a quiet year on Tour in which he had just one top-five finish and didn't factor at any of the majors. But the victory in Mexico City, three months before our coffee summit, had validated some of his unusual methods of reinvention. Our meeting spot was not a run-of-the-mill coffee shop but rather a java temple run by his friend Dave Phillips, the cofounder of the Titleist Performance Institute who was now traveling the world sourcing the most exotic beans. They were in the early days of forming what would become their coffee and dietary supplement company For Wellness, which Mickelson was already touting as a fountain of youth. (It's not the only magic elixir Mickelson has used to turn back the clock; a running gag on Twitter is showing old and current photos of Phil side by side to highlight how much less gray hair he suddenly has. Some folks in Mickelson's orbit have nicknamed him "Black Cherry" as that's the name of a popular color of hair dye.) A couple of years earlier, Mickelson had told me, "I went and got this food analysis from a doctor. Because I was getting sick six times a year, even though I was taking echinacea, which is an herb a lot of people take to help their immune system. I'd get sick immediately. It was awful. He said, 'You are extremely toxic to echinacea.' He says, 'The opposite of echinacea is coffee.' And I'd never been a coffee drinker. He says, 'You need to drink coffee and as much as you can.' Now I drink coffee all day long. I've not gotten sick one time in six years. So these are things that I've had to learn about that have really changed my life for the better." Did Mickelson really go six-plus years without a head cold? As with various things he says, it's un-fact-checkable but makes for good copy.

Now, in great detail, he laid out the strange brew he had invented for himself (a powder version of which is currently sold on the For Wellness website): coarse-ground Ethiopian Yirgacheffe coffee, almond milk, cinnamon, cacao nibs, collagen, and MCT oil. He had just begun embarking on his habit of doing three-day cleanses during which he eats no solid food, but drinks as much joe as he craves. Remarkably, in his late forties, Mickelson would get himself in the best shape of his life. "I look back to when I won the PGA Championship at Baltusrol in 2005, I was fifteen pounds heavier," he said. "I looked awful and here I am thirteen years older and I'm in better shape. I physically feel better. I eat better. I take care of myself better. Most people regress. I feel like I've improved over time." His old friend Rob Mangini is more expressive, saying, "He can curl a fifty-pound dumbbell like it's no big deal. He can bench-press a car, he can leg-press a house. He's become monster-strong, but no one knows it." Mickelson has found other ways to challenge himself. "Ten years ago, he spent a lot of time working with military snipers," says Mangini. "He wanted to learn their secrets for focus and mental discipline, and how to take that onto the golf course." This begs the question, Does Phil keep guns at his home? "I don't want to answer that directly because of the political dimension," says Mangini, "but put it this way: I've never heard of a guy who trains with military snipers who *doesn't* have his own firearms."

Sitting at the sidewalk table, Phil talked about how proud he and Amy are of their kids. Amanda is a cool, quirky young lady who preached tolerance in her valedictorian speech. (In her ensuing graduation photo from Brown, she would be turned out in a handsome suit and tie.) Sophia is a dancer and an artist who would go on to study film at Columbia. Evan is a coder and a member of a rock band who was occasionally spotted strumming his guitar at farmers' markets around town. As much as Mickelson loves being a very involved dad, the freedom of an empty nest loomed. "I'm looking forward to getting to date Amy again once the kids are out of the house," he said. The plan at some point is for him and his bride to live three to six months at a time in all of their favorite places around the world.

The Mickelsons' has long been the most scrutinized marriage in golf. Julie Crenshaw has observed them up close everywhere from Ryder Cup team rooms to casual hangouts. "The love they have for each other, that is genuine," says Julie, who hosted a baby shower for Amy at the 1999 PGA Championship. "It's not for show. They're the same way in private as they are in public. I've heard every rumor about them that's out there and people love to talk junk, but I know the real couple. They are so devoted to each other and he absolutely thinks she walks on water. Ohmylord, Phil is a grown kid and he thinks he knows everything about everything, but Amy brings him back down to earth."

Amy took on a lower profile as she became more immersed in their kids' busy teenage lives. Some close to her have detected a fatigue from a lifetime spent in the public eye. "What I have observed," says Amanda Leonard, "is that if she can't a hundred and ten percent be the lovely, happy, sparkly Amy that we all know, she won't show up. She'll just stay behind closed doors. It's one extreme or the other. And I say that without one ounce of judgment—I can't imagine being in her shoes. I love them both, but Phil is a tricky one. Super tricky. They're both complicated people and they have a big life. But I know Amy's number one priority is Phil and their marriage and staying together no matter what comes their way. Amy will do whatever she needs to do. She is incredibly devoted to him."

Back at the coffee shop, Mickelson's stomach was growling so we jumped in his souped-up golf cart, which has DirecTV and can touch fifty miles per hour. "Don't worry, it's perfectly safe and I'm a conservative driver," Phil said with a wolfish grin. In fact, riding shotgun with him is a terrifying experience. The tires were chirping on every curve and he admonished me for not leaning properly to combat the g-forces the cart was pulling. We brunched at the posh Bridges Golf Club, where Phil greeted every valet and busboy by their first name. (There is a no-tipping policy, but at the end of the meal he discreetly slipped a couple of Andrew Jacksons under the place mat.) The conversation meandered, with him often pressing pause on my tape recorder to talk shit about this or that. The TV in the grillroom was playing Clint Eastwood's *The 15:17 to Paris*, which led Mickelson to riff on his taste in cinema: "I'm not a very good movie critic in that I'm not critical. I like 'em all. Except the movies that win awards, like *The Shape of Water*—I just didn't care for that. A love story with a water alien? I just didn't get it. I actually had dinner with Clint Eastwood one time and he was raving about *La La Land*. So I watched it and I'm like, 'That was miserable. That was the worst frickin' thing I've ever seen.' So obviously my movie prowess is not very good."

I mentioned that a few weeks earlier, Brandel Chamblee had taken to Twitter to offer a passionate testimonial about *La La Land*. "Oh, see, that makes perfect sense because he and I don't see eye to eye on anything," Mickelson snorted. "I was afraid you were gonna say we felt the same way about something, and that would have thrown me for a loop."

I asked if he and Chamblee had some history I didn't know about. "I just like people who build up the game," Mickelson said. "I view this as, we're all in the game of golf together. We all want to grow the game. We all want to make it better. And I feel like he's made his commentating career off denigrating others. And I don't care for that."

Of course, this is a fundamental misreading of the role of the golf media. Reporters and analysts are not there to serve as Mickelson's cheerleaders, no matter how hard he tries to co-opt them. A couple days after Mickelson called out Tom Watson at the loser's press conference at the 2014 Ryder Cup, Chamblee was driving his kids to school when his cell phone bleated. It was Phil. "He wanted to tell me his side of the story," says Chamblee, who had been critical of Mickelson in the immediate aftermath of the Gleneagles rebellion. "He was very polite, he didn't get mad at me, he just went point by point and offered rebuttals to what I had been saying. In the following days I heard the very same things he told me come out of the mouth of numerous other media members, and I realized he had called them, too. It was a clever ploy, because we were probably less forceful in our arguments out of respect for Phil calling directly and debating the ideas. There is something Bill Clinton–ish about him in that he can use his charm and personality to wiggle out of things. He has a very cunning understanding of public relations."

Mickelson was working so hard to preserve his image because, into his late forties, as the wins became sporadic, he had morphed into an even more relentless corporate mercenary, which is saying something, given his long-standing shamelessness in pushing product. (At the 2010 Players Championship, he spent the whole week talking about how Five Guys burgers were fueling his good play, and only later did it come out that Mickelson was part of a group that had just bought the franchise rights to the burger chain throughout Orange County; the year before, Mickelson, Steve Loy, and another partner offered $20.2 million for 105 Waffle Houses in four states, but were outbid. Good thing Mickelson's foundation does not list combating obesity as part of its mission.) Now a guy who hates the taste and smell of beer is hawking Amstel Light.

At the 2018 Masters, a month before our brunch, Mickelson had created a huge buzz by playing a practice round with Woods, their first such game in two decades. But it was more about commerce than camaraderie: they were chumming the waters for the first of their made-for-TV spectacles, and Mickelson also used this high-profile spin around Augusta National to break out an awkward-looking oxford shirt made by a new endorsement partner. Now Mickelson stepped away from his avocado toast to take a couple of phone calls about details of *The Match*, each time returning to torture me with tantalizing details I was not yet allowed to print. The mano a mano versus Woods turned out to be a dud from a golf perspective, but it created another revenue stream that Mickelson has continued to exploit. (Not for nothing, the co-creator and producer of *The Match* is Phil's golf buddy Bryan Zuriff, who in 2013 pleaded guilty to his role in an illegal online gambling enterprise with alleged connections to the Russian Mafia.)

Brunch is over. Mickelson wants to show me the backyard practice area at his house, but stipulates there can be no photos. By way of explanation, he goes on a little monologue about how the general public has been conditioned to resent successful people and so he is cautious about showing off his lavish home. This calls to mind Mickelson's remarks in 2013 when he complained about the steep California state taxes, which led to such a backlash he wound up apologizing shortly thereafter. I agree to his conditions and we screech up in the golf cart to an expansive compound of lovely stone buildings that evoked a Tuscan village. Mickelson has a well-manicured tee box from where he can launch full drivers onto a vast lawn, though he has to hit them directly over a good-sized cottage that is used by staff. I ask if he's ever caught a drive a little low on the face and plunked the building. He looks at me as if I have three heads. Right, Hall of Famers don't do stuff like that. Nearby, there are greens with different grasses, bunkers with different varietals of sand, and three artificial-turf greens. We step to the artificial greens and Phil notes one is set at two degrees of pitch, the next at three degrees, and the third at four degrees. On each green, one of the holes is encircled by balls, and Mickelson works his way around, stroking putts to demonstrate how the ball will tumble in from different angles. It's like watching Michelangelo mix paint. He grooves the feeling of these different vectors and then, once on Tour, having spent decades absorbing the green-reading books that displayed the pitch of each putting surface, he has already cracked the code of how any given putt will break. I had always thought of Mickelson's short game as pure art—who knew there was so much science, too? He loves the seclusion of the setting, but Mickelson's privacy is occasionally compromised by the hot-air balloonists who traverse Rancho Santa Fe's lovely hills. At a dinner party at their home, Phil and Amy told the story of a balloon hovering overhead a bit too long while Mickelson was hitting balls . . . so he retrieved a firearm and sent a warning shot toward the heavens. According to two guests at the dinner, Amy was aghast about the tale while Phil seemed gleeful.

It was now deep into the lunch hour. Mickelson had a few calls to make and Sophia and Evan would soon be home from school. So we hopped back into his golf cart and roared back into downtown Rancho Santa Fe, where my rental car was parked. I thanked Phil for his time. "That wasn't too painful," he lied. With a wave he tore off down the street, headed for home.

To spend a morning with Mickelson is fun and exhausting. It reminds me of the time I interviewed Donald Trump back when he was merely a blustery real estate developer: the charm and hyperbole is relentless and disorientating. You can never tell what is real and what is pure puffery, and that seems to be the point.

The U.S. Open returned to Shinnecock Hills in 2018. It is one of Mickelson's favorite courses and represented perhaps his last best chance to win the national championship, given that he had contended there until the bitter end in both 1995 and 2004. The return to Shinnecock also gave the USGA a chance at redemption after having screwed up the golf course fourteen years earlier. That week, Mickelson played some of the best golf of his life, but was thwarted by the out-of-control conditions (and, to be fair, Retief Goosen's unflappable excellence). Mickelson's disenchantment with what the blue blazers did to Shinny began his cold war with the USGA. The feelings were inflamed in 2007, when he injured his wrist in Oakmont's over-the-top rough, and reached a boiling point at Merion in 2013, when Mickelson barked at executive director Mike Davis about the course setup in the middle of the final round as he was trying to win the tournament. "I think it's a very difficult job to find the line of testing the best players to the greatest degree and then making it carnival golf," Mickelson says. "I think it's a very fine line, and it's not a job I would want. And I know that the USGA is doing the best they can to find that line, and a lot of times they do, and sometimes they cross over it. It's not an easy job. It's easy for all of us to criticize. The difficulty is, when you dream of winning these tournaments as a child and you work hours and hours and you fly in days and days [early] to do all this prep work, and then you leave the outcome to chance, as opposed to skill, that's a problem. That's the problem that I have with it."

After the unpleasantness at Merion, the USGA leadership extended the ultimate olive branch: they offered Mickelson the Bob Jones Award to be presented at the 2014 U.S. Open at Pinehurst. The grace Mickelson had displayed in defeat there fifteen years earlier is exactly what the Bob Jones Award celebrates, as, according to the USGA, it "recognizes an individual who demonstrates the spirit, personal character and respect for the game exhibited by Jones." Presented annually since 1955, it is the highest honor bestowed by the USGA and the recipients include classic golfing gentlemen like Byron Nelson, Arnold Palmer, Jack Nicklaus, and Ben Crenshaw. But in an unprecedented act of pique, Mickelson turned down the award. According to someone very close to him, "Phil told the USGA to shove it up their ass."

Is that a direct quote?!

"No, but that was the gist of it."

All of this is necessary background to explain how and why Mickelson lost his mind—and the respect of swaths of the golf community—on the thirteenth hole of the third round of the 2018 United States Open. Mickelson drove the ball beautifully but putted poorly during opening rounds of 77-69. He had designs of going low on moving day, but by the time he arrived at number thirteen, he had bogeyed five of his previous eight holes and Mickelson's mood had soured considerably, even as the fans occasionally serenaded him with "Happy Birthday," as this was the day he turned forty-eight. It was hotter and windier than had been forecast, and the USGA put a couple of pins in spots that turned out to be dicey as the greens baked in the sun. At thirteen, the hole location was atop a crowned section of the green, tucked behind a bunker. Mickelson's approach shot raced over the green, and the ensuing pitch carried a little too far and his ball rolled (and rolled and rolled and . . .) all the way off the front of the green. He shook his head in disgust, but it was not yet clear if he was vexed by his imprecise play or the exacting hole location. Mickelson chipped past the flag again and then hit his eighteen-foot bogey putt too hard. As the ball trickled past the hole, Mickelson lumbered after it. Instead of letting his ball roll off the green yet again, he smacked it with his putter while it was still in motion. The crowd went silent with confusion. His playing partner, Andrew "Beef" Johnston, stared at Mickelson with a blank look. "I said, 'That's one of the strangest things I've ever seen,' and then just started laughing," said Beef. "I think it's just a moment of madness." Mickelson missed his ensuing putt for triple bogey and then tapped in for an eight. Moments later, a rules official dinged him with a two-stroke penalty for violating Rule 14-5 by playing a moving ball, bumping his score on the hole to a perfect 10.

This is where things got interesting. On the Fox telecast, former USGA executive director David Fay called for Mickelson to be DQed, citing Rule 33-7, which states, "A penalty of disqualification may in exceptional individual cases be waived, modified or imposed if the [tournament] Committee considers such action warranted." Clearly, Mickelson had violated the sanctity of the Open by flagrantly flouting one of the sport's most fundamental rules, which is to never touch a ball in motion. He probably could have gotten away with it if, as Beef suggested, he pled temporary insanity. "We've all been there," says Paul McGinley. "The red mist comes down and you lose the head. It's a difficult game and sometimes we snap. You apologize for it and people can accept that. But Phil had to double down and be a smart-ass about it. He tried to talk his way out of it, and that was more disappointing than what he did on the green. He brought the game, and himself, into disrepute."

After signing for his 81—tied for his worst score ever in a U.S. Open—Mickelson said, "Look, I don't mean disrespect by anybody. I know it's a two-shot penalty. At that time I just didn't feel like going back and forth and hitting the same shot over. I took the two-shot penalty and moved on. It's my understanding of the rules. I've had multiple times where I've wanted to do that, I just finally did it."

He had previously displayed petulant civil disobedience in other ways: at the 2010 Western Open, while facing a thirty-seven-footer for birdie on the fifteenth green at Cog Hill, he chipped with his wedge instead of employing his putter to highlight his displeasure with the ridgy greens that had been re-designed by Rees Jones, whom Mickelson has been bullying ever since Jones's unpopular reworking of Torrey Pines South.

"I think knowing the rules is never a bad thing," Mickelson continued at Shinnecock. "I mean, you want to always use them in your favor. It's a risk. I could have maybe hit a shot and somehow made the putt [if he had let his ball roll off the green]. I don't know if it would have saved me a shot or not, but I might have saved a shot doing it the way I did it, too."

Pressed on whether he had disrespected the national championship, Mickelson didn't exactly strike a conciliatory tone. "If somebody is offended by that, I apologize to them, but toughen up," he said, "because this is not meant that way."

The headline writers on various golf websites saw through the bad-faith filibustering: "Phil Mickelson Will Have to Live Down His Actions—and Words—at Shinnecock"; "Phil Mickelson's Rule Abuse Was Equal Parts Hilarious and Troubling."

Four days later, Mickelson issued a statement: "I know this should've come sooner, but it's taken me a few days to calm down. My anger and frustration got the best of me last weekend. I'm embarrassed and disappointed by my actions. It was clearly not my finest moment and I'm sorry."

Oh, by the way, the 2014 Bob Jones Award was awarded posthumously to Payne Stewart.

The golf gods ensured that Mickelson struggled in the immediate aftermath of Shinnecock, but he enjoyed another renaissance at Pebble Beach in February 2019, winning the Crosby Clambake for a record-tying fifth time. (Nunu's coin once again made its annual appearance.) It was the forty-fourth victory of his career, ninth all-time, and most memorable for a spicy conversation he had in the Sunday twilight with Paul Casey, who was in second place, three strokes back. The sun had already set, but Mickelson wanted to try to rush through the final two holes. Casey exercised his right to stop playing due to darkness and they finished out the tournament the next morning. "He was trying to bully me, but I can't be bullied," says Casey. "That was Phil flexing. He's allowed to flex—he's a Hall of Famer. Of course he can, but he was still wrong. The funny thing was Phil acting like a politician: he came out the next day and said I was right to have stopped play, but he never actually apologized."

As often happens with Mickelson, the good vibes from the victory were compromised by untoward headlines: a month after the win he publicly acknowledged that he and Amy had paid the disgraced college adviser Rick Singer to help get Amanda into Brown University. Mickelson insisted Singer did nothing unseemly on his daughter's behalf, and no evidence ever emerged to the contrary. But of all the players in golf, and all the college advisers on the planet, it had to be Mickelson who got mixed up in another scandal, even unwittingly.

However, in the battle for the hearts and minds of golf fans, he suddenly had a powerful new tool: social media. Mickelson reinvented himself yet again by joining Twitter and Instagram and playing a caricature of himself—jokey, goofy, swaggering, and eager to talk trash to fellow players and random followers. Given how stiff and stale most other Tour players are on social media, the public spooned it up.

At the 2020 PGA Championship, Mickelson conquered another medium when he visited CBS's eighteenth-hole tower for his first-ever stint as a guest commentator. He offered the viewers at home nuanced analysis of the course and various players and provided plenty of laughs as he thoroughly flummoxed Nick Faldo with his huge presence and quick wit. Golf Twitter lost its collective mind at the entertainment value and sheer cheekiness of Mickelson rendering Faldo obsolete in real-time. Sir Nick is only a little defensive about it. "I don't think he was trying to steal my job," says Faldo. "It was more like Phil just showing off, as he is wont to do anytime there is an audience, big or small. But having a free mic is very different than what we were doing. We have a system. We go to Frank [Nobilo] on one hole, then Ian [Baker-Finch] on the next, then they come back to Jim [Nantz] and I, et cetera. Phil just came bowling in with an open mic and talked right across everybody." Mickelson was even more uninhibited as the lead commentator of "The Match" that pitted Brooks Koepka against Bryson DeChambeau in November 2021. Coming off of that performance, there was zero doubt Mickelson had a future in television if he so desired; think Johnny Miller with more star power and a sharper needle. Longtime TV agent and publicist LeslieAnne Wade said Mickelson could command "Romo money"—former Dallas Cowboys quarterback Tony Romo is now making a reported $18 million a year as a wildly entertaining football analyst for CBS.

As he approached his fiftieth birthday, Mickelson began obsessing over his driving distance the way other men fret about a receding hairline. A large part of his social media schtick involved him woofing about the "bombs" and "hellacious seeds" he was now hitting with his driver, thanks to an emphasis on speed training. Off camera, Faldo buttonholed Mickelson to learn more about his methodology. "He said it starts with your mind, that you have to recondition your brain that you can do that," says Faldo. "Then you focus on mobility, then strength, then explosive exercises. Only then can you start swinging the club faster. It's not a five-minute gig or five weeks. It's months and years that you have to bring the commitment. To add six miles per hour more clubhead speed at age fifty, that's off-the-charts impressive."

Mickelson ended 2019 with a grace note. Tom Watson's wife, Hilary, succumbed to cancer that November; Phil and Amy flew to Kansas City for the funeral services. Watson was surprised to see them there and deeply touched by the gesture. "For a lot of us, that closed the door on the Ryder Cup stuff," says Ted Bishop, the former PGA of America president who tabbed Watson as captain and remains a good friend. "For Phil to come all that way to pay his respects, that showed a lot of class. In his own way I think that was Phil trying to make things right."

Mickelson struggled throughout 2020 as COVID took away the crowds, and this consummate showman seemed lost without an adoring audience. The weirdness with Bones was also becoming more apparent. Though Mackay forced himself to offer chipper insight about his former boss in his on-air commentary, they pointedly ignored each other any time their paths crossed at tournaments. The awkwardness was surely amplified by various whispers getting back to Phil, as Bones had begun telling intimates of the real reasons for their split. At the 2020 WGC in Memphis, Justin Thomas had to find a replacement caddie after his looper suffered dizzy spells, so he asked Mackay to moonlight on the bag. Inevitably, Thomas and Mickelson played together in the third-to-last pairing in the final round. Phil and Bones didn't so much as exchange a glance or a single word throughout the front nine as JT ran off a string of birdies to take control of the tournament. On the tenth hole, Thomas hit his approach to twenty feet, while Mickelson was in a greenside bunker. He played the ensuing shot and Tim Mickelson descended into the bunker to rake it. In such a scenario it is standard protocol for Bones to clean Phil's ball as a courtesy and to speed up play. Mackay started walking with his towel toward Mickelson to do his duty when Tim sprinted out of the bunker and wedged himself between them, like Moses Malone blocking out a would-be rebounder. It was odd and awkward and, since the PGA Tour is more insular and gossipy than high school, the story made the rounds at the speed of light. Mackay again caddied for Thomas the following week, at the PGA Championship, where they were paired with Woods. On the fourteenth hole, a repeat scenario played out when Tiger was in a greenside bunker. After his shot, caddie Joe LaCava raked the sand, so Bones strolled over to Woods to clean his golf ball. Without missing a beat, Tiger growled, "I'd rather have Tim clean it." Bones almost fell over laughing.

Mickelson's 2021 season got off to an awkward start when Donald Trump, in the dying hours of his presidency, commuted Billy Walters's sentence. ("Gambler Tied to Phil Mickelson Released from Prison Early" was the headline on GolfDigest.com.) The White House named three of the most popular figures in the game—Butch Harmon, David Feherty, and Peter Jacobsen—as among those who had sponsored the commutation on behalf of Walters. It was a reminder that Billy still had many friends in the golf world and, if folks had to pick sides, plenty of them were going to shun Phil. But what made the White House announcement all the more stunning was Mickelson being included in the list of Walters's sponsors. The simple explanation is that Trump's people screwed up; Mickelson had no role in the commutation process. "The press release referencing Phil Mickelson is erroneous," Mickelson's lawyer Glenn Cohen told ESPN. "The reason we are upset is because it's untrue." Walters returned to his life in Las Vegas. In his quiet time he has been working on a tell-all autobiography that is sure to give Mickelson (and Cohen) more heartburn when it is published.

Throughout the first half of the 2021 season, Mickelson appeared to be losing the battle with Father Time. Reluctantly, he made a few cameos on the Senior Tour, having turned fifty the previous June. He breezed to two easy wins but seemed unfulfilled without the bright lights of the big show. Mickelson continued to be a nonfactor when he played against the far tougher competition of the PGA Tour: in his first nine tournaments of 2021 he missed four cuts and failed to record a top-twenty finish. Augusta National seemed like the best bet as to where Mickelson could turn back time, but at the '21 Masters he had to fight to make the cut on the number. On the eighteenth tee, Mickelson smoked a drive that stopped one pace short of the fairway bunker. He cracked up the smattering of fans on hand by quoting Ben Stiller from *There's Something About Mary*: "Strong like bull." After the round, Mickelson excitedly informed a gathering of friends near the clubhouse that his drive had traveled 312 yards, uphill. And he offered a rosy assessment of his game: "It's close," he said. "It's very close. When it clicks I'm gonna go off."

This felt like wishful thinking. Two years earlier, Tiger Woods had defied belief with his epic victory at Augusta, but it seemed increasingly unlikely that Mickelson would get to enjoy his own such encore.

CHAPTER EIGHTEEN

Phil Mickelson's 70 in the first round of the 2021 PGA Championship tied him for eighth place but attracted scant notice. On Friday, when he birdied five of his last nine holes at the Ocean Course on Kiawah Island to surge into a tie for the lead, it felt like a curiosity. Following his 69, Mickelson said the key to his fine play was not his putting or ball striking, but rather more clarity in his mental game, which had increased after he recommitted to yoga and meditation earlier in the year. "I'm making more and more progress just by trying to elongate my focus," he said. "I might try to play thirty-six, forty-five holes in a day and try to focus on each shot so that when I go out and play eighteen, it doesn't feel like it's that much. I might try to elongate the time that I end up meditating, but I'm trying to use my mind like a muscle and just expand it because as I've gotten older, it's been more difficult for me to maintain a sharp focus, a good visualization, and see the shot."

This New Age juju dovetailed with Mickelson's age-defying efforts to remake his body and his swing in an effort to remain relevant. His obsessive quest for more distance off the tee felt like folly, or madness, until this PGA Championship, when he came to the brawniest major championship venue in history (7,876 yards) and bashed his way to the fifty-four-hole lead. "He's hitting it so long and straight it's incredible," said one of his playing partners, Louis Oosthuizen.

During the third round, Mickelson had been on the verge of a runaway until the tenor of the tournament flipped on one swing when he sniped a drive into the water on the thirteenth hole, leading to a buzzkill double bogey. That stirred the angst living inside every Mickelson fan, who have long been traumatized by the big miss. More wild shots ensued, but Phil the Thrill showed a ton of heart getting in the house without further damage, posting a 70 to lead Brooks Koepka by one stroke. Still, the existential dread lingered as Mickelson faced a date with destiny in the final round. Could golf's most wayward champion survive a booby-trapped course that severely punishes impudence? Five years removed from the last time he even contended at a major championship, could Phil become the oldest player ever to win one? Golf genius can be perishable; Mickelson's idol, Seve Ballesteros, is proof of that. Yet here was Phil, still bailing himself out with wizardly wedge shots on one of golf's toughest tests while his contemporaries were riding carts and battling the yips on the Senior Tour. It defied belief.

On the driving range before the final round, Mickelson's burden was palpable. He suffered through a sketchy warm-up session despite alignment sticks, an iPad, a launch monitor, and a hovering swing coach in Andrew Getson. Mickelson exuded an edgy energy when he arrived on the first tee, jaw clenched tight and his eyes hidden behind aviators as if they were the tinted windows of a limousine. The swollen crowd was already in a frenzy, desperate to witness the crowning achievement of a career of unsurpassed longevity. But Mickelson would have to tangle with big, bad Brooks, who rolled up to the first tee with his familiar cocksure swagger, like a heavyweight prizefighter confident he is going to land a few haymakers. A win would end two years of injury-related frustrations and give Koepka a whopping five major championship victories, tying him with a trio of all-time geniuses: Seve, "Lord Byron" Nelson, and the living legend with whom he was paired. Koepka has strained to brand himself an antihero and now he had a chance to ruin another Hollywood story line, having already done so at the 2018 PGA Championship when he thwarted Tiger's bid with a cold-blooded closing 66. He was clearly spoiling for a fight.

Koepka smashed a drive down the middle of the first fairway, taking the most aggressive of lines; over the first three rounds his ball striking had been so reliable it was boring to watch. As Mickelson stood over the ball, you could almost hear the *clack-clack-clack* of a roller-coaster car inching toward a summit. Sure enough, Phil lashed his drive deep into the left rough and then came up miles short with his approach, leading to a three-putt bogey. Brooks, with typical ruthlessness, brushed in a birdie and just like that snatched the lead. The ride had begun.

Mickelson steadied himself with a birdie on the par-5 second, thanks to an adroit up-and-down. But he bogeyed number three, a short par-4, after missing the green from thirty yards out. You could feel the tension, in the gallery at the Ocean Course and across Golf Twitter. On the tough par-3 fifth hole, Mickelson lost his tee shot into a bunker on the short side and it felt like the tournament was already slipping away. But he summoned some vintage magic, holing out for a game-changing birdie. It instantly joined the pantheon of Mickelson highlights.

Walking off the fifth green, Mickelson spied a fan named Kyler Aubrey positioned in the walkway in his wheelchair. Kyler has cerebral palsy, but that doesn't stop him from attending numerous tournaments each year with his father, Josh, a sportswriter for the *Statesboro Herald*. Mickelson pressed the ball into Kyler's hand, and for a split second their fingers were intertwined. "Thanks for bringing me some luck," he said. Kyler loosed a guttural grunt, which is his way of showing joy. That night, he would tap out a message on his iPad, every letter requiring great effort: *Golf ball. Meet Phil. Thank you Daddy.*

The sweetness of the moment faded when Mickelson bogeyed the sixth hole out of the rough. Walking off the green, his usually taciturn brother/caddie, Tim, got in his ear: "If you're going to win this thing, you're going to have to make committed golf swings." Says Phil, "It hit me in the head. I can't be passive. I can't control the outcome, I have to swing committed. The first one I made was the drive on [the par-5 seventh hole]. Gave me a chance to get down by the green and make birdie. That was the turning point for me. From then on, I hit a lot of really good shots because I was committed to each one. It was the perfect thing to say. I think that's why we work so well together—he knows how to say things that resonate. He doesn't say a lot. He says the right thing at the right time."

The birdie on seven pushed Mickelson's lead to two strokes. Across the front nine, he would hit only two fairways, suffer a three-putt, make three bogeys . . . and somehow double his lead. It was beginning to feel like the 2019 Masters all over again, when the crushing pressure and the palpable will of the golf gods overwhelmed every would-be contender except for a cagey Hall of Famer.

On the tenth hole, Mickelson stood in the fairway and deliberately assessed his options. With the pin tucked on the extreme left edge of the putting surface, behind a bunker, the safe play was to aim for the middle of the green and accept a par. But where's the fun in that? Mickelson played a low, hard draw with a sawed-off 7-iron. His ball tore through the wind and nearly knocked over the flagstick. "Now this was salty," he said afterward on Golf Channel, "because I had to start that over the bunker just left of the green because I couldn't cut it back into the wind—because it would take too much off it." Meanwhile, Koepka played the wrong shot shape, a towering fade that got gobbled up by the breeze and tossed into a bunker, woefully short. These two swings illustrated the difference between a modern, mindless basher and a crafty old-school shotmaker. Koepka's soft bogey and Mickelson's kick-in birdie gave Phil a commanding four-stroke lead and a time-share in Brooks's head.

On the back nine, Mickelson's routine became increasingly leisurely as he took long pauses before every swing, visualizing the shot he wanted to play. He was like a baseball closer strolling around the mound, going to the rosin bag, and shaking off the catcher; the game-within-the-game would be played at his pace. On the eleventh hole, Mickelson blew his drive left into the dunes and called for a rules official after a fan picked up the ball. While Phil worked the crowd, Koepka leaned on his club, exasperated. In the thirteenth fairway, Mickelson took so long going through his mental processes that Koepka slumped against his bag and shook his head ruefully. "A great example of gamesmanship is what Phil did to me at the PGA," Koepka said with a couple months of reflection. "I got trounced on that one. I thought it was pretty good what he was doing. It was tough for me to get into a rhythm [with] the timing of how things were going."

But Mickelson began playing prevent defense a little too early, and bogeys on 13 and 14 trimmed his lead to three strokes with a tough closing stretch ahead. Nick Faldo was calling the tournament for CBS; having won a Masters at age thirty-nine, he recognized the demons on Mickelson's shoulder. "People say you never forget how to win and that's true, but to do it you need trust in your game, and that's the hardest part," says Faldo. "You get deep into your career and you're experiencing failure a lot more. At the '96 Masters, I didn't have the same self-belief I used to. Mentally I had to walk myself through the process of hitting the shots. It used to be intuitive, now I had to force myself to do it. '*What do you want to do here, Nick?* Hit it fifteen feet right of the flag. *What about the pond?* I'm not going to hit it in the pond. *Yes you are.* No I'm not. *If you do, the wheels are coming off.* No they're not.' It was exhausting. You could see Phil having the same conversations with himself. He was working so hard to free his mind."

Oosthuizen finally showed some life with a birdie on the par-5 sixteenth hole, cutting Mickelson's lead to a tenuous two strokes. But on the sixteenth tee, Phil responded with an utterly fearless swing, uncorking a 366-yard piss missile that was the longest drive of the day by any player on that hole. That one swing validated years of quixotic speed training. He was a little too pumped up on the 6-iron approach shot, his ball rolling just over the green. Now Mickelson had to get up-and-down to salvage a crucial birdie. Was there ever any doubt? His delicate chip led to a tap-in birdie, and the crowd broke into delirious chants of "*Phil! Phil! Phil!*"

Mickelson faced one final test on the seventeenth green, with a knee-knocking three-footer to save par. He had recommitted to a conventional putting grip months earlier, but now, with the PGA Championship hanging in the balance, he switched to a claw grip. "The ball rolled into a low area and I wanted to launch it higher so it didn't push into the ground and shoot off-line," Mickelson tweeted the next day. "The claw allows me to angle the shaft vertical and eliminate my forward press." Yet another crafty veteran move. He rattled in the putt, setting up a delirious scene on eighteen.

Running, sweating, screaming, tweeting, the fans who swarmed the final fairway were not merely cheering for a golfer. They had been swept up in a communal experience that was bigger and grander than that. Mickelson wasn't just on the verge of winning the PGA Championship a month shy of his fifty-first birthday, he was exploding our collective notion of what is possible. The fans had become so unmoored that Mickelson had to shove his way through the crowd (with the help of a phalanx of cops). Finally, he reached the final green to tidy up his two-shot victory. "It was a little bit unnerving, but it was exceptionally awesome, too," he said of the crush of humanity. The gallery erupted at the sight of him, but it wasn't awe or reverence that fueled the cheers. It was unfettered joy. Mickelson has always had a deep connection with the fans, who appreciate the dignity he has displayed during slapstick losses and his class through forty-four victories . . . and counting. They cried along with him when he won the 2010 Masters for his cancer-stricken bride, and now they laugh at his deadpan, self-deprecating social media posts. They forgive his trespasses (meaty gambling debts and questionable stock transactions; talking smack about Tiger Woods's equipment; attempting hero shots on the seventy-second hole at Winged Foot) because even Mickelson's failings feed his image as an uninhibited thrill-seeker. Love him or hate him, Mickelson inspires emotion. In the Sunday twilight at the Ocean Course, Paul Casey stood on a hill behind the eighteenth green. He had finished his round nearly an hour earlier but stuck around to take in the scene. "This is cool shit," he said.

Jon Rahm, in a T-shirt emblazoned with DAD BOD, wormed his way to the edge of the green to get a better view of history. "If I know one thing about Phil," Rahm said, "he wants to make this putt." It wouldn't make a difference in the outcome but Mickelson is always looking to show off. He missed the birdie putt yet secured the trophy, a dizzying turn of events even he struggled to put into words. "Although I believed it, until I actually did it, there was a lot of doubt," he said. "Certainly one of the moments I'll cherish my entire life."

Mickelson had been stoic all week about what a victory would mean, part of the renewed emphasis on mental discipline, but in accepting the trophy he finally let a little emotion flow: "This is just an incredible feeling because I believed it was possible, yet everything was saying it wasn't. I hope that others find that inspiration. It might take a little extra work, a little harder effort, but it's so worth it in the end."

Says Faldo, "I think it's one of most remarkable achievements in golf, ever. How do you open the gates to do it again? How do you generate that amount of emotion and intensity and determination? You can't just flip the switch and generate that kind of want. We've all tried to and it hasn't worked. For Phil to actually do that, it's legendary stuff."

"It's so cool that a whole new generation of fans got to see what a stallion he is," says Keegan Bradley. "It just shows what kind of greatness Phil has inside of him. He hadn't played good all year"—in fact, the PGA Championship would be Mickelson's only top-10 finish of the season—"but drop him into that situation and he took total control of the tournament. What a gift to golf fans and, really, the whole game."

Mickelson's sixth major championship victory tied him with his diametric opposite, the fastidious Faldo, and Lee Trevino, one of the three or four greatest ball-strikers who have ever lived. If he can somehow steal another one—and at this point, how can you possibly bet against him?—Mickelson would join the immortals with seven majors: Arnold Palmer, Sam Snead, Gene Sarazen, and Harry Vardon. One measure of the greatness of a career is the span between a first and last major championship victory. Nicklaus, of course, leads the way at twenty-four years. Since the birth of the Masters, only Tiger Woods (twenty-two), Gary Player (nineteen), and Ernie Els (eighteen) can say they were big-game hunters longer than Mickelson (seventeen).

When it was all over, Mickelson marched triumphantly across the grounds of the Ocean Course, serenaded by the fans. It now takes two hands to count his major championships, but in victory he offered only one digit: a thumb raised triumphantly to the sky.

CHAPTER NINETEEN

Phil Mickelson's victory at the PGA Championship inspired many emotions, including wonderment. Thirty years after winning a Tour event as an undergrad, he had once again pulled off the improbable. The latest triumph led to a reexamining of Mickelson's place in the golf firmament, and the larger sports landscape. Among modern athletes, only Tom Brady and LeBron James can boast the same combination of longevity and excellence. Jim Nantz has had a front-row seat for Mickelson's and Brady's careers and become close to both men. "What I see are two guys who love what they do and it comes from a place deep in their heart and their soul," says Nantz. "They play with a boyish joy that never gets old for them. Whatever processes it takes that allows them to compete, that doesn't grow old. Think of when you're a little kid, bag over your shoulder, it's getting dark but you just want to play one more hole, and you're afraid your mom is going to be mad at you, but the pure joy of hitting a golf ball makes you keep playing—Phil has never lost that. Down the stretch at the Ocean Course, he might as well have been in his backyard with his dad, hitting flop shots. Just like Tom Brady, in the fourth quarter of the Super Bowl, it's as if he's slinging the ball around the backyard with his father. Tom still throws the football with the same intensity as when he was in his twenties. Phil still swings at the ball as hard as when he was in his twenties. They were both born to do it."

Mickelson's midlife burst made it impossible not to rethink the career-long comparisons with Tiger Woods. If Phil's 2021 was defined by triumph, Tiger's was marred by more catastrophe. There are twenty-six bones in a human foot, and, according to someone very close to Woods, he shattered twenty-one of them in the single-car accident that sent him to the hospital in February. This bracketed a dozen years of strife for Tiger, during which he broke his body and severely curtailed his career, throwing into sharp relief Mickelson's unparalleled longevity. "One of the reasons Phil has lasted so long is because he's had a joyful life," says Charles Barkley, who has been close to both Woods and Mickelson. "Tiger won a bunch of tournaments, but there wasn't much joy in it. Sure, Tiger is a better golfer. You're just in awe of his talent. But it's not fun to be around him. Everyone in his world is uptight and shit, afraid to say or do the wrong thing. Tiger himself has always acted like he's under siege. Gimme a fuckin' break—you're just a golfer, dude. When you're with Phil, you're guaranteed to have fun. He makes people feel good. Everyone around him is always smiling. That's a huge difference, man."

Mickelson's victory at the PGA Championship also demanded a reassessment of his place in the pantheon. My list:

1a. Jack Nicklaus (greatest champion of all time)

1b. Tiger Woods (most dominant golfer of all time)

3. Ben Hogan

4. Bobby Jones

5. Walter Hagen

6. Sam Snead

7. Gene Sarazen

8. Gary Player

9. Arnold Palmer

10. Tom Watson

11. Phil Mickelson

12. Lee Trevino

"He's inches from immortality," says Golf Channel analyst Arron Oberholser. "If he got a U.S. Open, he's easily top 10 of all time. How much of his cash do you think Phil would give for one U.S. Open? I think he'd give a kidney. He might give both of them. Would Phil go on dialysis for a U.S. Open? Maybe!"

For all that Mickelson has accomplished, it's impossible not to wonder if he could have been an even more prolific winner with a more disciplined and less unbridled style of play. "Oh, of course he would have," says Nicklaus. "He would have won a lot more. Right after he won the PGA this year I dropped him a note. I can paraphrase what I said: *Hey, you reined yourself in, you didn't try to do dumb stuff, and look what happened? You won.* When it comes to winning golf tournaments, it's not about your good holes—it's about minimizing your bad holes. Golly, he's cost himself so many tournaments over the years with the double and triple and quadruple bogeys."

"Listen, every good player, they have to do whatever is necessary to get their heartbeat in the right place for them to succeed," says Peter Kostis. "You know? Some people have to play very conservatively. When I worked with Tom Kite, that's the kind of player he was. He had to go from point A to point B and stay very structured and rely on his thousands of hours of practice to carry him. Phil has a style of golf that gets his heartbeat in the right place *for him.* He has a constant need to feel the excitement, feel the juice. And I commend him for understanding that and living that way. Could he have won more with another style of play? I'm not sure. If he tried to be someone he's not, it probably would have hurt his game more than it helped."

Brandt Snedeker recalls a long-ago Crosby Clambake when he was paired with Mickelson on Saturday. They were in the middle of the pack. Playing his second shot on Pebble Beach's par-5 14th hole, Mickelson aimed his 3-wood at the houses right of the green and tried to cut his ball back onto the putting surface. Instead, it sailed out-of-bounds, as did the reload. Mickelson made a 9 and missed the cut by one stroke. That night at dinner Snedeker asked him what the heck he had been thinking. "I was trying to win the tournament," Mickelson said, baffled by the question. "I was 9 back—I'm not going to lay up. If I make a 3 there and another one on eighteen, I could've given myself a chance to win." Says Snedeker, "It's an entirely different way of thinking about things. He was always, always playing to win. I respect that, even if he set himself on fire a few times as a result."

"You have to take the whole player as is, the whole package," says Hank Haney. "You can't swap out this piece or that piece, because if you change one thing you change everything. If Phil hit his driver straighter he would have been Tiger Woods. But you can't have everything. Phil had one weakness but so many other strengths. To make him play another way, that would be like putting reins on a racehorse. You just gotta let them go. That's how he plays golf, and it's helped him enjoy it for a really long time and kept him engaged and kept him going forward. You know what, when I was [commentating] at ESPN, it felt like I was always getting Jim Furyk's group. I fucking hate watching Jim Furyk play golf. It was like, Gawd anybody but fucking Furyk. He would hit every fairway, hit every green, and either make or miss the putt. That's it. Same boring shit hole after hole, and the entire time he has the same goddamn frown on his face. I used to beg them to let me watch Phil Mickelson. He's fucking fun to watch. He'll hit some wild shots, some great ones, he'll do some crazy shit, but he plays with so much personality."

In the end, maybe that's all that matters, not whether Mickelson won this tournament or that tournament. He had fun and so did we. And he did it his way.

In the wake of Mickelson's PGA Championship victory, the tributes and the outpourings of goodwill were unrelenting . . . until he again managed to be his own worst enemy. Five weeks after the PGA, Mickelson turned up at the Rocket Mortgage Classic in Detroit, his first time playing a recent addition to the schedule that has been trumpeted as a sign of the host city's ongoing renaissance. The *Detroit News* uncovered a juicy local angle: Phil's connection to "Dandy Don" DeSeranno, a Motor City character who was an alleged associate of the national Mafia organization La Cosa Nostra. Dandy Don favored gold medallions and shirts unbuttoned to his belly button, and had his pick of vintage Thunderbirds for tooling around town: red (1957), white ('55), or blue ('56). On Wednesday of tournament week, one of the newspaper's most decorated investigative reporters, Rob Snell, dropped a thoroughly researched story detailing how Dandy Don, having served as Mickelson's bookie, bilked him out of half a million dollars in winnings from sports wagering. "According to the trial transcript, DeSeranno was questioned about Mickelson after receiving immunity from federal prosecutors and testified as a government witness in the 2007 racketeering trial of Jack Giacalone, a reputed organized crime leader in Metro Detroit," the story said. "Giacalone's dad was the admitted mob captain Vito (Billy Jack) Giacalone, a suspect in the unsolved disappearance of Teamsters President Jimmy Hoffa." The trial transcript was reprinted in the story:

Giacalone's lawyer, Neil Fink, asked, "Did you cheat—do you know Phil Mickelson, the golfer?"

"Who?" DeSeranno said.

"Phil Mickelson, the golfer."

"Yes."

"Lefty?" the lawyer said.

"Yes."

"Did you cheat him out of $500,000?"

"I wouldn't say I cheated him."

"What would you call it?" Fink asked. "What did you do?"

"I couldn't pay him."

"You booked his action, correct?"

"Yes."

The story quoted Mickelson's lawyer Glenn Cohen, who confirmed the reporting. "Phil and a bunch of his buddies back then were betting on sports, and Phil was the guy placing the bets," Cohen said. "They got this guy's name and had no idea what his background was." U.S. attorney Keith Corbett made it clear in the story that Mickelson had done nothing worse than exercise terrible judgment. "We never looked at him," Corbett said. "I don't know what the laws were in Vegas, but from a federal standpoint, it is not a crime to be a bettor."

Despite the fair and balanced reporting, Mickelson went on the offensive, taking to Twitter to rip the story and telling reporters at the tournament, "I feel that Rob Snell made an article this week that was very opportunistic and selfish and irresponsible. I was looking at some ways that my foundation might be able to get involved. When you have a divisive voice like that, it's very hard to bring people together, and that needs to change because the people here are great. But when that's your voice, it's hard for me or somebody else to come in and get other people and bring other entities involved to help out because you're constantly being torn down as opposed to brought together and built up. It was so much effort for me to be here to have that type of unnecessary attack. Not like I care, it happened twenty-something years ago, it's just the lack of appreciation. Yeah, I don't see me coming back. Not that I don't love the people here and they haven't been great, but not with that type of thing happening."

. Mickelson wanted to dismiss the story as old news but it was built on new revelations: the trial transcript did not appear in Giacalone's court file until 2018, and it wasn't until June 2021 that the connection to Mickelson was discovered, as Giacalone faced prison time in a new case connected to an overdue tax bill of $537,222. Mickelson's ire may have been less about the timing of the story than the fact that it made him look like a putz and a pigeon and a palooka. All the whinging was certainly not crafty public relations: The original article had been locked for subscribers to the *News*, giving it only a small regional audience, but once Mickelson made it big news, the paper tore down the paywall so the whole world could read (and retweet) it. Things took a turn for the absurd when a local golf fan created a petition at Change.org to try to convince Mickelson to come back to Detroit. Sensing that his threats to boycott a feel-good tournament over a lone newspaper story made him look small and thin-skinned, Mickelson quickly backtracked and said he would return if the petition garnered fifty thousand signatures and each signer agreed to do "one random act of kindness for another member of the community." (Insert eye roll emoji here.) Flailing for further damage control, Mickelson donated $100,000 to the Detroit-based Children's Foundation.

He hadn't teed it up in the state of Michigan since 2008, so the locals weren't used to the Mickelsonian bobbing and weaving. "The way he handled it was stunning, frankly," says Gary Miles, the editor and publisher of the *Detroit News*. Fighting for a spot on the U.S. Ryder Cup team, Mickelson finished in seventy-fourth place, third from last, fifteen strokes behind winner Cam Davis. How did his act play with local sports fans? Miles is too polite to answer directly, but he says, "Detroit prides itself on work ethic, and as a sports town, the folks who tend to retain stardom are not flamboyant—they just put their head down and deliver. You score a touchdown and you hand the ball to the referee and don't say much afterward. As for Mickelson, Barry Sanders he isn't."

Dandy Don wasn't the end of Mickelson's bad press in 2021. Throughout the year, he was linked to a controversial plan by Golf Saudi to create a new golf circuit that would be a direct competitor to the PGA Tour. Mickelson has always been loathe to travel overseas for tournaments, but in February 2021 he jilted the Phoenix Open—what used to be his hometown event—and flew halfway across the world for the Saudi International, a tournament affiliated with the European Tour (which has since been rechristened the DP World Tour, the naming rights having been sold to a behemoth Dubai corporation). Steve Loy made the trip with Mickelson. He was the talk of the driving range, as word quickly got around that Loy had gotten himself in a pickle at the airport for trying to bring in bottles of wine as gifts to top Saudi officials; alcohol is forbidden by law in the Kingdom. (Loy did not respond to a request for comment.) Whatever his flaws may be, Coach remains a powerful force in Mickelson's life. His role transcends merely being an agent and has come to include partnering with Mickelson on a variety of investments. "It's more like a marriage than a business relationship," says Davis Love. Someone who is close to both Loy and Mickelson believes the bond is stronger than that; after all, marriages can be dissolved. "They're like blood brothers," says this person. "They know all of each other's secrets and they're going to take them to the grave."

Not long after Mickelson spent a week pressing flesh in King Abdullah Economic City, word began to leak out that the proposed LIV Golf Invitational Series would feature tournaments with $20 million purses—the 2021 PGA Championship offered a record $12 million—and there were whispers that number would increase significantly year over year. Some of Mickelson's colleagues were revolted by the idea that Saudi Arabia, which birthed fifteen of the nineteen 9/11 hijackers, would become a home of professional golf. Rory McIlroy had already turned down seven-figure appearance fees to play in the Saudi International, saying, "There's a morality to it." Now he deemed LIV "a money grab" and added, "I would like to be on the right side of history with this one."

Mickelson refrained from saying anything of substance publicly about LIV, but his involvement in the birth of the tour is much more extensive than has been previously known; he laid out all the details for me in an hour-long phone call in November 2021. Mickelson said he had enlisted three other "top players" he declined to name and that they paid for attorneys to write LIV's operating agreement, codifying that the players would have control of all the details. He didn't pretend to be excited about the prospect of making his professional home in Saudi Arabia, admitting LIV was nothing more than "sportswashing" by a brutally oppressive regime. "They're scary motherfuckers to get involved with," he said. "We know they killed [*Washington Post* reporter and U.S. resident Jamal] Khashoggi and have a horrible record on human rights. They execute people over there for being gay. Knowing all of this, why would I even consider it? Because this is a once-in-a-lifetime opportunity to reshape how the PGA Tour operates. They've been able to get by with manipulative, coercive, strong-arm tactics because we, the players, had no recourse. As nice a guy as [Tour commissioner Jay Monahan] comes across as, unless you have leverage, he won't do what's right. And the Saudi money has finally given us that leverage. I'm not sure I even want [LIV] to succeed, but just the idea of it is allowing us to get things done with the [PGA] Tour."

Indeed, Monahan quickly treated LIV—and a less well-capitalized would-be start-up tour, the Premier Golf League—as an existential threat, and he warned that any player who signed on with the competition would be banned for life by the PGA Tour. (This is a legally dubious position but reflected Monahan's siege mentality.) The Tour quickly began pumping money to the players to try to blunt the Saudi incursion, jacking up the 2021 Players Championship purse to $15 million and introducing the new $40 million Player Impact Program (PIP), which was billed as a bonus pool for the players who had the biggest media reach and best engaged with fans through social media. The Tour alluded to shadowy algorithms and unspecified metrics but refused to make public how the money was distributed, leaving no doubt it was merely a slush fund for Monahan to try to buy the loyalty of his superstars. The day after Mickelson called me, word leaked about the Tour's continued efforts to purchase its players' happiness: in 2022, the PIP would be raised to $50 million; the FedEx Cup bonus pool increased from $60 million to $75 million; two spurious season-long bonus programs would hand out a total of $20 million more; and tournament purses increased $60 million to $427 million, with the Players Championship payout rising to $20 million. (Where have we heard that latter number before?)

Mickelson's machinations with the Saudis had clearly worked, to the benefit of all, but he remained unsatisfied despite the influx of so much funny money. In his mind, two larger battles remained: the players being able to take possession of their media rights and a wholesale restructuring of how the players are governed. The Tour's draconian policy has long been that they own absolutely the media rights to its members. So Turner Sports has had to pay the Tour a $1 million licensing fee every time Phil teed it up in an iteration of *The Match*, though Mickelson himself has made upwards of $15 million from the franchise. "I don't want to say it's infuriating, but it is definitely more than frustrating," he says. A bigger deal is that the players don't own the broadcast highlights of their own shots. Each of these moments could potentially be turned into an NFT and sold to fans or collectors. (Over the last year, more than $600 million of NFTs of NBA players have been sold, with individual NFTs fetching upwards of $200,000. Every player shares equally in the 5 percent transaction fee.) "The Tour is sitting on multiple billions of dollars worth of NFTs," says Mickelson, his voice rising like a revivalist preacher. "They are sitting on hundreds of millions of dollars' worth of digital content we could be using for our social media feeds. The players need to own all of that. We played those shots, we created those moments, we should be the ones to profit. The Tour doesn't need that money. They are already sitting on a eight-hundred-million-dollar cash stockpile. How do you think they're funding the PIP? Or investing two hundred million dollars in the European Tour? The Tour is supposed to be a nonprofit that distributes money to charity. How the fuck is it legal for them to have that much cash on hand? The answer is, it's not. But they always want more and more. They have to control everything. Their ego won't allow them to make the concessions they need to."

Is it about the money or the principle? With Mickelson, you can never be sure. Given the scale of his gambling losses—and we don't know what we don't know—it's possible the Saudi seduction is born of necessity. Mickelson raised eyebrows by selling his Gulfstream in 2019. "He loved that plane so much it was like his fourth child," says someone very close to him. "I was absolutely shocked that he sold it. The only reason I could possibly imagine him doing that was him feeling serious financial pressure." The Mickelsons have purchased land on Jupiter Island, in Florida, and have been interviewing architects; Phil may yet get the haven from state income tax he has long lusted after. "I was interviewing him one time," says John Feinstein, "and he said, apropos of nothing, 'You always think of me as a right-winger, but I'm actually pretty liberal on social issues like abortion.' I said, 'But your number one issue is taxes.' He said, 'No, no, no, my number one, two, three, four, and five issues are taxes.'"

But Mickelson's second outstanding issue with the Tour has nothing to do with money. It's about control. "The Tour likes to pretend it's a democracy, but it's really a dictatorship," he says. "They divide and conquer. The concerns of the top players are very different from the guys who are lower down on the money list, but there's a lot more of them. They use the top guys to make their own situation better, but the top guys don't have a say." At that moment, the players were a minority on the all-powerful PGA Tour Policy Board, holding only four of the nine seats, with the other five being filled by luminaries of the business world who, by age and experience, have more in common with the commissioner than the jocks; the pros would later be granted a fifth seat on the board.

Mickelson's idea for governance is, he says, based on the United States Congress: the Tour's vast middle class would be like the House, voting on ideas that would then be rejected or tweaked and ultimately ratified by a much smaller Senate-like body comprised of the game's biggest stars. "That way nothing will get done without the approval of both sides," Mickelson says. It is an idealistic vision. Phil says he has spent at least a dozen hours on the phone talking through these issues with Monahan, but found him to be unresponsive. Is Mickelson really ready to blow up the PGA Tour if he doesn't get his way?

"I know twenty guys who want to do this," he says of LIV, "and if the Tour doesn't do the right thing, there is a high likelihood it's going to happen." It felt like he was bragging.

Just before Christmas 2021—a month after Mickelson uttered those words—an internal memo leaked with the news that the PGA Tour was creating a new NFT platform for its players to provide them a source of "long-term, incremental revenue." Once again, Mickelson's brinkmanship had worked. And then, on December 29, he tweeted that he had received the ultimate Christmas gift: the $8 million bonanza for winning the Player Impact Program. Twitter sleuths immediately pointed out that Mickelson's declaration of victory was premature, given that the algorithm numbers would continue to be crunched until the ball dropped in Times Square. Golf writer Sean Zak tweeted, "Claiming that you've won the PIP before final standings have been tabulated . . . just to juice your mentions even more. Chess, not checkers from @PhilMickelson." To which Mickelson replied, with a smirking emoji: "Last minute move. Checkmate."

Phil loved *The Queen's Gambit*—"It fits his obsessive personality," says Amy—but he is not quite the master strategist he fancies himself. When the official PIP standings were announced in March 2022, Woods was the actual winner, leading him to masterfully troll Phil on Twitter . . . which got so much engagement from fans it probably guaranteed Tiger will repeat as PIP champ.

The Saudi gambit failed in a much more spectacular fashion. In February 2022, Mickelson blew off Pebble Beach—sorry, Nunu—and returned to the Kingdom for the Saudi International. While over there, he ripped his home tour to writer John Huggan, leading to a provocative GolfDigest.com headline: "Phil Mickelson says PGA Tour's 'obnoxious greed' has him looking elsewhere." According to multiple sources, Mickelson's militance caused considerable angst among his endorsement partners, particularly at KPMG and Callaway, which are deeply invested in the PGA Tour in ways that go far beyond sponsoring one aging left-handed Hall of Famer. Mickelson's deal with Workday was set to expire shortly before the 2022 Masters; in the aftermath of Phil's comments to Huggan, a top executive at Workday confided that Mickelson's increasing stridence had made it an easier decision for the company to not renew the deal. Mickelson's disparaging remarks about the PGA Tour did not play well on Golf Twitter, either. Reporters, fans, and even fellow pros filled his mentions with sharp critiques, leading Phil to go on a well-publicized blocking spree, which further eroded goodwill.

In the days after Mickelson returned home from Saudi Arabia, two longtime agents whispered to me that LIV had signed its twentieth player, reaching the threshold its leadership had set to publicly announce the creation of the

234 // ALAN SHIPNUCK

tour. A splashy kick-off press conference was purportedly being organized for the week of the Players Championship in mid-March. With the Saudi question coming to a boil, Mickelson's role in helping to organize LIV, and his true feelings about it, felt too important to the future of professional golf to leave buried in the pages of this book, Woodward-style. For over a year, one of the biggest questions in the sport had been: What does Phil want? Among professional typists, only I knew. In mid-February—three months before the release date for this book—Mickelson's comments to me about Saudi Arabia and the PGA Tour were excerpted on the website of the Fire Pit Collective, at which I am a partner.

His sneakiness and callous indifference to Saudi atrocities ignited a firestorm. Nearly 300 websites linked to Phil's incendiary quotes, including many across Europe and the Middle East. Golf's chattering class savaged him for being a rapacious mercenary. The blowback was so extreme that the two other most prominent players linked to LIV in press reports, Dustin Johnson and Bryson DeChambeau, immediately ran for the hills, releasing carefully worded statements pledging their fealty to the PGA Tour. Mickelson was holed up at the Yellowstone Club skiing with Amy—"The snow is just too good," he had told me—but various players blasted him in absentia, led by McIlroy, who didn't try to disguise his disdain while speaking to reporters at the L.A. Open. "I don't want to kick someone while he's down," McIlroy said, nevertheless winding up like Pelé, "but I thought they were naïve, selfish, egotistical, ignorant—a lot of words to describe that interaction he had with Shipnuck. It was just very surprising and disappointing. Sad. I'm sure he's sitting at home sort of rethinking his position and where he goes from here."

Indeed, Mickelson released a statement five days after his comments were published, claiming they were off-the-record. I will go to my grave knowing that's not true. The backstory is telling: our phone call had been more than a year in the making. I first told Mickelson I would be writing this book at the PGA Championship at Harding Park in August 2020. "Cool!" was his very first reaction, and it almost sounded like he meant it. I asked if he would be willing to sit for interviews. Edging away, Mickelson added, "Let's talk more about it soon." I approached him at Torrey Pines, in January 2021, and asked again if we could sit down to discuss his life and times. Now he was more circumspect, saying, "I'm flattered you're doing it, but I'm nervous because it's you." He again demurred about doing interviews. I made another run at Mickelson a few weeks later at Pebble Beach, and this time he said he wouldn't do any interviews because he didn't want it to appear as if this biography was "authorized." (The cover of the book should clear that up.) I let it go, but just before Thanksgiving, Phil texted me out of the blue, asking if we could have a conversation about media rights and his battles with the Tour. "I believe it could be a deciding factor on a decision I need to make," he wrote. That seemed highly unlikely—Mickelson had access to people far better versed than me on these subjects. But I was happy to humor him.

When we spoke, Mickelson inquired about my kids, the high school girls basketball team I coach, and the new golf media company I am helping to build. I was impressed and amused by the effort. At one point he couldn't resist his version of flattery, saying, "As much as you scare the shit out of me, I think you're one of the most talented writers ever. You're really good at getting shit out of people and creating interesting story lines. So that's scary as fuck for me." Mickelson did indeed ask for my thoughts regarding the Tour's position on NFTs and media rights, which inevitably led to his provocative thoughts about Saudi Arabia. Not once in our texts or when we spoke on the phone did Mickelson request to go off-the-record, and I never consented to it; had he asked, I would have pushed back hard, as this was my one chance to speak with him for this book.

After blowing me off for more than a year, why was Mickelson suddenly so eager to tell all? He inquired when this book was coming out and I told him May 2022—by then the Saudi question was sure to be settled. My take is that he wanted his true feelings to be known but, as always, was working both sides of the street. If he wound up signing with LIV, at least his quotes to me would serve as a signal to American golf fans that he knows the Saudis are bad actors and that it's strictly a business decision. If he remained in the fold with the PGA Tour—what could have been perceived as a political defeat for Mickelson—he would have preemptively made it clear that he did so only after extracting many of the concessions he wanted, thus fulfilling his need to always be seen as the smartest guy in the room. Of course, Mickelson could have revealed his inner self to any number of reporters. Why on earth did he ring up the one person he knew was writing a biography about him, after having previously refused to talk? It remains baffling, even to me. But Mickelson has spent his career charming, and manipulating, the media. If he was going to make LIV Golf his home, shaping public perception was going to be almost as important as the size of the checks.

Mickelson's blunt words to Huggan and to me—and the ensuing sharp criticism from his peers and most of the golf press—gave cover to the corporate overlords who were already unnerved by his dalliance with the Saudis: KPMG and Amstel Light abruptly ended their relationships with him, and Callaway put their deal on "pause." In his public statement, Mickelson allowed that his comments were "reckless" but couldn't resist making himself both the victim and the hero of his narrative, writing, "Golf desperately needs change, and real change is always preceded by disruption. I have always known that criticism would come with exploring anything new. I still chose to put myself at the forefront of this to inspire change, taking the hits publicly to do the work behind the scenes."

The most interesting part of his press release was when Mickelson wrote, ". . . I have often failed myself and others too. The past 10 years I have felt the pressure and stress slowly affecting me at a deeper level. I know I have not been my best and desperately need some time away to prioritize the ones I love most and work on being the man I want to be." To me, this last bit had little or nothing to do with Saudi Arabia—it sounded like a cry for help. As this book goes to print in early March, Mickelson remains out of sight. A variety of players, caddies, agents, Tour wives and reporters have reached out to me with tips and speculation (and wild gossip) about why exactly Phil might be trying to better himself. More revelations may be forthcoming. Or maybe it's just noise, which often envelops Mickelson.

Plenty of commentators have already opined that he tarnished his legacy with his craven flirtation with the Saudis, and perhaps even compromised his chances at being a future Ryder Cup captain or TV commentator. That shows a very short collective memory. Woods, while married and hawking family cars on TV, became entwined in the most salacious of sex scandals, and later his addled mugshot and damning dashcam video went around the world after he was arrested for a DUI. Yet Tiger is now more beloved than ever. Mickelson has often been engulfed in controversy but somehow always emerges with his vast fanbase intact. Sports fans love a comeback and a redemption story. A more humble, more human, less cartoonish Mickelson figures to be more popular than ever. Come what may, he will survive, because he survives everything.

Only Phil Mickelson could dominate a Ryder Cup without hitting a single shot. In September 2021, the United States beat Europe 19–9. It was a blowout seven years in the making, dating back to Mickelson's rebellion at Gleneagles. After two decades of utter futility, the U.S. has now won two of the last three Cups. With a squad full of young superstars, compared to Europe's aging core, the Americans are poised for a long run of dominance. Everything Mickelson had pushed for at the dawn of the Task Force era played out at Whistling Straits: cohesive leadership, empowered players, and more institutional support. The formerly stingy PGA of America had kicked down for a team of statisticians to run models on potential pairings, sprung for private jets to ferry the U.S. team to Wisconsin for two days of practice rounds, and even built a special gym on-site so the Yanks could stay in fighting shape during Ryder Cup week. In the glow of victory, Vice Captain Davis Love hailed the changes that Mickelson had set in motion: "The Phil thing [with Tom Watson] was the boiling-over point. It had been simmering for a while. Phil was the only one with enough nerve to say it. Now, he could have said it in the [private] debriefing, but it wouldn't have been as impactful."

Mickelson watched this legacy play out from the sidelines, as his post-PGA swoon cost him a spot on the U.S. team, the first time he wouldn't be competing in a Ryder Cup since 1993(!). But as vice captain, he still had a big voice, including the nonstop profane chatter he spewed into his walkie-talkie for the enjoyment of the rest of Team USA. "Anything Phil said during this whole competition I cannot repeat," said Captain Steve Stricker. "No, he was really wonderful to have around. His lightness, his demeanor with the guys made the whole atmosphere in our team room that much better."

Mickelson paid particular attention to DeChambeau, a finicky personality who bloomed in the team setting. "He has been instrumental to my whole experience," DeChambeau said. "He is the most positive human being you could ever be around. He always says the right thing at the right time. It's had a big effect on me, for sure."

Ryder rookie Scottie Scheffler recalled a quintessential Mickelson moment during the Saturday afternoon better-ball matches. He and DeChambeau had lost the twelfth hole to go one-down, and Mickelson was waiting for them when they arrived on the thirteenth tee. Said Scheffler, "He just smiled and looked at us and goes, 'Man, this is great, isn't it?' And in my head I was like, *Phil, get the F away from me, this isn't great—we just bogeyed number 12.* But it was exactly what we needed at the time." They rallied to win the match.

Everywhere Mickelson went, he was hailed by the swollen crowds, even as he tried to hide behind his aviators. He would respond with a trademark thumbs-up, but more often than not wound up shushing the gallery. He didn't want to be a distraction, and that included going the entire week without being part of a single press conference.

Amy was by his side every step of the way. They were only a couple of months away from celebrating their twenty-fifth wedding anniversary, but they seemed as smitten as newlyweds. There had been some chatter about Amy not being on hand for her hubby's triumph at the PGA Championship. In fact, their son, Evan, had been on the verge of his high school graduation and she was back in California tending to all the details. Throughout Ryder Cup week, Phil could be seen draping an arm around Amy, whispering in her ear, squeezing her shoulder, and rubbing her back. He was practically petting her. If it was for show, Phil is a better actor than the young Marlon Brando.

On Saturday evening, as play was ending and the members of Team USA were scrambling to get back to the clubhouse, I bumped into the Mickelsons. I asked how their week was going. "It's different, but I'm enjoying it," Phil said.

"Oh, this is great!" Amy interjected. "All the fun but none of the stress."

They were standing near the eighteenth tee, and suddenly a big, thick, fuzzy caterpillar materialized in the long grass. The Mickelsons inspected it with childlike wonder. It was a sweet stolen moment, but for some reason I thought of something Bones had recently told a friend, which was relayed to me during Ryder Cup week: "Nobody knows Phil Mickelson. Nobody. I spent twenty-five years standing next to the guy and he's still a total mystery to me." It has been a singular life, yet after three decades in the spotlight, Mickelson remains enigmatic. A low roar always follows him, going all the way back to his conceding Jeff Thomas's forty-footer at the U.S. Amateur or the dissing of the Irish lasses at the 1991 Walker Cup. So much tumult has followed—the Black Baby rumors, talking trash about Tiger's golf clubs, calling out the PGA Tour commissioner on live TV, cancer scares, very public gambling debts, shady Mob-adjacent associates, throwing Tom Watson under a Greyhound, an insider-trading escapade, the bust-up with Bones, losing his mind at Shinnecock Hills, Dandy Don, the Saudi self-immolation, and God knows what else. No doubt more controversies await, and probably more triumphs, too. Mickelson has already given us some of the most iconic moments of the last quarter century in golf: receiving Payne Stewart's tender embrace at Pinehurst; a walk-off birdie putt to win the Masters; tapping the Nicklaus plaque at Baltusrol and then the exquisite chip that followed; an impossible 6-iron out of the trees in Amen Corner; the tearful hug with Amy behind the final green at Augusta National; the curling putt on the final green at Muirfield to clinch the Claret Jug; a win for the ages on the Ocean Course. But all of that felt very far away on Saturday evening at the Ryder Cup. There was Phil, holding hands with his sweetheart. The applause had died down and it was just the two of them, strolling down the final fairway and straight into the sunset.

AFTERWORD

On March 16, 2022, barrels of Saudi money officially arrived in professional golf, and nothing would ever be the same. Greg Norman, in his guise as CEO and commissioner, announced the launch of the LIV Golf Invitational Series, with a slate of seven tournaments featuring $25 million dollar purses and double that for the decadent season finale. The name borrowed the Roman numerals for 54, which is the perfect score if you birdie every hole in a round of golf. (But what if the course is a par 71? And wouldn't a perfect round feature at least one eagle on a par-5 and a hole-in-one? Eh, never mind.)

The arrival of LIV Golf was cataclysmic, but one man was missing in all the hoopla around its unveiling: Phil Mickelson. He remained in the exile that began with the published excerpts from this book in February 2022. The Masters came and went three weeks after LIV's public unveiling but there was no sign of Phil, a stunning development given his love of the tournament and popularity around Augusta National. At the traditional Tuesday night champions dinner, Gary Player ruffled a few feathers by offering a passionate defense of Mickelson; the Black Knight represented South Africa throughout the apartheid years so he knows what it feels like to be a golfing pariah. Under the famous tree behind the Augusta National clubhouse, golf's chattering class tried to decipher exactly why Mickelson was not on the grounds. It was widely assumed Phil had been suspended by the PGA Tour, and that would later be confirmed in court documents. (According to the Tour's player handbook, "Public comments that a member knows, or should reasonably know, will harm the reputation or financial best interest of PGA TOUR . . . shall be considered conduct unbecoming a professional.") The PGA Tour recognizes the Masters as a sanctioned event but has no jurisdiction over how the tournament is actually run. The green jackets quite plainly do whatever the hell they please when it comes to their little invitational and are under no obligation to uphold a Tour disciplinary action. In his annual pre-tournament press conference, chairman Fred Ridley said, "We did not disinvite Phil. He made a personal decision." In fact, the decision was largely made for him: According to sources with close ties to Augusta National, multiple club members reached out to Mickelson and discouraged him from playing in the Masters, offering variations of the opinion that making his return to public life in Augusta would be a sideshow that would besmirch the tournament.

So Mickelson remained in hiding, though not entirely: On April 27, FirePitCollective.com posted a video of Phil taking an almighty rip with his driver at Rancho Santa Fe Country Club. (It had been shot by a visitor to the club.) Mickelson looked heavier and sported a scraggly beard, befitting his new status as golf's Yetti. The Mickelson sightings continued at the private clubs around San Diego; he was playing a lot of golf, with some of his old brio. It felt like he was gearing up to defend his PGA Championship title. But among PGA of America officials a spirited debate erupted as to whether their tournament was compelled to honor Tour disciplinary sanctions. A vote of the board of directors loomed when a top PGA of America official called Mickelson and encouraged him to remain in hiding. Phil acquiesced, so on May 13, six days before the tournament commenced, the PGA's Twitter handle reported that Mickelson had "withdrawn." That he declined to make the announcement himself reflected how woebegone he had become in the year since his glorious triumph at Kiawah Island.

Mickelson was barely mentioned during the PGA Championship broadcast, but he inevitably hovered over the proceedings in absentia. His old caddie Bones Mackay had begun working full-time for Justin Thomas in September 2021, and they wound up in a playoff versus Will Zalatoris to decide the PGA Championship. The reporting in this book had made it known throughout the golf world that the breakup between Mackay and Mickelson was not nearly as amicable as they had portrayed it publicly. After Thomas dispatched Zalatoris to win the PGA—the second major championship victory for a superstar in waiting—his caddie found himself encircled by reporters. Bones had walked off the final green at Southern Hills carrying not only the flag but the stick too. I said to him, "Looks like you've got a death grip on that thing." It had been a long journey for Mackay since his split with Mickelson. He wiped away a lone tear and loosed a long, deep, satisfied laugh but words would not come.

The prized possession he cradled in that moment is now displayed in Mackay's dining room, the only flag in the whole house.

Three weeks after the PGA Championship, LIV Golf held its first tournament, outside London, featuring a $20 million purse plus $5 million more for the concurrent team competition. The slate of players initially announced underwhelmed, to say the least; Dustin Johnson was the only blue-chipper in the 48-man field. But the tournament had saved a couple of spots for surprise entrants, and on June 6th, three days before the first round, Mickelson announced via social media that he was going all-in with LIV, lured by a payday widely reported to be $200 million over the life of the multi-year deal. "First and foremost, I want to again apologize to the many people I offended and hurt with my comments a few months ago," his statement began. "I have made mistakes in my career and in some of the things I have said and done. Taking time away and reflecting has been very humbling. I needed to start prioritizing the people that I love the most and work on becoming a better version of myself. I have spent this time with Amy and loved ones. I have been engaged and intentional in continued therapy and feel healthy and much more at peace. I realized I still have a long way to go, but I am embracing the work ahead. I am ready to come back and play the game I love but after 32 years this new path [LIV Golf] is a fresh start, one that is exciting for me at this stage of my career and is clearly transformative, not just for myself, but ideally for the game and my peers."

The new and improved (?) Mickelson continued to bare his soul. In a phone interview with Bob Harig on the eve of LIV London, Phil indirectly confirmed this book's reporting about the scale of his gambling losses, saying, "My gambling got to a point of being reckless and embarrassing. I had to address it. And I've been addressing it for a number of years. And for hundreds of hours of therapy. I feel good where I'm at there . . . The anxiety, the other things that come with gambling off the course and addiction off the course, I really needed to address." *Addiction* is a powerful word, and one Mickelson had never used to describe his destructive urges. It takes bravery to publicly take ownership of such a deep-rooted problem, and Mickelson should be applauded for confronting it head-on. (The cynic would say he is trying to soften the blow of any damaging revelations in Billy Walters's forthcoming autobiography.)

I had not planned to cover LIV London; my kids' summer vacation had just begun, and I would be away the ensuing week for the U.S. Open. But once Phil announced his return to public life, I felt compelled to be there. I scrambled to get an overnight flight and landed in London on the morning of the first round. Jane MacNeille, LIV's senior vice president of player communications, met me at the entry gate of the Centurion Club to hand-deliver both my media credentials and a message: "Just so you know, Phil doesn't want to talk to you." Other than a pithy text message he sent me in February on the day the book excerpt dropped I had not enjoyed any contact with Mickelson since this book altered both of our lives. But I was noncommittal with MacNeille. I had crossed an ocean to do my job and wasn't going to let LIV or Mickelson dictate the terms.

The first round had a fun and chaotic energy. Fans repeatedly ducked under the ropes to get closer to the action. Reporters scurried about to post iPhone videos of the action, unencumbered by LIV's social media policies, which are far less restrictive than the PGA Tour's. Mickelson looked surprisingly sharp during an opening 69 and he repeatedly flashed his familiar thumbs-up and aw-shucks smile for the decent-sized gallery.

After the round Mickelson journeyed to an interview area outside of the press tent. I had my credential scanned to gain access to this roped-off spot, like every other reporter. I arrived just as Mickelson stepped to the microphone. Reporters and cameramen were already standing two- and three-deep against a metal railing, so I took my spot in the back row. Just as Mickelson began answering the first question, I felt some jostling to my right. I ignored it, assuming this was a persnickety cameraman trying to squeeze into the front row, which happens. Then a meaty hand squeezed my arm. Annoyed, I pulled it away without even looking back. Then someone grabbed my *other* arm. That was when I realized that I had been bracketed by a pair of neckless security goons.

"We need to scan your badge," one of them said.

I kept my eyes on Mickelson and said, "I'm good, it just got scanned two minutes ago."

They tried to pull me backward but, drawing upon the swim move taught by my high school basketball coach, I wriggled free and stood my ground. Now these ear-pieced thugs grabbed me harder.

"Don't fucking touch me," I growled.

This worked, momentarily, and they loosened their grasps. But the balder, uglier of the two gents elbowed his way directly in front of me and said, with some heat, "We're going to need to scan your badge. *Right now*."

I suddenly became aware that some of the nearby reporters were ignoring Mickelson and were now watching me and my antagonists. In that split-second I ran a quick cost-benefit analysis in my mind. The preceding four months—from the publication of the excerpts and then the release of this book and corresponding hoopla—had been an exceptionally turbulent time. A reporter's job is to tell the story, not become it, but the revelations in this book and the upheaval it wrought for Mickelson put me at the center of the storm. The last thing I wanted was to make more headlines by rolling around in the dirt with a couple of security guards in front of the global golf press, so I decided to play peacemaker. I walked on my own volition about twenty steps to the nice young woman in charge of scanning the badges; the security henchmen shadowed my every move. My credential got zapped and it confirmed what each of us already knew: I had every right to be in the interview area. I strode back toward Mickelson, but the shorter, fatter security guard stepped directly in front of me, blocking my path.

"This is fucking ridiculous," I said. "Who told you to pull this shit?"

"I don't have to answer that," he said, his breath reeking of tuna and onions.

We stood there talking in circles for a few more minutes. To his everlasting credit, the Welsh sportswriter James Corrigan—a frequent antagonist of mine on Twitter—wandered over and began heckling the security guards.

About then Mickelson ended his press conference and exited stage right. The security dudes suddenly became unconcerned with the state of my media credential and skulked away.

I was pissed. I didn't get to listen to Mickelson's comments or ask him a question. I texted Greg Norman, "Are you aware that I just got muscled out of Phil's press conference by a couple of your goons?" He didn't respond right away.

I retreated to the press room to put the final coat of polish on my dispatch about the debut of golf's new world order. I didn't mention the incident with the security guards because I didn't want to make myself the story. After filing the article, I caught an Uber back to my hotel, closing my eyes for a few minutes at the end of a long, crazy day. When I connected to the wifi at the hotel my phone began dinging like a slot machine. A video had begun making the rounds of my confrontation with the security guards. Shot by Alex Thomas, the sports anchor for CNN International, it captured the moments when I was being obstructed by the meatheads after having my badge scanned. Its Zapruder-like value comes from what can be glimpsed in the background: standing directly behind me was Greg Fucking Norman. His face was contorted into such a scowl he looked like the Grim Reaper, only more devoid of a soul. I had no idea he had been standing right there, a witness to the tomfoolery of his security lackeys.

I was watching the video for a third or fourth time when my phone bleated again. It was Norman finally responding to my text, an hour and a half later: "Did not hear," he wrote. "Thanks for letting me know."

I really hadn't wanted to go public with the events of the press conference because the whole thing was so dumb. But Norman's bald-faced lie was too outrageous to let stand. I responded to him with an image from the video showing him lurking right behind me and then screenshot the whole exchange and put it on Twitter. *Hooo boy.* The tweet went global, overshadowing the first round of the tournament. It got so much traction because it confirmed the widespread belief that Norman is a schmuck. My ejection from an otherwise innocuous press conference also fed the all-too-easy narrative of the Saudis' aggressive disdain for a free press.

The next day, when I arrived at the course, MacNeille came to my desk to apologize for what had happened and say that, to her knowledge, no one at LIV had been responsible. She made the credible point that the last thing LIV execs wanted was more bad press so none of them would have been stupid enough to toss me out of a presser in full view of all my peers. In watching the video snippet, I had noticed that standing in the background, simpering, was Mickelson's swing coach, Andrew Getson. At one point he leans in and whispers something to Norman, looking a little too pleased with himself. After subsequently unwinding the events with various involved parties, I believe that it was Mickelson, or his people, who sent in the clowns, not LIV. Sure, Norman could have interceded, but, charitably, he might not have grasped what was happening until it was too late. I confronted Mickelson's manager, Peter Davis, with my theory. With his preppy wardrobe and slicked-back hair, Davis has the vibe of the punchable bad guy from every teen movie. He denied any culpability, but his smarmy smirk told a different story.

The whole kerfuffle is noteworthy not because one brave and hardworking reporter was mistreated but for what it apparently said about Mickelson and those around him: Despite the carefully worded press releases and cloying public statements, they still felt the rules didn't apply to them, and that they could warp their reality, and public opinion, through bullying. When Mickelson returned from his suspension, he paid a lot of lip service to being a changed man. The early returns suggested otherwise.

The war between LIV Golf and the PGA Tour escalated during the London tournament when LIV announced it had signed former U.S. Open champion Bryson DeChambeau and former Masters champ Patrick Reed. Unlike most of the original signees, DeChambeau, 29, and Reed, 32, are not well past their prime. These high-profile defections and the wild rumors about who would bolt next guaranteed that the United States Open, at The Country Club outside Boston, would be overheated.

Beset by putting problems, Mickelson finished a distant 33rd at LIV London and then flew to Beantown. He was greeted by the public release of a letter written by Terry Strada, the national chair of 9/11 Families United; Strada's husband, Tom, had worked on the 104th floor of the North Tower of the World Trade Center and died in its collapse. Strada had sent the letter to LIV golfers Mickelson, DeChambeau, Reed, Dustin Johnson, and Kevin Na. "As a 9/11 widow, I feel compelled to help you understand the level of depravity the Kingdom engaged in when it knowingly sent government agents here to establish the support network needed for those hijackers," Strada wrote. "As you may know, Osama bin Laden and 15 of the 19 September 11 hijackers were Saudis. It was the Saudis who cultivated and spread the evil, hate-filled Islamist ideology that inspired the violent jihadists to carry out the deadly 9/11 attacks. And, most egregiously, it is the Kingdom that has spent 20 years in denial: lying about their activities, and cowardly dodging the responsibility they bear. Yet these are your partners, and much to our disappointment, you appear pleased to be in business with them.

"Given Saudi Arabia's role in the death of our loved ones and those injured on 9/11—your fellow Americans—we are angered that you are so willing to help the Saudis cover up this history in their request for 'respectability.' When you partner with the Saudis, you become complicit with their whitewash, and help give them the reputational cover they so desperately crave—and are willing to pay handsomely to manufacture. The Saudis do not care about the deep-rooted sportsmanship of golf or its origins as a gentleman's game built upon core values of mutual respect and personal integrity. They care about using professional golf to whitewash their reputation, and they are paying you to help them do it."

This was the harsh reality now facing Mickelson: many people considered him a traitor not only to the PGA Tour but also his fellow Americans. On Tuesday of U.S. Open week, Mickelson met the golf press in a hot, sweaty tent adjacent to The Country Club's clubhouse. In the moments before Mickelson arrived there was an unmistakable electricity in the air. He showed up dressed in black, as if for a funeral. For twenty minutes, Mickelson got pounded with questions about the outrage of the 9/11 families, Saudi sportswashing, how much he had been heckled in his practice rounds, how the move to LIV might besmirch his legacy, the frosty reception from his colleagues, LIV's alliance with Donald Trump, and sundry other unpleasant topics. Mickelson spoke in a deadened monotone; there was no mirth from showman who had always treated press conferences as performance art. Mostly, Mickelson looked forlorn and defeated. Removed from the enablers and apologists on his payroll and away from the carefully cultivated artificial reality of LIV, he seemed to be feeling, for the very first time, how much ill he had stirred up.

More public rebukes were to come. In July, Mickelson traveled to St. Andrews for the 150th Open Championship. The week was full of pomp, but the LIV awkwardness cast a dark shadow. The Royal & Ancient had already publicly disinvited Norman, a two-time Open champ, from attending any of the week's events, noting (accurately) that his polarizing presence would be a monumental distraction. Open week began with the R&A Celebration of Champions, featuring a total of 38 male and female winners of various British Amateurs and Opens. Jack Nicklaus, Tiger Woods, Tom Watson, Lee Trevino, Nick Faldo, and Rory McIlroy were among the legends who played in the four-hole exhibition. So did amiable Louis Oosthuizen, who had pledged his allegiance to LIV. But noticeably absent was Mickelson. He also skipped the ensuing past champions dinner, having been made to feel unwelcome at both. "(The R&A) said, 'Look, we don't think it's a great idea you go, but if you want to, you can,'" Mickelson said. "I just didn't want to make a big deal about it, so I said fine. We both kind of agreed that it would be best if I didn't." One of the most enduringly popular golfers of the preceding three decades had suddenly become radioactive.

A couple of weeks after the Open, Mickelson did enjoy rich vindication: *Forbes* named him the highest paid athlete in the world, estimating that he had earned $138 million dollars in the preceding 12 months. (Tiger Woods, who in his heyday topped the list 10 years running, was surpassed by four LIV golfers despite weighing in at $68 million.) Professional golf had never been awash in so much funny money, and then the spigot was opened even further. At the Tour Championship, in August, embattled commissioner Jay Monahan announced that in 2023 the PGA Tour would roll out a super schedule of a dozen "elevated" tournaments with $20 million dollars purses, double or more what these events had previously been paying out. Some would not bother with 36-hole cuts. It was LIV Lite, and in the wake of the announcement one veteran golf writer tweeted simply, "Phil was right." Okay, that was me. With more nuance: Mickelson had long nursed the suspicion that the PGA Tour was not giving the players their fair share of the revenue. He cited the Tour as having cash reserves of $800 million, an exaggerated number that hinted at the truth. Faced with the LIV threat, the Tour created the nebulous Player Impact Program as a way to funnel money to the top players, and in less than a year the pot has ballooned from paying 10 players $40 million to distributing a whopping $100 million among 20 players. (One of the Tour's selling points had been that it is a pure meritocracy versus LIV's corrupting guaranteed money, but the PIP now offers lavish compensation that is not-tied to on-course performance.) Asked at the Tour Championship where all this fresh money would come from, Monahan said existing tournament sponsors would help defray the costs, but he also cited the primary source of this new largesse: "Reserves." Phil was right, and even his shrillest critic begrudgingly admitted it. "As much as I probably don't want to give Phil any sort of credit at all," said McIlroy, "yeah, there were certain points that he was trying to make. Some of these ideas, did they have merit? Of course they did."

Mickelson had resolved to not publicly discuss Tour matters and was clearly trying to shed his smart aleck tendencies, but he couldn't resist noting, "The guys on Tour are playing for a lot more money—that's great that they magically found a couple hundred million."

The sense of vindication, or righteousness, finally put a little pep in Mickelson's step. He had looked utterly lost on the golf course since returning from exile, including woeful missed cuts at the U.S. and British Opens. But Mickelson tied for eighth at LIV Chicago and fifteenth at LIV Bangkok, and then flew from Thailand to Saudi Arabia for LIV Jeddah. This was Mickelson's first visit to the Kingdom since he had been quoted calling its people "scary motherfuckers." He channeled all that anxiety into a relentless charm offensive. A fellow LIV golfer, who spoke on the condition of anonymity, says, "If you think Phil is a bullshit artist normally, this was another level. You've never seen anyone kiss so much ass with that kind of enthusiasm and skill. He was 'on' from the second he got off the plane and he never broke character. I'm pretty sure by the end of the week he could have been elected mayor of King Abdullah City, if they actually held elections over there."

Mickelson ramped up his rhetoric in his pre-tournament press conference, saying, "Pretty much all the best players played on the PGA Tour, at least for the last 20 years. That will never be the case again. I think going forward you have to pick a side. You have to pick what side do you think is going to be successful. And I firmly believe that I'm on the winning side of how things are going to evolve and shape in the coming years for professional golf."

Those were fighting words, but another question in the presser offered a chance at reconciliation: "You made some comments about this country last year which you've apologized for. I wondered how you feel about it now that you're here? Have you changed your opinion?" This was the ultimate softball, a chance for Mickelson—who at that moment was adorned with a temporary henna tattoo he had received the night before at a tournament party—to wax about the wonders of Saudi Arabia and the hospitality of its people. Instead, he responded, "So I will reiterate, I never did an interview with Alan Ship*nick*. And I find that my experience with everybody associated with LIV Golf has been nothing but incredibly positive and I have the utmost respect for everybody that I've been involved with."

Once again, Mickelson was trying to be too cute by half, suggesting in this little semantic game that our hour-long phone call that informs the preceding chapter of this book had not been an actual interview. At least, that's how I took it, but fans and reporters less learned in the black art of Mickelsonian misdirection thought he was claiming I had made up the whole thing. (In that case, what the heck was he always apologizing for?) Instead of some warm, fuzzy remarks about his host nation, Mickelson touched off another frenzied news cycle about his weirdness and duplicity. He was forced to clarify his remarks the next day to Harig: "We agreed multiple times that I was not going to be interviewed or a part of the book. He obviously took a conversation differently and we're going to have to agree to disagree." This was utterly nonsensical. *Not be part of the book?* He is the book! We had no such agreement that he wouldn't be interviewed; that's why I kept asking him to sit for questions. And then *he* called *me*.

A funny and ridiculous postscript came by way of a phone call from someone very close to Mickelson, who told me, "When he said your name wrong in Jeddah, I know him well enough to know that he intentionally mispronounced it. That way he has a technicality he can fall back on: 'I didn't say Shipnuck, I said Shipnick.' I know it sounds crazy but that's how smart he thinks he is."

After a middling finish at LIV's season finale in late-October, at Trump Doral, Mickelson faded into the off-season. It should have been a chance to catch his breath and find his game after the most contentious year of a controversy-filled career. But a week after Doral, Pat Perez went on Claude Harmon's podcast and told the world, "I have a different hate for Phil than most people. People won't know the story—I'm not going to go into the story again—but Phil crossed the line with me that is just uncrossable and unforgivable. He knows that he screwed up. He apologized for the action, but I cannot forgive him for it because I've known Phil for a long, long time. I've known the guy forever. And the fact that when he made this action, not only was it—he had intentions of doing it; he knew it was going to happen before it happened and when he did it—I was hurt, for one. I was like 'How can this guy do this?'"

The incident to which Perez referred is an open secret on Tour, mostly because Perez himself has told so many people. A handful of folks conveyed details to me while I was reporting this book, so in November 2021, I approached Perez to see if he wanted to discuss it publicly. He declined, but clearly is still nursing a throbbing, turgid grievance. According to one source who had a long heart-to-heart with Perez—"he had tears in his eyes," this person says—Mickelson invited Pat and his wife, Ashley (a buxom, outspoken redhead), to dinner during the 2015 Barclays tournament, which was played at Plainfield Country Club in Edison, New Jersey. Mickelson stayed nearby at Liberty National Golf Course, where he is a member. He hosted the Perezes for dinner in the clubhouse, apparently an exciting development for Mickelson. "He was completely enamored with Ashley Perez," says the source. "He talked about her a lot." As the story goes, when Pat excused himself to use the restroom during dinner, Mickelson whipped out his phone to allegedly show her a photograph of himself that she found offensive. Mickelson and his representatives declined a detailed request for comment. Approached again in December 2022, Pat Perez would only say, "It's a matter between us. We handled it."

If the PGA Tour is high school with money, LIV Golf is boarding school with trust fund money; it is a cloistered, incestuous world populated by the spoiled and entitled. That two of the biggest personalities on tour are now openly feuding does not portend well. At the Portland event, before he went public with his grievances about Phil, I asked Perez what he liked so much about LIV. "It's an incredible family atmosphere," Perez said. "Everyone is looking out for each other. We're all in this together."

It was at LIV Portland that I chased down Norman in the parking lot. We hadn't had any interaction since London. He was apologetic and we had a long, animated, productive conversation. At one point I asked if he considered Mickelson an asset or liability, since at that time Phil was rarely speaking to reporters and almost entirely absent from LIV's social media and promotional offerings. "Of course he's an asset," Norman said. "But it's a complicated time."

And Phil Mickelson remains a very complicated person.

SOURCE NOTES AND ACKNOWLEDGMENTS

This book was three decades in the making. I first began covering the PGA Tour in 1994, Phil Mickelson's second full season. That was the era of Corey Pavin and Mark O'Meara and Lee Janzen; thank gawd we had Phil, who is many things, but never boring.

Even as I have shadowed Mickelson throughout his career, I've never been one of his boys. There are sportwriters with whom he's played recreational rounds of golf or had long, discursive dinners—we've enjoyed neither together. I would characterize our relationship through the years as an amused wariness. At the 2020 Masters, after I had already told Phil this book was happening, he journeyed to the cavernous press building for a pretournament press conference. Given that he had won only one tournament in the preceding seven years, I commandeered the mic and said to Mickelson, "You don't do many pretournament press conferences anymore—is it fun to come in here knowing that you have a big stage on which you can perform?"

He replied, live on Golf Channel, "I just don't think my views are that much desired during this era, and it's been easy to kind of just slide in and out. But I always love to come and see you, Alan."

These little digs always make me laugh, just as it's been undeniably fun (if occasionally combative) to chronicle Mickelson through the years. I remain upset that he impugned my professionalism by claiming his comments about Saudi Arabia and the Tour were off the record, but at some point in the future I hope we will bury the hatchet, just as we did after he wanted to brawl at Medinah all those years ago. We have spoken often in the past, including sitting down together for an hourlong podcast in 2015, taped in his secret lair within the clubhouse of the Madison Club in Palm Springs. While Phil and I had only that one fraught phone call for this book, I was in frequent touch with two of his lawyers, who offered their perspective on a variety of subjects. Over the years I have had many conversations with Amy, Bones, Steve Loy, Phil's father and father-in-law, his trainer and sports psychologist and publicist and assorted swing and putting coaches. For this book I've drawn upon all of this previous reporting as well as the accompanying game stories and features I typed for the Fire Pit Collective, *Sports Illustrated,* GolfDigest.com and *Golf Magazine.* The material is used here with the permission of each outlet.

Researching a book during the COVID era had its advantages and drawbacks. Access to players was severely restricted at PGA Tour events but throughout the pandemic many folks were stuck at home, bored, and happy to entertain phone interviews. It was common for these chats to stretch for an hour or more. During a single day in December 2020, I interviewed Paul Azinger, Mark Calcavecchia, Luke Donald, Tom Kite, Hale Irwin, and Brendan Steele. (That's four U.S. Opens, a British Open, a PGA Championship, 131 total victories across the PGA and Champions Tours, and more than $170 million in career earnings.) By the end of that day I was sipping tea with honey and lemon because my voice was failing. In all, I conducted nearly two hundred interviews for this book: players, caddies, swing coaches, Tour wives, ex-wives, nannies, Tour officials, tournament directors, corporate sponsors, agents, lawyers, federal investigators, reporters, broadcasters, civilians. Some would speak only on the condition of anonymity. (They are not listed below.) Others are not quoted in the book but informed my thinking. Except where noted in this chapter, every quote is from my own reporting or taken from press conferences or similarly public utterances. Among those I interviewed: Azinger, Mark Baldwin, Michael Bamberger (who also offered much helpful advice on the direction of the manuscript), Charles Barkley, Chip Beck, Ted Bishop, Keegan Bradley, Mark Brooks, Calcavecchia, Tom Candiotti, Paul Casey, Brandel Chamblee, Cam Champ, K. J. Choi, Stewart Cink, Roger Cleveland, Fred Couples, Ben Crenshaw, Julie Crenshaw, John Daly, Bryson DeChambeau, Jaime Diaz, Donald, Mike Donald, David Eger, Ernie Els, Harris English, Nick Faldo, David Fay, John Feinstein, Tony Finau, Tim Finchem, Steve Flesch, Jerry Foltz, Rickie Fowler, John Garrity, Brian

Gay, Kimberly Gay, Matt Ginella, Paul Goydos, Hank Haney, Tim Herron, Harry Higgs, Charley Hoffman, J. B. Holmes, Steve Hulka, Irwin, Peter Jacobsen, Dustin Johnson, Zach Johnson, Christina Kim, Tom Kite, Peter Kostis, Bernhard Langer, Lehman, Amanda Leonard, Justin Leonard, Luke List, Davis Love, Sandy Lyle, Hunter Mahan, Casey Martin, Bob May, Scott McCarron, Gary McCord, Graeme McDowell, Paul McGinley, Shaun Micheel, Johnny Miller, Francesco Molinari, Jay Monahan, Jim Nantz, Jack Nicklaus, Greg Norman, Andy North, Arron Oberholser, Sean O'Hair, Jose Maria Olazabal, Neil Oxman, Ryan Palmer, Gary Player, Tom Purtzer, Rick Reilly, Dean Reinmuth, Chris Riley, Jimmy Roberts, Xander Schauffele, Scottie Scheffler, Webb Simpson, Vijay Singh, Rick Smith, Brandt Snedeker, Jordan Spieth, Steele, Dave Stockton, Kevin Streelman, Steve Stricker, Paul Tesori, Bo Van Pelt, Jimmy Walker, Bubba Watson, Matthew Wolff, John Wood, Gary Woodland, Ian Woosnam, and Manny Zerman.

When the manuscript was completed, I emailed Phil a series of questions requesting comment. He never responded, instead referring me to one of his lawyers, who spoke to me only off the record.

NOTES

CHAPTER 1

This chapter could have been a book unto itself. I felt strongly that every story should be exclusive to me but Harry Higgs's tale about the "nasty" drive was simply too good to leave out. It's from the *Fore Play* podcast on November 23, 2021.

CHAPTER 2

The Al Santos backstory owes much to Bamberger's excellent feature on Nunu, which posted on golf.com on June 6, 2019. I borrowed the quote about pirates shooting at the fishing boat and Santos's maxim regarding the silver dollar.

The Steinbeck quote is, of course, from *Cannery Row*, first published by Viking in 1945.

Following his win at the 2004 Masters, Mickelson wrote (with Donald T. Phillips) a quickie autobiography entitled *One Magical Sunday (But Winning Isn't Everything)*, published by Warner Books in 2005. It has the gee-whiz tone of a *Leave It to Beaver* episode but is a useful document for a biographer. I pulled from there the wording of Mickelson's birth announcement and his

258 // SOURCE NOTES AND ACKNOWLEDGMENTS

father recounting Phil's first swings as a toddler and the subsequent reconfiguring of his first golf club.

My research included reading two dozen books, hundreds of newspaper and magazine articles, and even more press conference transcripts. I also listened to easily fifty hours of podcasts that were even tangentially related to Phil. Interesting material popped up in unexpected places; from what I can tell, the best explanation Mickelson has ever given on the benefits of a right-hander playing lefty came in a short video with Tron Carter on the "No Laying Up" YouTube feed on March 11, 2021. That quote is used here.

CHAPTER 3

The quotes "Rainy days were my favorite time . . ." and "After a while, I began to notice . . ." are from *One Magical Sunday*. I love the parallels between Phil's golfing education and the natural way Seve Ballesteros learned the game. The book I quote from is *Seve: The Official Biography*, published by Yellow Jersey Press in 2007.

Part of the fun of research is revisiting old friends. I haven't seen the great old-timey sportswriter Bob Verdi in a while but loved rereading his 2009 *Golf Digest* Q&A with Mickelson, which included the quote, "Problem was, you could always get bumped . . ."

Other quotes used in this chapter:

"You don't realize at the time": Karen Crouse, "Fortune Smiles on Phil Mickelson on Way to Hall of Fame," *New York Times*, May 5, 2012.

"That's going to help the team immensely": Dennis Brown, "The Fairways Are Greener: South African Manny Zerman Moves to United States for Golf Opportunities," *Los Angeles Times*, April 3, 1988.

"I was impressed with him": Chris Ello, "Mickelson Follows His Hero and Nearly Catches Him," *Los Angeles Times*, Feb. 19, 1988.

"I don't really know what happened": Ibid.

CHAPTER 4

This is one of my favorite chapters in the book, a cross between *Animal House* and *Follow the Sun*. Mickelson's former Arizona State teammates are great talkers but I supplemented their tales with various other sources:

"Hi, Phil. I'm Steve Loy": Mickelson with Phillips, *One Magical Sunday*, 42.

"If I play the way I've been playing": Gary Baines, "Phil Being Phil, 1990 Edition," colorodagolf.org, August 24, 2020.

"I'll never forget the look he gave me": Dave Shedloski, "After a series of close calls, the ASU All-American beat friend, fellow San Diego native Zerman, 5 and 4, in final at Cherry Hills C.C.," usga.org, July 31, 2012.

I didn't quote from it but Amy Ellis Nutt's feature on Jeff Thomas ("The Natural Who Self-Destructed"), from an August 2003 edition of the *Newark Star Ledger*, was indispensable background. It is archived on her personal website, amynutt.com.

"No thanks, Coach": Mickelson with Phillips, *One Magical Sunday*, 41.

I interviewed both Manny Zerman and Arizona coach Rick LaRose about the denied drop/hole-out for eagle but Gene Wojciechowski, in the *Los Angeles Times*, had the cleanest quote on the subject, in his 1991 story that ran under the memorable headline, "His Dirty-Ball Trick Leaves Opponent with Egg on Face."

Imagine the young Amy McBride lives an apartment above your friend's place and he is trying to set you up with her, but you'd prefer to work on your flop shot—is that madness or genius? Phil's quote on the matter ("I never took the time . . .") is from *One Magical Sunday*.

CHAPTER 5

As the golf writer at the *San Diego Union-Tribune*, T. R. Reinman was the O. B. Keeler to the young Mickelson's Jones. Reinman parted ways with the *Union-Trib* as the newspaper industry contracted, and eventually Mickelson hired him as his PR guy. It seemed like an act of friendship as much as a business decision, and it certainly didn't hurt Mickelson's standing in the press room that he took care of one of our lodge brothers. The details about Mickelson's first victory as a pro are from Reinman's newspaper account on February 22, 1993.

I love the story about Phil's awkward phone call to Amy's father. She told me one version of it years ago but the Gary McBride quote is from *One Magical Sunday*.

Verdi was such an avuncular presence in Mickelson's life that his kids referred to him as "Uncle Bob." That intimacy helped him land one of the first big features on Jim Mackay, for ESPN.com in March 2006, from which I used the funny details about Bones's college match versus Florida and James Blanchard still waiting for him to report to work.

CHAPTER 7

Steve Williams is on the short list of people I regret not getting to interview, as he politely declined my overtures. His play-by-play from the 2001 Masters is drawn from the HBO Sports documentary *Tiger*.

"You know how it is": Mickelson with Phillips, *One Magical Sunday*, 95.

"In my mind": "A Conversation with Lefty," *Golf Magazine*, March 2003.

"Philip, this is your year": Mickelson with Phillips, *One Magical Sunday*, 128.

CHAPTER 8

Before the internet changed everything, one of the best assignments on the golf beat was to write the "game story" for *Sports Illustrated*. Like playing center field for the Yankees, it came with a legacy: the game story was handed down from Herbert Warren Wind to Dan Jenkins to Rick Reilly. In the late '90s, when Reilly took over the magazine's back-page column, I got a few at-bats on the game story, but in 2002 and 2003 I worked as an editor out of *SI*'s Manhattan offices. I returned to the golf beat as a typist in 2004. At that year's Masters, I had a strong premonition Mickelson would win and started walking with his group during the first round, filling my notebook by chatting with Amy, Phil's father, and swing coach Rick Smith. When Mickelson made his triumphant walk-off birdie I was ready to write the best game story of my life. Only one problem: Reilly. He wanted to make Phil the centerpiece of his column, too. I love Rick, and he has many talents, but sharing isn't one of them. We were staying in neighboring houses (on Medinah Lane!) and late that Sunday night we met on one of the front lawns for a freighted negotiation:

"You can have the dead grandpa but I get the kid almost croaking in the delivery room."

"Fine, you can have the victory party but I get the scene around the last putt at 18."

We went our separate ways to grind, and a couple days later shared billing on the cover. (The headline to my story and my byline were above Rick's in slightly larger font, and it gives me joy to know that it surely still bothers him.) The quotes "Honey, I miss you lately . . ." and "I don't mean to be disrespectful. . ." are from Rick's typically excellent column.

CHAPTER 9

Credit to Dave Shedloski for his enterprise on the story about the pebble in the Shinnecock bunker that complicated Mickelson's bid at the 2004 U.S. Open. It ran on golfdigest .com in June 2018 and the quotes on that subject are taken from Shed's story. Hal Sutton's kvetching about the 2004 Ryder Cup is from the *No Laying Up* podcast on April 3, 2020.

CHAPTER 10

When I sit next to a middle-aged dude on an airplane and he asks what I do for a living I always say, "Commercial real estate." (The two times that a seatmate responded "Me, too!" I mumbled that I was transitioning out of it.) But inevitably I'm drawn into conversations about golf with strangers, and across the last three decades the most common question has been, "Who's the biggest asshole on Tour?" This tells you something about human nature. I shit you not, the second-most asked question has always been, "Is Phil Mickelson a phony?" It was fun to dig into that question. Hunter Mahan's quotes on the topic are from Teddy Greenstein's 2010 story that appeared in the *Los Angeles Times* under the headline, "The Real Truth About Phil Mickelson? . . . He's a Good Guy."

"It's pitch-black dark out there": *No Laying Up* podcast, March 28, 2018.

"A semi-shank, half-flier": Dan Jenkins, "It Ain't Over 'Til It's Over," *Sports Illustrated*, July 30, 1984.

"I had a very bad flight home": Colin Montgomerie, *Monty: An Autobiography*, Orion Publishing, 2012, 187.

"There was never even a consideration": Mark Cannizzaro, "Mickelson's Caddy: Driver Was Only Choice," *New York Post*, June 20, 2006.

CHAPTER 11

I was blessed to have a fantastic editor on this project, Jofie Ferrari-Adler. Our only disagreement concerned the passages in this chapter about Phil's philanthropy; Jofie thought it went on a bit too long but ultimately deferred to my wishes to keep all the material, which I find touching and compelling. If you were at all bored in that section, know that Jofie is on your side.

"If we can get him to play out of the fairway": Doug Ferguson, "Mickelson Spectacular in Victory," golfchannel.com, May 13, 2007.

"It's hard for me to interpret": Doug Ferguson, "Mickelson a Man of Mystery On and Off the Course," golfchannel.com, September 4, 2007.

"An angel without wings": Dave Shedloski, "For former NFL star, Mickelson 'an angel without wings,'" pgatour.com, June 6, 2007.

"I wouldn't call Mickelson a great player": Murray Hills, "Stevie on Phil: 'I Hate the Prick,'" stuff .co.nz, December 12, 2008.

"It's a small locker room": *Fore Play* podcast, March 9, 2021.

CHAPTER 12

Across a very public life, Mickelson has done a remarkable job bottling up his emotions. The only time I've ever seen him shed a tear was behind the final green at the 2010 Masters. What a scene.

In my recounting of Phil's epic shot out of the tree on the 13th hole, Bones's quotes are from the *No Laying Up* podcast on April 5, 2021.

CHAPTER 13

Billy Walters did not want to be interviewed for this book. Actually, he did want to—he has quite a bit to say about Phil Mickelson. But Walters is working on his autobiography (with Armen Keteyian as a cowriter) and they are saving Billy's words for their own book. But Walters allowed a surrogate to express Billy's views to me and provide fact-checking.

"I was born a gambler": Mike Fish, "Billy Walters on His Conviction, Gambling—and Ex-Friend Lefty," ESPN.com, March 28, 2018.

"money laundering of funds": Mike Fish and David Purdum, "Millions from Phil Mickelson Tied to Money Laundering, Gambling Case," ESPN.com, June 29, 2015.

"owed similar debts to Mr. Walters": Jeffrey Toobin, "Phil's Insider-Trading Escape," golfdigest .com, June 27, 2017.

CHAPTER 14

Mickelson's triumph at Muirfield still feels overlooked, perhaps because many Americans were asleep when he was making all of those birdies. To me, that three-week stretch in the summer of 2013 perfectly captures who Phil is as a player: bitching at Mike Davis at Merion; blowing that U.S. Open with a series of sloppy mistakes; rallying to conquer one of the best courses in the world with one of the most dazzling final rounds in major championship history. The guy is so maddening/exhilarating.

"I'll tell you about these Opens": Matt Long, "Lessons from Merion," podiumsportsjournal .com, July 6, 2013.

CHAPTER 15

I had so much material on Mickelson from covering him for so many years it wasn't a big deal that he didn't want to sit for interviews for this book. But of all the things I wished I could have pressed him on, the numerology/astrology business is near the top of the list. Hopefully I'll get to do it in future. Maybe Phil can predict that for me? The quotes from Ted Bishop on the subject are from his book, *Unfriended: The Power Brokers, Political Correctness and Hypocrisy in Golf*, published by Classics of Golf in 2016. So are the Tom Watson quotes "When are one of you guys . . ." and "You guys suck at foursomes . . ."

CHAPTER 16

"We talked for about two hours": Tim Rosaforte, "Phil Mickelson flew to Las Vegas to break up with Butch Harmon in person," golfdigest.com, November 4, 2015.

"The FBI and the Securities and Exchange Commission": Matthew Goldstein and Ben Protess, "Golfer Mickelson's Role Said to Be Overstated in Insider Inquiry," *New York Times*, June 11, 2014.

"In July 2012, Walters called Mickelson": "SEC Announces Insider Trading Charges in Case Involving Sports Gambler and Board Member," SEC.gov/news/pressrelease, May 19, 2016.

"I just lost the biggest bet of my life": Mike Fish, "Billy Walters on His Conviction, Gambling— and Ex-Friend Lefty," ESPN.com, March 28, 2018.

"It was clear from the pleadings": Ibid.

"Here is a guy that all he had to do was come forward": Ibid.

"Held that recipients of inside information": Toobin, "Phil's Insider-Trading Escape."

"Oi, Darren, it's the end of the Ryder Cup": Martin Rogers, "European players take aim at Phil Mickelson, but all in good fun," *USA Today*, October 2, 2016.

CHAPTER 17

Jim Mackay declined to comment for this book. His views were conveyed, and the details about his time with Mickelson were fact-checked, by sources close to him.

CHAPTER 18

I still can't believe Mickelson won the PGA Championship. Unreal. Just a few weeks before that, I had told Ferrari-Adler that, overwhelmed by helping to launch the Fire Pit Collective, I needed more time to finish this book and perhaps we should bump the publication to 2023, or even '24. Then Phil pulled a Phil. Thanks to my bulldog agent David Black for helping me keep my eyes on the prize.

"Thanks for bringing me some luck": Bamberger, "How this small gesture from Phil Mickelson made a lasting impact," golf.com, October 31, 2021.

"Now this was salty": "Live From the 2021 PGA Championship," Golf Channel, May 23, 2021.

"A great example of gamesmanship": Matt Rudy, "Brooks Koepka doesn't hold back in our exclusive poolside interview," golfdigest.com, September 14, 2021.

CHAPTER 19

"According to the trial transcript": Rob Snell, "Lefty and Dandy Don: How a Grosse Pointe bookie allegedly cheated Phil Mickelson," *Detroit News*, June 20, 2021.

"There's a morality to it": "McIlroy not interested in Saudi event: Doesn't excite me," golf channel.com, December 9, 2019.

"a money grab": Ewan Murray, "'A money grab': Rory McIlroy denounces Saudi-backed breakaway golf tour," theguardian.com, May 5, 2021.

The first sentence of Mickelson's autobiography goes, "As in life, golf is a game of circles." This brings us back to Phil's central statement in this book, from the Introduction: "You think you know me, but you don't." If you've come this far, gentle reader, hopefully you know him a little better now.